JARB
6'

NIGEL SLATER

Real Fast Food

350 RECIPES READY-TO-EAT IN 30 MINUTES

THE OVERLOOK PRESS

WOODSTOCK • NEW YORK

To John Zentner and Tony Richardson

First published in the United States in 1996 by
The Overlook Press
Lewis Hollow Road
Woodstock, New York 12498

Library of Congress Cataloging-in-Publication Data

Slater, Nigel
Real fast food / Nigel Slater.
p.   cm.
Includes bibliographical references and index.
1. Quick and easy cookery.   I. Title.
TX833.5.S59   1996
641.5′5—dc20
95-34602
CIP

Manufactured in the United States of America
ISBN: 0-87951-642-9
First American Edition

CONTENTS

INTRODUCTION

T his is a book of ideas for everyday eating, a
collection of recipes for simple food that is easy to
prepare and quick to cook. It is written for anyone who
enjoys good food eaten informally, and should
particularly appeal to those who lack the time to cook it.
Most of the recipes are based on fresh food with as little
as possible done to it. There are no complicated
procedures, no dithering around with affected arrange-
ments on oversized plates, and no effete garnishes. It is a
set of straightforward recipes for fast food with bold
flavors, cooked in minutes, and served without
pretension.

There are three types of fast food I think worth
eating. Firstly, there is street food, such as the crisp
Indian *samosas,* sold hot from their pans of crackling
fat, or the robust and smokey Greek *souvlakia,* grilled
over charcoal and wrapped in comforting pita. Then
there is takeout food, some of which can be very fine
indeed. What can beat a crisp-based and deeply savory
Italian pizza, or a fillet of fresh fish fried in light, rustling
batter with homemade fries?

Thirdly, there is fast home cooking, the sort of food
you throw together when you come home tired and
hungry. At its worst this can come from the "101 ways
with condensed mushroom soup" school of cooking, or
be a bland, ready-made dinner chucked in the
microwave, but at its best fast home cooking can mean
fresh food, bright flavors, and relaxed eating. That is
what this book is all about.

The recipes are easy and within the grasp of all but
the most ham-fisted of cooks. While most of the recipes
included here are fast, I make no claims for five-minute

feasts or ten-minute dinner parties. I think that good food can be measured only by its flavor and freshness, not by a stopwatch. That said, most of the recipes in this book can be completed in under 30 minutes, which is, after all, the time it takes a supermarket ready-made dinner to heat through. Many of them take just half that time. The ingredient lists are short, and most of the recipes require only one or two fresh ingredients that can be bought on the way home. I like the idea of buying one ingredient that looks particularly good, then mixing it with some pantry staples, and seeing what happens.

The ideas behind the recipes are a hodgepodge of the original, the borrowed, and the stolen. It would be an arrogant writer indeed who suggested that all his recipes were his own. Many of the recipes here are classics whose origins are obscure, if not totally lost, to all but the most thorough of food historians. Some of the recipes are mine (whatever that may mean), some have been adapted from others, and a few have been previously published in another form in *marie claire* magazine.

There are a few indulgences. I stand accused of using some things to excess: extra virgin olive oil, Parmesan cheese, garlic, basil, olives, and bitter salad leaves. I will accept criticism, too, for my overuse of berries, fruits, and soft fresh cheeses, and I might as well admit addictions to anchovies and to dark, bitter, and absurdly expensive chocolate, though thankfully not together.

If there is one thing I hope will emerge from this book, it is that fast food is not just about pizzas, hamburgers, and noodles, good though they can be (and they are all here); fast food can also mean a slice of truly ripe, aromatic melon eaten with a hunk of salty Feta cheese and a few black olives, or perhaps a juicy white peach sliced and dropped into a glass of chilled, deep-yellow wine.

Think of a piece of chicken brushed with aromatic herbs and lemon, then char-grilled, and stuffed into a crisp roll slathered with garlic mayonnaise, or a comforting bowl of oatmeal with blackberries and heather honey. Imagine shredded, peppery basil leaves stirred into buttery mashed potato, a slice of pork pan-fried with fennel, or a plate of purple-yellow muscat grapes and ripe figs. All this is fast food.

Whether it is Elizabeth David's immortal omelet and a glass of wine, a hot bacon sandwich when you return from the pub on a cold night, or a plate of pasta with slices of soft white goat cheese and leaves of pungent fresh thyme, there is nothing like real, fast, food.

A FEW NOTES FOR THE FAST COOK

Most of the recipes are enough for two. I know this is slightly unusual, but I am certain that more people eat this sort of food in twos than in fours. Although four is a popular number for dinner parties, it is less practical for everyday eating, with different members of the same family eating at different times. But it is easy to double the recipes in order to serve four. Those traditional complicators of recipe multiplication, such as gelatin and cornstarch, have no place in this book. I also believe that many of us eat alone, particularly the young and elderly, and it is easier to halve a recipe successfully than to quarter it.

The dietary balance of the recipes in this book is based on the World Health Organization's recommendations; the bulk involve fresh vegetables and fruit, and most main dishes are accompanied by a salad (the W.H.O. suggests we eat 400 grams, or about 14 ounces, of these per day). A good number of the recipes include starches in the form of bread, pasta, and potatoes. (The W.H.O. recommendation is that they should provide 50-70 percent of our energy.) The remaining recipes using red meat, cream, and high-fat cheeses should provide no more than 30 percent of your daily food intake. Over two-thirds of the recipes are suitable for non-meat eaters, and the majority of them are distinctly frugal in meat quantities.

These recipes are not definitive. I should hate to think of anyone following them slavishly. I would prefer that they are used as a starting point, a springboard if you like, for your own ideas. I cook in a relaxed way that would probably raise eyebrows with the house-proud or the more efficient of cooks. I believe that no recipe should appear in a book until it has been tested, but I should add that I rarely enjoy the triple-tried-and-tested style of cooking, where recipes have been tested to death. They may be guaranteed to work, but have more often than not lost their heart and soul along the way.

Timings

The majority of these recipes can be on the table within 30 minutes or less. If waiting even that long is beyond you, there is a section of pantry Quick Fixes at the end of the book. It is difficult to give accurate timings for recipes. Everybody works at a different pace, ovens do not have identical thermostats, and one person's idea of a minute can differ from the next's (even with one eye on the clock). My timings therefore should be taken as approximate. All recipes point to a clue other than just time whether a dish is ready or not, that is, firm to the touch, tender to the point of a knife, black around the edges, and so on, which is a more reliable guide than the clock.

Accompaniments

Many of the snacks in this book can become a complete meal by serving them with a salad and following with cheese and fruit. I cannot think of a fish or meat dish that I would not accompany with a salad of various green leaves.

Although most of the recipes will stand up for themselves as a light meal, I have included suggestions with some recipes for accompanying dishes, should you wish to combine them in a more traditional fashion. This particularly applies to the meat sections where some hearty eaters may find my ubiquitous accompaniment, "a salad of baby green leaves," insufficient.

Ingredients lists

The lists of ingredients that precede the method of each recipe are generally quite short. I have tried to include no more than one or two that you will need to go out and buy, while the rest of the list is made up of things you will probably have hanging around anyway: lemons, mustard, spices, herbs, and the like. Some recipes include nothing that is not in a reasonably well-stocked pantry. And by that I mean an average kitchen cabinet as opposed to a country house pantry or a student's windowsill.

When listing ingredients I have attempted to be as helpful as possible, that is, extra virgin olive oil or peanut oil rather than just "oil." Likewise, I have stated boiling or baking, whole wheat or *ciabatta,* or cherry or plum, rather than simply potatoes, bread, or tomatoes. My suggestions, though, are probably the ideal rather than a necessity. For example, 4 medium cloves of garlic is not a world away from 2 plump cloves. I have put 2 large ones because they are easier to peel and sometimes both fresher and sweeter. Just use the best you can get hold of.

I have tried to find a balance between the practical and the absurdly persnickety. If, for instance, I have listed English or Dijon or tarragon mustard in the ingredients, then that is what I consider to be right for the recipe; if I have just said "mustard" then the type is of less importance to the finished dish. Use what you have on hand.

When I say butter, I mean unsalted. When I say flour I mean all-purpose and when I say salt I mean sea salt. By butter I do not mean margarine or a lowfat spread. And stock comes fresh in cartons from the supermarket or from a wine bottle or, if there is no other aromatic liquid around, the tap. Never a cube. If you will not take my advice, then at least try Marigold Swiss Vegetable Stock Powder, to my taste the least offensive.

Herbs

When I list herbs in the recipes you can take it I mean fresh ones. Dried herbs, with the possible exception of oregano, are of little use to the quick cook as they need slow cooking in order to give up their flavor to the dish. Many dried herbs, in particular parsley, chervil, and basil, are a complete waste of time and money, though I will concede that thyme and rosemary have their uses-but not here.

Measurements

I have to admit to rarely measuring anything. My cooking is not so finely tuned that a *soupçon* more or less of anything will cause much grief. If I am cooking for myself I forget all about cups and spoons, and just go with whatever tastes and looks right. If you were to use this book as a stepping stone to adopting the same method I would be a very happy man.

In measuring ingredients I have tried to be accurate; generally speaking, teaspoons and tablespoons are lightly heaped, *and not level,* unless it says otherwise, and they are standard measuring spoons. A glass of wine means a normal Paris goblet, about ½ cup. "A small bunch of" means the size of a child's posy, and "a handful" refers to the amount that can comfortably be held in the palm and fingers of the average hand.

Where I feel scrupulously accurate measurements are essential to the balance of flavors, then I have said so; if not, then a little more or less is unlikely to end in tears. But I wouldn't take any of it as gospel.

Shopping

Be prepared

I have mentioned before that many of the ingredients listed in each recipe are probably to be found in a reasonably stocked kitchen cabinet. It is worth spending a little time every now and again stocking up on oils, spices, dried pasta, rice, and condiments such as soy and chili sauces.

Daily food shopping can then be cut to a minimum—a few fish fillets, a green vegetable, or some fruit. Shopping, however limited your time, becomes less of a hassle if most of the heavy stuff is already at home, giving you time to find the ripest fruit and the pick of the vegetables.

A word about prepared food. Supermarkets stock an increasing number of prepacked labor-saving ingredients. Some of these I approve of: fillets of fish (though I wish they would put a few bones into the pack for stock) and washed potatoes, for instance. Bags of ready-washed spinach and salad leaves save time. Despite the fact they appear expensive, I find *mesclun* or other mixed leaves cheaper than keeping several different types of leaves and herbs in the refrigerator. I draw the line at sliced vegetables, though. Can anyone really be too busy to slice a zucchini?

Organic foods

I want food that is as fresh and as pure as possible. My first stop in any food market is the organic section. Food labeled "organic" has been produced without the use of chemical pesticides, herbicides, and fungicides normally used in today's intensive farming methods. These chemicals can leave residues in the food, about which the longterm effects on the body are not known. Some of the big food chains are taking the organic movement seriously, and there are often potatoes, tomatoes, mushrooms, and wonderful green-topped carrots available.

Food grown in this natural way is more expensive because the farmers' yields are lower and less reliable. Organic farming is a massive growth area, and given encouragement from the consumer it will go from strength to strength.

Quality

The better quality an ingredient the more use it is to the cook whose time is short. By quality, I mean flavor and freshness. After a couple of decades, when food quality seemed to be on a downward spiral, I think it is safe to say that the choice has never been better. Where some greengrocers, grocers, and fish merchants are still reluctant to offer us anything new, there are many who set a shining example, stocking all manner of interesting things. I look to these people first, before I tackle the supermarkets because I think it would be sad to see specialist food stores disappear in favor of the big chains.

The supermarkets, though, are responding quickly to consumer interest in good food. Among buyers, flavor, rather than yield, reliability, and shelflife, is the buzzword of the 1990s. Some chains work directly with the growers and farmers to produce a better product. In the U.K., for instance, one supermarket chain has been rekindling interest in old English apple varieties. Things are looking up.

How to speed up your Cooking

Check the ingredients

It is worth spending a couple of minutes checking that you have all the ingredients before you start cooking. Many times I have found that the butter I "knew" I had has mysteriously disappeared. If you get halfway through a recipe and find that the crucial ingredient is missing, then you must experiment or starve. Improvization is a wonderful thing. It is how cooking moves forward.

In the kitchen

It really does help to assemble all the ingredients first. I do not mean measuring out the tablespoons into quaint little bowls like some demonstration cook, but bringing the olive oil to the stove, grating the cheese, and rummaging through the spices for the fennel seeds will save some time. When you have to chop and sweat an onion, I suggest you do that first and then prepare the other ingredients while it cooks.

A place for everything

I am as suspicious of a tidy kitchen as I am of a tidy desk. I hate the sort of kitchen (they are usually white) that if you so much as turn the egg-timer over will look like a bomb has hit it. But I have to admit that everything in my kitchen has its place. This is not due to some manic do-it-and-dust-it side of my nature, but partly because my kitchen is so small. The oils, vinegars, and mustards all live in the same place, and the salt and pepper haven't changed place in years. This is a great boon when time is short. It can take forever to locate the coriander seeds if they are not put back in the same place each time.

The right tools

I hardly even need to mention that sharp knives and good-quality, heavy-based pans make cooking quicker, safer, and more enjoyable. You know that. But I shall point out that it is useless, not to mention dangerous, to throw those sharp knives in the dishwashing water. I also cannot resist saying that I recommend Le Creuset enameled cast iron pans. I have had mine for years, and swear by them rather than at them. The best woks, incidentally, are the thin, one-handled ones from Asian shops, rather than the designer numbers from kitchenware stores.

Get on with it

There is little point in standing over a pot or constantly peering into the oven. Unless a recipe insists that you should keep an eye on the food while it cooks, or that something requires constant stirring, you can do something else while it cooks, such as toss the salad, finish the crossword, or brush the cat.

Taste, taste, taste

I suggest you taste your cooking at every stage. If you like the taste of a dish before you are supposed to add the cream or the lemon juice, then stop right there. Try adding salt and pepper only after tasting the dish first, because some foods, cheese for one, can vary enormously in saltiness. Remember that many of us eat too much salt, so try to cut back a bit as it is not always necessary; in fact, quite a few of the recipes in this book do not contain it at all. Taste continuously, and use your finger—it's quicker.

The table

Good food is good food, and no amount of pretentious table settings will make it taste any better. My motto is, the less fuss the better, but little things do make a difference. A white linen napkin and a fruit knife can turn eating an apple (if it is a good one) into a special occasion. But if I have time to spare I use it to cook with rather than to starch napkins. Flowers on the table are delightful, but I think they are far more beautiful when naturally arranged (for which read "just stuck in the vase"). Flower arrangers have a great deal to answer for.

Food looks much more appetizing on a plain white plate (preferably with a deep rim to hold any pan juices or sauce) than on some artful designer number. The Italians and the French make good sturdy plates for everyday eating. The fickleness of fashion means that heavy, deep-bowled white plates are now available in the designer stores.

Ignore anyone who tells you that every meal should be a "performance," and be suspicious of those who tell you they iron a tablecloth and arrange the flowers when they come in from work, exhausted, at eight o'clock. They are trying to hide something. Probably the food.

And remember that any fast food, be it a sandwich eaten while standing in the kitchen, or a sauté of chicken with olives and herbs, tastes even better with a glass or two of wine.

THE FAST FOODIES' PANTRY

It was Patience Gray and Primrose Boyd who pointed out, in their delightful little book *Plats du Jour,* that the main object of the pantry is: "to provide meals at short notice without shopping, and, equally important, to leave one free to select the piece of beef for *gulyas* or *boeuf à la mode* without having to search at the last moment for paprika pepper or a handful of juniper berries."

To the quick cook a sufficiently stocked pantry is not just a time-saver but a source of inspiration. On countless occasions I have come home and made a meal from the contents of the kitchen cupboards. *Pappardelle* cooked with olive paste from a jar, canned salmon fishcakes and bottled sweet peppers char-grilled, then served warm with a drizzle of olive oil and sprinkled with garlic, have all been the results of rummaging through the kitchen cabinets.

I have a small kitchen. It has probably less room than many closets. Cupboard space is at a premium, and large bottles of olive oil and vinegar tend to migrate to the already cluttered work surfaces. Rolling out pastry or making bread demands that everything be relocated to the floor. This is not my dream kitchen.

My pantry is lean and restricted to essentials rather than groaning with all manner of "things that may just come in useful." I am ruthless about just how many jars and bottles I have open at one time, so there are perhaps three different mustards and pickles on the go rather than the five or so I really wish for. I have no facilities for hoarding "little bits in bags," and will have no truck with unfamiliar ingredients that glare accusingly at me every time I open the refrigerator door. Not for me the packages of rock candy or exotically flavored tea that clutter so many shelves for months, even years, on end.

If I had to choose only three ingredients for my desert-island pantry, and assuming that a few staples such as rice, dried pasta, and some potatoes had been washed ashore with me, they would probably be lemons, olive oil, and Parmesan cheese. Allowed to take six and I would probably add anchovies, dried mushrooms, and then agonize over a block of fine dark chocolate or a wooden box of rose or lemon Turkish Delight. I detail below some key ingredients that will form a strong backbone to the fast cook's kitchen. I have kept it short and somewhat personal, knowing that this list has worked for me for years.

Oils I have three, sometimes four, oils open at once: two olive oils, one bland oil, and one fancy nut oil. I like a light olive oil for general cooking—the French James Plagniol brand is one I like—and a smart, fruity, extra virgin oil from Italy for pouring over salads and vegetables. I prefer a bland peanut oil for frying and stir-frying, using the deeply fragrant walnut and hazelnut oils, bought in small cans and bottles, for mixing with lemon juice for dressing salad leaves and goat cheeses. Toasted sesame oil is good for finishing stir-fries, but I can live without it.

Vinegar I use wine vinegar, red or white, for almost everything (I like the *Badia a Coltibuono* one available in good specialty food stores). I have both sherry and cider vinegar for salad dressings, and I have paid a king's ransom for rich, mellow balsamic vinegar to which I am becoming addicted. Forget the cut-price supermarket blends and go for broke.

Mustard I have three jars open at once, all from Dijon. A great favorite both for spreading on sandwiches and cooking with is a smooth tarragon mustard from any of the leading French importers. A jar of grainy French mustard made crunchy by the inclusion of seeds or the smooth yellow variety are types I also find invaluable. I avoid the fancy mustards, the ones with honey and heaven knows what else, as I find a straightforward mustard hard to beat.

Dried Pasta Lots. Something flat such as *fettuccine* or, better still, the wider *pappardelle.* A variety for picking up copious quantities of sauce, such as shell-shaped *conchiglie* or corkscrew-shaped *fusilli,* and a vacuum bag of *gnocci* are pretty much essential. Look out for brands such as de Cecco.

Salt, Peppercorns, and Spices Maldon sea salt with its large, flat crystals is my first choice. Black peppercorns are the most essential spice; it is hard to think of cooking without them. I rarely use hot white peppercorns, preferring the aromatic black ones, and grinding them as I need them in a wooden peppermill. Other spices to have handy include dried hot chilies, whole coriander, chili powder, ground cinnamon, ground cumin, a good proprietary curry powder or your own ground and stoppered, and ground paprika.

Dried herbs are rarely used in quick cooking as they do not keep well and rarely bear any resemblance to the fresh thing. They can be used to good effect in casseroles when the slow cooking time can extract their flavor.

Bottled Sauces These are useful when you have no time to make your own or to visit the market for freshly made ones. Essential are creamed artichoke, pesto, and black and green olive pastes for pasta, hot red *harissa* for couscous, and dark soy for stir-fries and light soy as a condiment.

Canned Foods Some things survive the canning process well enough to be included in the pantry. Chick peas (garbanzos), tomatoes, and sardines in olive oil are obvious contenders. Some flageolet and cannellini beans can be okay, though they lose the bite of the dried ones when cooked. Salmon is quite sufficient for fishcakes and bakes, and tuna even better. The sardines in tomato sauce in my cupboard belong to the cats, who will not eat any other sort.

I use little flour in my cooking so buy it in small bags, stocking large amounts only when I am going through one of my baking sprees. When I do, I buy unbleached, organic, stoneground flour, which is available in many health-food stores and wholefood markets. I have been caught without sugar in the house many times, but I try to remember to keep a small bag of granulated for sprinkling on *crêpes* and making *brûlees*. I always have a box of French *A la Perruche* cane-sugar cubes for coffee.

A Few Extras I mention some ingredients I keep for instant snacks in Quick Fixes on page 311, but here are a few other foodstuffs. These are hardly essential, but I like to have them in the cupboard if possible. They are: tapenade for spreading on toasted rounds of French bread. Salty *anchoïade* for smearing thinly on toast. Sun-dried tomatoes for snacking on straight from the jar. High-fruit, low-sugar jams to make a satisfying sweet snack when spread on French bread or stirred into yogurt, (apricot and greengage are usually the most successful for keeping a true fruit flavor). Unfiltered flower honey and Marmite for spreading on fingers of toast, and thick, crunchy peanut butter for sandwiches.

CHAPTER ONE

BAKERY GOODS *and* DRINKS

I find something intrinsically "right" about eating food while holding it in my hands. It is as if this is how food was meant to be eaten all along, with knives, forks, and chopsticks being part of a parlor game that somehow got out of hand. I certainly enjoy the feel of the food in my fingers, and no doubt aspire to the primitiveness of it all.

Handheld food is not just for the street and the picnickers' meadow, but an established alternative to eating at table. For comfort and convenience, most of it is enclosed in an edible wrapper—sometimes warm, sometimes not, but almost invariably dough-based.

The snatched sandwich of a working lunch, the croissant stuffed with melted cheese for a light supper, even the soft chapati used to mop up a spicy stew, are instances of how a starchy envelope is used to cradle the scorchingly hot and the rich and messy. Examples can be found in almost every culture. The Chinese have their sweet pork stews wrapped in thick balls of steamed dough, and the Mexicans their tortillas. The Cornish choose a strong pastry case for the traditional pastries in a miner's lunch, while within the pita pockets of the Middle East lurk all manner of savory things. The Greek *souvlakia,* the French baguette, and the Indian *samosa* share a *raison d'être* with both the American hamburger and the Russian blini with its precious freight of caviar.

I love the idea of swapping fillings and wrappings to suit my mood and what is available at the time of my hunger. I can see no reason why the fluffy apples and thick cream of a French *crêpe* cannot sit on an English muffin, or why the moist and fragrant tikka-spiced chicken of India should not lie between slices from a good loaf of white bread.

I did not know that strawberries and cream were better suited to a flaky French croissant than a substantial shortcake biscuit until I tried it. Neither was I aware of how perfectly Chinese spiced pork sat in a floury Scottish bap, or bun. But those bound by tradition and prejudice will no doubt disagree.

The sandwich, bagel, English muffin, and pita fillings that follow are merely suggestions. Chop and change to suit your predicament. But do not skimp. The dainty triangular sandwich, with its scraping of butter and thin line of ham, makes an uncomfortable bedfellow alongside the generously filled flat bread of the Middle East, stuffed to bursting with its hot and spicy cargo. Only the generous can make a sandwich worth eating.

BREAD

BRUSCHETTA

Bruschetta is garlic bread. Not the sort made from French bread and dripping with garlic butter, but the Italian version made with slices from a coarse-textured country loaf and thick, unctuous, extra virgin olive oil.

Grill a slice of coarse-textured white bread on both sides. You can do this over a charcoal grill or under the broiler, or bake it in a very hot oven. Loath to heat my oven for a piece of toast, I often just zap it on my preheated, ridged Le Creuset grill pan.

When crisp on both sides, cut a juicy clove of garlic in half and rub it over one side of the bread. Drizzle the bread with olive oil. Use your best oil, something deep green and fragrant.

BRUSCHETTA AL POMODORO

FOR 2

4 slices of white bread, cut from a crusty loaf, ½ inch thick
1 clove of garlic, peeled
4 ripe tomatoes, roughly chopped

salt
freshly ground black pepper
extra virgin olive oil

Grill the bread on both sides. Cut the garlic clove in half and rub the cut edge all over one side of the toasted bread.

Spread the tomatoes over the garlic toast and sprinkle with a little salt and a grinding of black pepper. Trickle olive oil over the tomatoes, and eat the toast while still hot.

A Few Good Things to Put on *Bruschetta* or *Crostini*

Crostini are small rounds of bread toasted and then brushed with olive oil much as in *bruschetta*.

Eggplant, Feta, and Mint

Spread the oiled and garlicked bread with eggplant purée from the deli counter, crumble over some salty Feta cheese, and sprinkle with a little chopped fresh mint.

Creamed Eggs and Grilled Scallions
Brush trimmed scallions with olive oil and grill (on the grill pan) till golden, about 3 minutes on each side. Scramble eggs with a little butter in a pan, then fold in a spoon or two of *fromage blanc.* Place the grilled scallions on hot *bruschetta,* and spoon the creamed eggs on top. Serve hot.

Gorgonzola
Mash together an equal quantity of Gorgonzola cheese and softened unsalted butter. Mix in a little brandy and spread over the hot toast.

Broiled Radicchio and Goat Cheese
An idea from Frances Bissell. Cut a head of radicchio into thick slices, about four per large head. Brush each slice with olive oil, season, and cook under a preheated broiler, turning it occasionally. Top each slice with a round of goat cheese and broil till bubbling.

PAIN PERDU OR FRENCH TOAST

FOR 2 AS A SNACK

4 slices of white bread, crusts removed	*2 tablespoons sugar*
⅔ cup milk	*1 medium egg, beaten*
	butter, for frying

Cut the bread into triangles. Sweeten the milk with the sugar. Dip the bread into the milk, then into the egg, and fry it on both sides in hot butter till crisp, which will take around 3 minutes on each side. Remove, sprinkle with sugar, and eat hot.

MOZZARELLA IN CARROZZA

FOR 2 AS A SNACK

6 ounces Mozzarella cheese, sliced
  ¼ inch thick
4 slices of white bread, ¼
  inch thick, crusts removed
2 tablespoons milk

a little flour, seasoned with salt
  and freshly ground black pepper
1 medium egg, beaten
fresh bread crumbs
peanut oil, for deep-frying

Place the sliced Mozzarella on two of the slices of bread and top with the remaining slices to make two large cheese sandwiches. Brush the sandwiches on both sides with the milk, then dust with flour. Dip into the beaten egg and then into the bread crumbs. Fry in hot oil, about one finger's depth, till crisp, about 3 minutes on each side. Cut into quarters and serve.

TOASTED CHEESE AND HAM

I make this snack from time to time, sometimes omitting the onion, and occasionally adding chutney instead of mustard.

FOR 2 AS A SNACK

4 slices of bread, cut thick
English or other hot mustard
½ cup chopped cooked ham

1 scallion, trimmed and minced
½ teaspoon Worcestershire sauce
¾ cup grated cheese, whatever you have

Toast the bread on one side. Spread the untoasted side thinly with mustard. Mix the other ingredients and spread on top. Place under the preheated broiler for a couple of minutes till the cheese has melted.

SANDWICH JAMBON DE PAYS

A good ham sandwich is a rare thing. I have found more of them in France than anywhere else. But then, the French have a knack of getting the simple things right.

A ham sandwich can be good when only ham and bread are used, as long as both are the best of their type. It does not require mayonnaise, tomatoes, chutney, or lettuce, though I really do think a fine spreading of hot mustard enhances the ham. The bread should be cut from a thin baguette. It must have a crackling crust that shatters when you bite. The ham must be carved from the bone and not, absolutely not, peeled from a package of wet, pink, rectangular slices. I do not believe that fine, sweet ham can come out of a package.

Choose baked or boiled ham, with a cure that suits you. Ask to taste the ham before you buy, just as you taste cheese. Have it carved thinly; it is much better sliced thin and piled high. Spread just a little mustard on the bread, a hot English one rather than a mild French variety. Pile on the ham in slender, small pieces, then top with the second half of the bread.

Some good things to put in a Ham Sandwich

However good your bread and ham may be, you may want to gild the lily a little. Perhaps in order to turn a snack into supper:

► Cover the ham with creamy scrambled egg (see page 46) into which you have stirred a spoonful of fresh chopped chives

► Toast the bread and spread it with tapenade, the olive and anchovy paste. Cover that with the ham, then add thin slices of good melting cheese, such as Gruyère or Mozzarella. Flash it under the broiler till the cheese melts

► Shred some radicchio leaves. Toss them in olive oil and broil till they start to wilt. Return them to their bowl, and while still warm toss them with the thin slices of ham. Pile on the bread

► Toss the ham with sliced bottled artichoke hearts that have been drained and broiled till tender and browned

► Brush baby leeks with olive oil and broil till they are soft and lightly browned. Sprinkle with grated Parmesan cheese and broil a little more till the cheese smells savory. Lay them on top of the ham

► Toss the ham with bottled red pimientos, cut into strips, that have been broiled till sweet and browned at the edges

► Sauté dandelion leaves till they wilt, then toss in a few pine nuts and slightly fewer raisins. Pile on the bread and top with the ham

ITALIAN PROSCIUTTO SANDWICH

Prosciutto is dry-cured Italian ham. Parma is the most famous variety. It is usually sliced very finely, and has a generous proportion of fat around the edge. Its flavor is piquant, and as with most cold meats it is best sliced just before it is bought, rather than ready-sliced and vacuum-packed.

I prefer an open-textured bread with ham sliced this thin. A French baguette is good enough, but the best is Italian *ciabatta,* which has a floury crust and huge holes, or other Italian bread.

► One of my favorite sandwiches is a split piece of *ciabatta,* spread with a little mayonnaise, then stuffed with alfalfa sprouts, watercress sprigs, and Parma ham

► A substantial sandwich I made recently consisted of an open-textured bread, split and spread with black olive paste from a jar. I then filled it with baby arugula leaves tossed with lemon and olive oil, and thin slices of Taleggio cheese. Topped with a slice of prosciutto and a handful of black olives, it satisfied both my addiction to olives and my love of cheese and bitter leaves

THE HOT DOG

Frankfurter sandwiches, better known as hot dogs, are an American institution. Like all such things, feelings run high about how they should be eaten. Apparently, the frankfurter was born in the 1850s, when a German butcher stuffed a long bun with a smoked sausage in honor of his pet dog. The idea went to America in the 1860s with one Charles Feltman, who sold them in the street from a charcoal stove on Coney Island, Brooklyn.

Purists insist that the sausage be grilled over charcoal or boiled, then stuffed into a long, soft bun. Mustard is piped along the entire length of the frankfurter. These views apart, I think hot dogs make a fine late supper, especially after a movie. Buy them in cans or vacuum packs. Split the bun in half (it should be a bit longer than the sausage and soft). Stuff it with warm sauerkraut, which you have transferred from its jar to a pan and heated gently. Spread a little mild mustard on a hot grilled frankfurter and push it inside the bun. Eat with a cold beer.

Bacon Sandwich

Feelings run high about bacon sandwiches. White bread or brown, toasted or untoasted, smoked or unsmoked bacon, butter or not. Then there's the ketchup question. For me the bread should be white, and untoasted. Somehow it is better made with what I call "plastic bread." I like the bacon to be smoked, and cooked just short of crisp. The bread should be dunked in the hot bacon fat. I tend to give the ketchup a miss.

The British love of the bacon sandwich is looked on with amazement by Americans, who, of course, have the sublime BLT (see below). But the bacon sandwich remains the quintessential after-pub nosh. Like Chinese takeouts, it only really comes into its own when you are slightly drunk.

For each sandwich:

FOR 1. BEST EATEN ON A COLD WINTER'S NIGHT, AFTER A TRIP TO THE PUB

*4 thick slices of lean
   smoked bacon (or
   Canadian bacon)*

*2 medium-thick slices of white
   bread*

Fry the bacon, in a little fat if the bacon is very lean, until it starts to show signs of crisping. I think the edges should be just turning golden. Push the slices to the side of the pan. Dunk one side of each slice of bread into hot bacon fat. Sandwich the bacon between the bread and eat while still very hot.

Pastrami on Rye

Pastrami on rye is the most chic of all sandwiches. Pastrami is a wood-smoked brisket of beef that has been first cured with sugar, salt, and several spices. Garlic, ginger, and pepper are the most obvious, but the recipes vary. They are almost always secret. All that really matters is that the spiced pink meat is juicy and very garlicky.

As I understand it, the definitive pastrami on rye is made with hot beef (it is steamed to keep it moist) and light rye bread. There should be mustard, but no butter, and a garnish of a lightly pickled cucumber.

To make the authentic Manhattan-style kosher sandwich at home is difficult. Good pastrami is difficult to find and can be expensive. (I am not keen on the commercial brick-shaped blocks with their paprika coating, preferring the original peppercorn-coated variety.) To buy a block of it large enough to steam and slice would be very expensive indeed.

The next best thing is to eat it cold. Secure a quarter-pound of pastrami per sandwich. You will find it, apart from at kosher delis, in specialist food stores. Make sure it is moist before they slice it for you, particularly important as you are eating it cold. Cut slices from a light rye loaf, no thicker than ¼ inch. Spread them with English mustard and pile on thin slices of pastrami. Add a second slice of mustard-spread bread, and serve a pickle on the side.

THE CLUB SANDWICH

A true feast that the late American writer James Beard described as one of the "great sandwiches of all time." Surprisingly, this Gargantua among snacks was not of the monstrous proportions we are now led to believe, as it was traditionally made with only two rather than the assumed three layers. Here is a reasonably authentic version, saved from being definitive only by my suggestion of whole wheat toast, which will no doubt ruffle a few feathers. Butter a crisp piece of toast cut from a white or light brown loaf. While this is still warm, layer crisp lettuce, long oval-leaved romaine for preference, with slices of tomato, cooked sliced chicken, and slices of bacon with mayonnaise. Finish with a second piece of toast.

A few rules that one is wise, but not obliged, to bow to: the toast and bacon slices should be crisp, the chicken moist from a freshly roasted bird, and the mayonnaise homemade or Hellmann's at the very least. You can garnish the sacred sandwich with little green olives without offending anyone.

COLD ROAST PORK SANDWICHES
WITH PICKLED WALNUTS AND CRACKLING

My father liked pickled walnuts, and cold roast pork with its crackling almost more than anything else. This is for him.

FOR 1 AS A SNACK

1 teaspoon mild mustard

2 tablespoons mayonnaise

3 inches or so of pork crackling (roasted pork skin), crushed into fragments

a small handful of finely shredded white or red crisp cabbage

2 slices of soft whole wheat, grain, or nut bread

2 slices of cold roast pork, about as thick as silver dollars

salt

1 large pickled walnut, sliced into rounds

Mix the mustard into the mayonnaise, tasting and adding more mustard as you wish. Fold in the crushed crackling and the shredded cabbage. Spread half of the cabbage on one slice of bread. Lay a slice of pork on top. Add a little salt and the sliced pickled walnut. Lay the second slice of pork on top and cover with the remaining dressed cabbage. Top with the second piece of bread.

SPICED TUNA ON RYE

Have you noticed how celery seems to be *de rigueur* in tuna sandwiches?

MAKES 2 SANDWICHES

a 7-ounce can line-caught tuna, drained

⅓ cup mayonnaise

2 tablespoons minced celery

1 tablespoon minced sweet onion

a clove of garlic, crushed to a pulp

¼ teaspoon paprika

¼ teaspoon cayenne pepper

1 teaspoon lemon juice

salt

a bunch of watercress, fresh and green, trimmed

4 slices of rye or white bread

Flake the tuna, not too finely, with a fork. Mix with the mayonnaise, celery, onion, garlic, and spices. Stir in the lemon juice. Taste and add salt if necessary. Pile between the bread with sprigs of watercress.

► There has been a lot of fuss about tuna lately. Rightly so. Some tuna are netted, causing the dolphins, which are sometimes picked up with them, to be killed. Check that any tuna you buy is line-caught, and save a dolphin.

HOT SANDWICHES

Pan-Fried *Anchoïade* and Camembert Sandwich

SERVES 1

2 slices of white bread
olive oil
2 teaspoons anchoïade *or*
   tapenade

2 ounces Camembert, thinly sliced
freshly ground black pepper

Brush the bread on both sides with olive oil. Spread one side of each piece with *anchoïade* or tapenade and one with sliced Camembert. Season with pepper. Heat a little olive oil in a frying pan. Place one piece of bread on top of the other and fry in the hot oil over a low heat till golden, turning once. The sandwich is ready when both sides are golden brown and the cheese is oozing.

Toasted Tofu, Cheese, and Chili Sandwich

SERVES 1

5 ounces pressed tofu, cut into
   ½-inch cubes
2 slices of whole wheat bread

½ teaspoon hot chili spread
¾ cup grated melting cheese such
   as Gruyère

Fry the tofu in a nonstick pan till golden on all sides. Toast the bread on one side only under a preheated broiler. Slather with the chili spread, using a little more if you like things really spicy. Cover with the cubes of tofu and scatter with the grated cheese. Broil till bubbling, then cut into fingers.

Pan-Fried Mushy Pea and Bacon Sandwich

SERVES 1

4 slices of white "plastic" bread
2 thick slices of bacon, crisply fried
¼ cup mushy peas (these canned puréed marrowfat peas are an institution in the north of England, often served with fish in batter and jellied eels!)

salt
freshly ground black pepper

Fry the bread in the bacon fat till crisp on one side. Warm the mushy peas in a small saucepan, stirring so that they do not burn. Spread the untoasted sides of two of the slices of bread with the mushy peas, top each with a bacon slice, season, and cover with the remaining bread. Cut into rectangular halves to serve.

A FEW SWEET SANDWICHES

French Bread with Goat Cheese and Fruit
Split a baguette in half, spread with a creamy soft goat cheese, and top with whole and sliced summer berries.

Toasted Chocolate *Panettone* with Hot Prunes and Armagnac
Chocolate *panettone* and fruits bottled in alcohol are treats stocked by Italian grocers and specialist food stores at Christmas.

Toast a flat, round slice of *panettone* under the broiler, then drizzle with a little Armagnac or alcohol from the bottled fruits. Warm the prunes in a small pan. Pile on prunes, which you will of course have first pitted, and eat while warm. Have a scoop of vanilla or coffee ice cream on the side.

Peanut Butter and Banana Sandwich
This is simply white bread, spread thickly with crunchy peanut butter and covered with sliced bananas. Top with a second slice of bread. To be taken with a glass of milk.

Malt Loaf with Warm Fig Jam and Clotted Cream

*4 slices of malt loaf
(a sweet fruited bread) or
use rich, dark fruit cake
½ cup Turkish or French
fig jam*

clotted cream

Warm the jam in its jar in a small pan with enough water to come halfway up the side of the jar. Very lightly toast the bread, just enough to heat it and heighten the flavor. Spoon the warm jam over the slices of malt bread and add a dollop of thick, yellow clotted cream at the side of the plate.

PITA

A few good things to stuff into Pita Bread

Fried Potato with Spices and Basil Vinaigrette

Fry a couple of scallions, minced, in a little butter. When they are soft, stir in 2 leftover boiled potatoes, chopped into ½-inch cubes. Cook till the potatoes are golden. They will probably break up a little. Add a tablespoon of lemon juice, a teaspoon of *garam masala,* and a pinch of cayenne. Fry for 1 minute, then pile into the warm pita with finely shredded bulb fennel or white cabbage dressed with vinaigrette to which you have added half a dozen or more shredded basil leaves. Enough for 1.

Deep-Fried Zucchini with Turkish Tarator Sauce

To make the tarator sauce, which is a Middle-Eastern garlic and nut sauce, dunk a thin slice of white bread in water and squeeze dry. Crumble it and whizz slowly in the blender with 2 cloves of garlic and ⅓ cup pine nuts or walnut pieces. Add salt, about ½ teaspoonful, and 4 tablespoons olive oil. Taste, and sharpen with a tablespoon lemon juice or wine vinegar. Slice each of 2 plump, medium zucchini into three lengthwise. Dust them with flour and deep-fry in very hot peanut or sunflower oil till crisp. Drain on paper towel, and pile into the warm pita with generous drizzles of the tarator sauce.

Cauliflower and Bacon with Cilantro-Cream Sauce

Broil or fry 4 thick slices of bacon till crisp. Steam a handful of cauliflower florets until quite tender (about 6 minutes). Whizz a handful of fresh cilantro leaves with ½ cup light cream, 3 tablespoons peanut oil, and a tablespoon Dijon mustard in a blender. Taste and add lemon juice, salt, and freshly ground pepper. Snap the bacon into pieces and mix with the hot cauliflower. Dress while hot with the cilantro-cream sauce. Pile into the warm pita. Enough for 2.

Labna Balls with Eggplant and Chili

Labna is a Middle-Eastern cheese made from drained, salted yogurt; the balls of cheese can be bought in jars from Middle-Eastern grocers. Slice a small eggplant into disks as thick as silver dollars. Fry them in peanut oil till soft and golden, about 4 minutes on each side. Drain. Toss them with 2 sliced labna balls and a tablespoon of dressing from the jar, a minced clove of garlic, and a little minced fresh hot chili. Toss with shredded romaine and stuff into the hollow warm pita.

Hot Mackerel, Tomato, and Sweet Onion

Place a mackerel fillet in a buttered baking dish, season with salt and freshly ground pepper, and bake, skin-side up, in a preheated 425 °F oven for 6 minutes, till golden and crisp. Break the hot fish into large chunks and pile into the warm pita with sliced tomatoes, sweet onion rings, and finely shredded crisp lettuce that has been tossed with lemon and a little olive oil. Enough for 1.

A few more good things to stuff into Pita Bread

► The Warm Cod, Parsley, and Potato Salad on page 68

► The Fresh Plum *Tabbouleh* on page 196 with slices of cold roast duck or chicken

► The Sautéed Chicken Livers on page 232 with a handful of baby spinach leaves and the pan juices from the livers

► The Spiced Lamb Kofta with Pine Nuts and Red Cabbage on page 243

► Softly scrambled eggs, and melted butter in which you have fried a teaspoon of good-quality curry powder

ENGLISH MUFFINS AND CRUMPETS

I am delighted by the knowledge that a "muffin-worry" is a collo-quialism for an old ladies' tea party. The expression conjures up fireside gossip of scandalous goings-on in the neighborhood. English muffins are the soft, doughy rolls that you split in half, while a crumpet is thinner and full of little holes.

Muffins make sound bases for poached, scrambled, or fried eggs, and for melted cheese and baked beans. There is a certain etiquette concerning muffins and their toasting. But we are not obliged to follow it. In her *Book of Breakfasts,* Marian McNeill writes, "The correct way to serve them is to open them slightly at their joint all the way around, toast them back and front, and butter the insides liberally. Serve hot."

I can find no reason for not splitting the muffin first and toasting it in the toaster. You will get a different texture, of course, with the dough toasted crisp, but I like that very much. Crumpets I prefer toasted and smothered, absolutely smothered, in butter. You may like to consider these toppings.

► Thick orange-blossom honey and thickly sliced bananas

► Blackberry jelly and *fromage blanc*

► Cottage cheese with chopped fresh mint and sliced fresh apricots

► Blue cheese, such as Stilton, and pan-fried apple slices

► Squares of the darkest, bitterest chocolate you can find placed on the toasted bun and allowed to melt ever so slightly

Hot Cheese Muffins

My mother died when I was quite young. My father was left with the daunting task of feeding a somewhat finicky child. Apart from vast quantities of fruit and vegetables (even spinach), there was very little I would eat. His greatest, and possibly only, success was this simple dish. Needless to say, he soon gave up and installed a housekeeper, of whom I shall say no more.

FOR 2 AS A SNACK

a walnut-sized piece of butter
the whites of 2 small scallions,
*   trimmed and chopped*

1½ cups grated Cheddar cheese
2 hot, toasted English muffins,
*   split*

Melt the butter in a small heavy-based pan over a low heat. Add the chopped scallions and fry till soft and slightly golden in color. Stir in the grated cheese and let it melt slowly over a low heat. Slide the whole lot onto toasted muffins and eat while still very hot.

► Spread the muffin with homemade pickle relish or chutney before you coat with the molten cheese

► Sandwich the muffins together with crisp bacon

The Bagel

The bagel is different from other bread rolls in that it is both baked *and* boiled. It is the brief boiling, or more often steaming, that gives the bread its chewy texture. Bagels are round, about 4 inches across, with a hole in the center. They originated in Austria, where *beugeln* means ring.

The close-textured bread rolls landed in America with the first Jewish immigrants, and at first were rarely known outside the Jewish community. Now they are found all over, eaten warm and stuffed with all manner of unorthodox things. I buy mine at Brick Lane in London's East End. The lines are long, but the shops are open 24 hours a day, and at least you can watch the dough being prepared and the bagels being baked.

A few good things to put in a Bagel

Lox and Cream Cheese

Smoked salmon, cut thicker than usual, and a generous spreading of cream cheese is the most famous filling for a bagel. If I fill them at home I always add a little lemon juice.

Smoked Mackerel

Creamy smoked mackerel works well with the close-textured bread. A dill pickle, minced, can be added if you wish.

Cinnamon and Raisins

Split and toast the bagel, then spread with butter, and dust with ground cinnamon. Scatter over a few raisins and add a dollop of cream cheese.

THE CROISSANT

A really flaky, buttery croissant is satisfying enough to eat on its own, but can be stuffed quite successfully for a more substantial snack. In Paris, they are to be found warm, filled with thin slices of ham and melted cheese.

The supermarket variety, which are often not as flaky as they might be, crisp up well under a hot broiler. Slice the croissant in half horizontally, losing as few crumbs as possible. Fill with any of the following.

Fromage Blanc, Thyme, and Sun-Dried Tomato

Remove the tomato from its oil and slice it thinly. Season the *fromage blanc* with a little freshly ground black pepper and fold in some chopped leaves of fresh thyme. Spoon mounds of the *fromage blanc* on the bottom half, dot with slices of sun-dried tomato, and top with the other half.

Roquefort and Walnut

Crumble the Roquefort and pile on the bottom half of the croissant. Scatter over a few broken walnuts and broil, with the top half, till the cheese has just melted and the nuts are fragrant. Do not overcook: the cheese should just start to ooze. Eat hot.

Apple Purée and *Crème Fraîche*

Warm the croissant gently under the broiler. Split carefully and spoon on a layer of apple purée, scented with cinnamon if you like. Cover with dollops of unctuous, very cold *crème fraîche* and top with the other half. Eat while the pastry is hot, and the cream has just started to run.

PIZZA BASES

A homemade pizza base, given character with rye flour and made light and crisp by its two risings, is a fine thing. But it is not a serious contender in the fast-food stakes. Commercial vacuum-packed pizza bases are not so bad. They store well, and can be filled, baked, and on the table in 15 minutes.

ARTICHOKE AND GREEN OLIVE PIZZA

Canned or bottled artichoke hearts in oil can be found in Italian grocers and delis. Often sold by weight from a bowl, they make the finest of all pizza toppings, not to mention the quickest.

FOR 2

1 pound artichoke hearts in oil
½ lemon

⅓ cup green olives, pitted
fresh parsley
1 pizza base

Drain the artichokes from the oil that comes with them. Sharpen the oil with the lemon juice and brush this over the pizza base. Slice the artichokes and their soft stems in half, and lay over the pizza. Dot with green olives and bake in a preheated 425 °F oven for about 20 minutes, till the outer rim of the pizza base is golden and crisp. Scatter parsley over the pizza as it comes from the oven, and eat while hot.

Good things to put on a Pizza Base

Char-Grilled Red Pepper, Eggplant, and Goat Cheese Pizza

Brush the base with olive oil. Cover with quarters of red bell pepper (broiled till sweet and slightly charred, then peeled), broiled slices of eggplant, and thick wedges of goat cheese. Brush with olive oil again and bake in a preheated 425 °F oven for about 20 minutes. Top with a large spoonful of chopped black olives and fresh flat-leaf parsley.

Cheese and Garlic Pizza

Mozzarella is traditional and melts smoothly, but other cheeses are interesting, too. I often use up ends of cheese, grating or slicing anything from goat cheese to Gorgonzola. Brush the pizza base with olive oil and minced garlic, then add grated cheese, mixed or in separate sections. Cook as above.

Salami and Black Olive Pizza

Cover the pizza base with a thin layer of tomato sauce—homemade or from a jar—the thicker the better, leaving just 1 inch of rim bare. Top with a layer of thinly sliced salami and scatter over a handful of black olives. Drizzle with oil. Bake as above.

Four-Tomato Pizza

Over a layer of thick tomato sauce, homemade or from a jar, arrange sliced plum tomatoes, whole cherry tomatoes, and sliced sun-dried ones. Brush with oil and bake as above. Scatter with torn fresh basil leaves and coarse-ground black pepper.

Pissaladière

A quick version of the famous Provençal tart. Brush the base with garlic oil, then cover with sautéed onions, anchovy fillets, chopped tomatoes, and black olives. Drizzle with oil and bake as above.

TACOS

Tacos, the crisp Mexican corn tortillas, are ideal for holding a slightly sloppy cargo such as beans in a spicy sauce or ground beef with hot chilies. The idea is to pile the wet filling into the taco shell, then top it with grated cheese, yogurt, and a spiced sauce.

BEEF TACOS WITH SALSA CRUDA

Fay Maschler is now the London *Evening Standard*'s restaurant critic, but before that she wrote the daily recipe column. Just as my collection of her cuttings was becoming too sticky to read she cleverly issued them all in book form. The result, *Eating In,* has since become one of my most-used books, sitting with half a dozen others next to the stove. This recipe is from her book.

FOR 4:

1 large onion, minced
2 cloves of garlic, minced
a little vegetable oil
1 pound ground beef
1 teaspoon ground cumin or cumin
   seeds
1 teaspoon dried oregano

1 tablespoon chili powder, or 1
   chopped fresh hot chili, or 1
   teaspoon hot pepper sauce (to taste)
dash of soy sauce
salt
freshly ground black pepper
pinch of sugar

FOR THE SAUCE:

4 tomatoes
2 teaspoons wine vinegar
½ onion, minced
2-3 canned jalapeño peppers, chopped

¼ teaspoon fresh oregano
salt
12 taco shells, reheated in a
   350°F oven for 2-3 minutes

Fry the onion and the garlic in the vegetable oil. Add the beef and stir until browned. Season with cumin, oregano, chili, and a dash of soy. Season with salt, pepper, and sugar. Keep warm.

To make the salsa cruda, broil the tomatoes until the skins blister and can be removed, then mix the chopped flesh with the wine vinegar, onion, jalapeños, oregano, and salt. Put out the heated taco shells, a bowl of the spiced beef, and another of the sauce alongside bowls of shredded lettuce, grated cheese, ripe avocado mashed with a peeled, seeded, and diced tomato, lemon juice and hot pepper sauce, and yogurt or sour cream. Assemble your own tacos with the constituent parts.

BLACK BEAN TACOS WITH TOMATO-CHILI SALSA

A non-meat alternative filling for tacos, which takes about half an hour to prepare. Add a chopped avocado to the salsa if you have one ripe.

FOR 4

2 16-ounce cans black beans
   or black-eyed peas, drained
   and well rinsed
3 tablespoons olive oil
1 bay leaf
2 onions, sliced
2 plump cloves of garlic, finely
   sliced
2 teaspoons paprika

½ teaspoon cayenne pepper
2 16-ounce cans chopped plum
   tomatoes
1 canned jalapeño pepper,
   seeded and minced
salt
freshly ground black pepper
approximately 2 teaspoons white
   wine vinegar

FOR THE TOMATO-CHILI SALSA:

3 large tomatoes
2 cloves of garlic, minced
1 large or 2 medium canned
   jalapeño peppers, minced
1 tablespoon roughly chopped fresh
   cilantro

12 taco shells
1 lime, for serving
1 cup grated cheese

Put the rinsed beans in a pan with a tablespoon of the oil and the bay leaf and cover with water. Bring to a boil and simmer for 10 minutes. Warm the remaining oil in a shallow pan, add the onions, and cook till soft and golden. Add the garlic, paprika, and cayenne and cook till the garlic is soft, about 4 minutes. Add the tomatoes with their juice and the jalapeño and simmer for 10 minutes. Drain the beans, and add to the sauce. Taste and season with salt, pepper, and wine vinegar. Simmer rapidly till thick, about 10 minutes.

To make the tomato-chili salsa, chop the tomatoes roughly, including their skins and seeds but not their cores. Dump them in the food processor or blender with the garlic and the jalapeños. Whizz briefly to produce a rough sauce, then stir in the cilantro. Warm the taco shells for 3 or 4 minutes in a 350 °F oven, or for 2 minutes under the broiler, then fill them with the bean stew. Spoon over the salsa, squeeze over a drop of lime, and top with cheese.

Drinks

There are a few drinks that are sustaining enough to call a snack in a glass: a spicy Bloody Mary, a rich dark Hot Chocolate, and a Banana Milk Shake. I have also added a couple of fruity yogurt drinks, one made with orange juice, the other with puréed mangoes.

Bloody Mary

Sunday morning is my usual time for one of these. Made with love it can be substantial enough to be considered a snack. At the risk of sounding pathetic, I actually prefer it without the alcohol, when it should really be known as a Virgin Mary.

FOR 1

1 fluid ounce vodka
1 cup tomato juice
Worcestershire sauce

hot pepper sauce
2 teaspoons lemon juice

Mix the vodka with the tomato juice. Season with the spiced condiments and lemon juice to taste. Serve chilled, over ice cubes.

Mango Lassi

One sniff of mango and yogurt and I am immediately transported back to Goa, and the palm hut on the virtually deserted beach where I took breakfast and lunch almost every day during my stay there.

FOR 1

1 cup plain yogurt
1 cup chilled water
2 teaspoons lemon juice

⅔ cup chopped ripe mango flesh,
   juice reserved
a little salt

Whizz together all the ingredients, apart from the salt, in the blender. Salt to taste.

HOT CHOCOLATE

Real hot chocolate, made with the finest, darkest chocolate, is far removed from the sweetened powdered stuff. Real hot chocolate is very rich, and is best served in small cups rather than mugs. This recipe is based on one by the Chocolate Society which, like me, suggests that Valrhona chocolate is the most suitable.

FOR 4

3 ounces good-quality dark chocolate, such as Valrhona Manjari

½ cup light cream
2½ cups milk

Break the chocolate into bits, put in a small saucepan, and allow to melt in the cream over a medium heat. Bring the milk to a boil and pour over the melted chocolate. Whisk lightly to prevent a skin from forming, and drink while hot.

MEAL-IN-A-GLASS

Whizz equal quantities of plain yogurt and orange juice, freshly squeezed if possible, in the blender with 1 egg yolk and 1 peeled banana per 1¼ cups liquid. Stir in a few ice cubes, plus a teaspoonful of wheatgerm if the idea grabs you.

BANANA MILK SHAKE

1 cup milk
1 banana, peeled and sliced

⅓ cup heavy cream
squeeze of lemon juice

Whizz all the ingredients in a blender till really smooth. Pour over ice cubes and serve cold. A scoop of vanilla ice cream would be a divine way to gild the lily. The shake should be very cold and very smooth; there is nothing more difficult to swallow than a warm and lumpy banana milk shake.

EGGS

The egg must be the most convenient of all foods. A couple of eggs and a few pantry staples, and you have a meal. Add butter to make an omelet, herbs to produce *oeuf en cocotte,* a red bell pepper and a few tomatoes to make *chakchouka* or *pipèrade,* and you have a feast.

Eggs are possibly the ultimate fast food because they have only to set rather than actually cook. It takes less than five minutes to make scrambled eggs with potted shrimp, and little more to make a version spiked with Eastern spices. Those who do not have the time to cook can toss an egg yolk into fruit juice and yogurt for an instant, nourishing drink.

Unless otherwise labeled, eggs are gathered from a battery unit, in which birds are stored in cages, so small the creatures can hardly turn around. They are fed automatically and spend their lives in total confinement. Having seen such an operation, it amazes me that people are still prepared to buy eggs produced in this way, so patently cruel is the system and artificial the birds' existence.

Eggs marked "range" or "free range" (or "cage free") come from birds that do have a certain opportunity to roam. Usually there is a warm hen house and reasonable access to the outdoors. Of course it is not always the case that the birds want to leave their cosy house to peck around outside.

When looking for free-range eggs it is worth reading the label on the carton carefully. Some producers give quite a lot of detail about the birds' welfare, feed, and living conditions. The egg recipes in this book were developed for large free-range eggs, unless a larger egg is specified.

▶ Eggs keep surprisingly well, as long as they are refrigerated. But I rarely keep eggs longer than a week, to ensure best flavor and cooking quality

▶ Eggs should be stored with the most pointed end of the egg down. Although many refrigerators have special egg containers, it's best to leave the eggs in the cartons in which they came, to prevent damage and exposing them to odors from other foods

▶ To test an egg for freshness, gently drop it into a glass of water. If it sinks it is fresh. The less fresh the egg is, the more likely it is to float

▶ The color of the egg's shell has nothing to do with how the egg will taste, or its nutritive value. It's determined by the breed of the bird

A Plain Boiled Egg

Allow 2 very fresh large eggs per person, and make sure that they are not too cold, or they will crack in the water.

Bring a large pan of water to a boil. Carefully slide in the eggs, cover the pan, and simmer for 3½ minutes. They will have a barely set white and a runny yolk. Eat them immediately, with "soldiers" (fingers) of brown toast.

Scrambled Eggs

At their best, scrambled eggs should form soft, creamy curds, barely set. This is quite easy to achieve if you cook them slowly over a low heat and ignore any interruptions. Friends and family must wait for their scrambled eggs and not, most emphatically not, the other way around.

FOR 2 AS A SNACK

4 eggs	*freshly ground black pepper*
salt	*2 tablespoons cold butter*

Break the eggs into a bowl and add a little salt and 3 or 4 twists of the peppermill. Beat with a fork for a few seconds, just to mix the yolks and the whites.

Melt most of the butter in a small saucepan or skillet. Pour in the eggs. Stir with a wooden spoon, scraping the bottom of the pan and bringing the outside edges to the middle. Continue this for 2 minutes, then remove from the heat but don't stop stirring (the eggs are still cooking). Check to see if they are done; if some of the egg is runny, return the pan to the heat and stir for another minute till just set.

Remove the pan from the heat, drop in the remaining cold butter to arrest the cooking, and tip gently onto a warm plate (not a hot one, which would allow the eggs to continue cooking).

SCRAMBLED EGGS WITH SWISS CHEESE

As an apprentice, one of my jobs in the kitchen was to prepare various "reductions," usually of wine and herbs, to be added to sauces. Any of the concentrated liquid that was left over usually found its way into midnight feasts, such as these cheesy scrambled eggs.

FOR 2

1 wineglass of dry white wine
1 large or 2 small cloves of garlic
4 healthy sprigs of fresh tarragon
3 extra large eggs
½ cup coarsely grated
  Emmenthal or Gruyère cheese

salt
freshly ground black pepper
a piece of butter, about the size of
  a walnut
2 slices of toast

Pour the wine into a small saucepan, preferably one with a heavy base, and place it over a medium heat. Flatten the garlic clove(s) with the flat of a knife blade and drop it, with the tarragon, into the wine. Let simmer for 5–7 minutes at quite a pace, until half has evaporated. Remove from the heat.

Break the eggs into a bowl, stir them about a bit with a fork to break them up, and then stir in the grated cheese. Season with about ¼ teaspoon of salt and several turns of the peppermill. Remove the garlic from the wine, and beat the wine into the egg mixture with a fork. Throw away the garlic and tarragon.

Tip the mixture into the saucepan that you used for reducing the wine, add the butter, and cook over a gentle heat, stirring gently with the fork. The eggs will start to set. When they are creamy and still a little liquid, tip them over the toast.

SCRAMBLED EGGS WITH POTTED SHRIMP

Potted shrimp are sold in little waxed cartons similar to the ones in which you buy ice cream at the movies in this country. The shrimp freeze well and are handy to have around. Use the butter in which they are potted to cook the eggs.

FOR 2

2 cartons of potted shrimp (6–8 ounces)	*salt*
4 eggs	*freshly ground black pepper*

Remove the butter from the top of the shrimp, reserving half and melting the other in a small heavy-based pan. Break the eggs into a small bowl, season with salt and pepper, and beat them for a few seconds with a fork.

When the butter has melted, pour in the beaten eggs and stir with a wooden spoon, scraping the bottom of the pan and bringing the outside edges to the middle.

Cook the eggs for 2 minutes, then toss in the shrimp. Remove the pan from the heat and keep stirring while the shrimp warm through in the creamy egg. If any of the egg is still liquid, then return to the heat for a minute till just set. Drop in the remaining shrimp butter to stop the eggs cooking, and tip gently onto warm, rather than hot, plates.

PARSEE SCRAMBLED EGGS

These spiced eggs are made all over India. I have been offered them for breakfast there, but chickened out. I usually prefer my morning kick-start to come from espresso rather than hot chilies. This makes an exceedingly good supper dish, though.

FOR 2 AS A PRINCIPAL DISH

2 tablespoons melted butter, oil, or clarified butter or ghee	*½ teaspoon ground cumin*
1 small onion, minced	*1 tomato, seeded and chopped*
½-inch piece of fresh ginger, peeled and minced	*4 eggs, beaten with 2 tablespoons milk*
1 fresh hot green chili, about 2 inches long, seeded and chopped	*salt*
	freshly ground black pepper
½ teaspoon ground turmeric	*1 tablespoon chopped fresh cilantro*

Melt the butter, oil, or ghee in a deep-sided frying pan and cook the onion, ginger, and chili until the onion is golden, about 5 minutes.

Add the turmeric and cumin and fry for 2 minutes. Add the tomato and cook for 2 minutes longer, then add the egg and milk mixture. Season with salt, pepper, and cilantro, and stir gently until the eggs start to set in place—probably 30 seconds or less. While the eggs are still creamy and with a tinge of runniness to them, slide them onto warm plates. Serve with toast or fried bread.

Scrambled Eggs with Cheese and Chives

Any cheese that melts well is good for this, in particular Gruyère, Emmenthal, or Edam. I have had success, though, using up scraps of assorted cheeses, grated and mixed together.

FOR 2

¾ cup grated melting cheese	*3 extra large eggs*
1½ tablespoons butter	*1 tablespoon chopped fresh chives*
salt	*3 English muffins, split and*
freshly ground black pepper	* toasted*

In a small heavy-based saucepan cook the cheese and butter with the seasonings over a low heat until the cheese has melted.

Beat the eggs with a fork, add the herbs, and pour into the cheese. Cook over a low heat, stirring constantly. The mixture will become creamy and start to thicken. Serve it with the toasted muffins.

Good Things to Add to Scrambled Eggs

► A tablespoon of juices from roasting meat or poultry

► A spoonful of mustard—a crunchy one full of seeds

► Fresh tarragon, chopped and stirred into the eggs before beating

► Green olives, pitted and chopped

► Fresh cilantro leaves and a splash of chili sauce

► A spoonful of bottled or homemade basil pesto sauce

► Shredded smoked salmon, chopped fresh dill, a generous grinding of black peppercorns, and sea salt

► Watercress, wilted in a frying pan with a drop of olive oil, and sprinkled with a drop or two of sweet rich vinegar, such as balsamic or sherry

► A handful of cooked brown or green lentils and a spoonful of chopped fresh parsley

► Dark-green Savoy cabbage, shredded very finely and steamed for 30 seconds, then dressed with a splash of olive oil

CREAMED EGGS AND ASPARAGUS

This is my variation of Jane Grigson's recipe from *English Food* for scrambled eggs with asparagus.

½ pound fresh asparagus tips
4 slices of whole wheat bread
1½–2 tablespoons butter
8 eggs

salt
freshly ground black pepper
2 tablespoons heavy cream

Cook the asparagus tips in boiling salted water. Drain and keep warm. I find the best way to do this is by wrapping them in a dish towel.

Toast the bread and butter it. Put it, buttered-side up, in a warm dish. Beat the eggs with salt and pepper and melt the butter in a small, solid saucepan. Tip the eggs into the pan and scramble them, stirring to stop the egg sticking around the edges of the pan, until soft, creamy, and still slightly liquid. Stir in the cream.

Place the asparagus tips on top of the toast and spoon over the creamed eggs. Eat immediately.

PIPÉRADE

I spent part of my wandering apprenticeship in England's West Country, with Kenneth Bell at Thornbury Castle. This dish, originally from the Basque region of France, was something he mastered when at The Elizabeth restaurant in Oxford, and it appeared from time to time on the menu at Thornbury. Diners generally came to the castle for something slightly grander, and the dish became a favorite for the staff midnight suppers.

FOR 2

2 tablespoons olive oil
2 red bell peppers, cored, seeded, and
   cut into narrow strips
2 small onions, finely sliced
2 cloves of garlic, chopped
1 cup canned plum tomatoes,
   drained, seeded, and chopped

4 extra large eggs
salt
freshly ground black pepper
fresh basil leaves
chopped fresh parsley

Heat the oil in a frying pan and add the bell peppers and onions. Cook them over a medium heat until they are tender and the onions golden, about 5–7 minutes. Add the garlic and cook a minute or two longer. Tip in the tomatoes and simmer the mixture until it thickens.

Beat the eggs, season them, and pour them into the mixture, stirring as you would for scrambled eggs. Shred the basil leaves and stir in with the chopped parsley. Serve while the eggs are creamy.

Parmesan and Anchovy Eggs

Good though this is by itself, it makes a more substantial snack on toast or toasted English muffins.

FOR 2

4 eggs
freshly ground black pepper
4 tablespoons butter
2 tablespoons grated Parmesan
  cheese

8 anchovy fillets, drained of their
  oil and chopped

Break the eggs and beat them gently with a little freshly ground pepper. Melt half the butter in a small, solid saucepan, turn down the heat, and pour in the seasoned, beaten eggs.

Stir the eggs with a wooden spoon, making sure that you get around the edges of the pan. While the eggs are still slightly liquid, remove the pan from the heat and stir in the remaining butter. Stir in the grated Parmesan and chopped anchovies. Serve immediately, on toast.

A Plain Omelet

FOR 1

3 eggs
salt
freshly ground black pepper

2 tablespoons butter, cut into
  small chunks

Break the eggs into a small bowl and add a teaspoon cold water, some salt and pepper, and half of the butter. Beat them a little with a fork.

Melt the rest of the butter in a small frying pan, or omelet pan if you have one. It will start to sizzle and then to foam; just as the butter starts to smell nutty, swoosh in the egg.

Quickly stir the egg three or four times with the fork; it will start to set on the bottom of the pan. Lift the edge of the omelet nearest the handle with the fork, tilting the pan as you do, and gently flip one half of the omelet over the other. Slide the finished omelet onto a warm plate.

COLD OMELET WITH VINAIGRETTE

If you have made and eaten an omelet, then I suggest that you make another while you are still in the mood. Keep it in the refrigerator—it will come to little harm overnight—then eat it cold, with a strong chive dressing.

FOR 1 OR 2 WITH SOME SALAD ON THE SIDE

a cold omelet, brought to room temperature
1 shallot, finely diced
1 tablespoon and 1 teaspoon red wine vinegar

4 tablespoons extra virgin olive oil
2 teaspoons chopped fresh chives
salt
freshly ground black pepper

Put the omelet on a serving plate. Mix the shallot and the vinegar in a small bowl and pour in the olive oil. Whisk gently with a fork, stir in the chives, and season with salt and pepper.

Pour the dressing over the omelet. Slice the omelet into thick diagonal strips and eat with a fork, pushing the slices around the plate to soak up the chive dressing.

Good Things to Put in an Omelet

► Wine vinegar, or better still, balsamic vinegar

► Onions fried in butter till golden and slightly caramelized, and moistened with a drop or two of wine vinegar

► Leeks, sliced into thin rounds, steamed for a few minutes, and sprinkled with chopped fresh tarragon

► Cubes of bread fried in butter, hot from the pan

► Sorrel leaves softened for a couple of minutes in butter

► Feta cheese, crumbled, mixed with fresh thyme leaves

► Fresh flat-leaf parsley, roughly chopped with a rinsed anchovy fillet, stirred into the beaten egg

► Canned artichoke hearts, drained, rinsed, sliced, and dressed with a little olive or walnut oil and lots of chopped fresh parsley

► Sun-dried tomatoes, patted dry of their oil and sliced thinly

► Goat cheese, crumbled, with a few chopped fresh thyme leaves

► Basil leaves, torn into shreds, stirred into the beaten egg

More Good Things to Put in an Omelet

► Nasturtium leaves and flowers, shredded, dressed with a squeeze of lemon juice

► Arugula, roughly chopped, wilted in a spoonful of oil over a gentle flame

► Fava beans steamed till tender and (if you have the time and patience) peeled of their papery outer skins

► Blue cheese, such as the exquisite French Fourme d'Ambert, a creamy Italian Gorgonzola, or a melting Irish Cashel Blue, sliced into soft chunks and tossed with toasted walnut halves

► Unsmoked bacon fried to a crisp and crumbled

► Or, if you know your supply and are feeling brave, quiveringly fresh raw mussels, torn straight from the shell

FRITTATA

A *frittata* is an Italian omelet. Unlike its soft and creamy French cousin, a *frittata* is cooked slowly over a very low heat. It is sautéed on both sides and cut into wedges like a cake. This is the basic recipe, flavored with grated cheese and a generous grinding of black pepper. Like the omelet, though, it can be filled with almost anything that takes your fancy.

FOR 4

6 extra large eggs	*a large handful of grated Parmesan*
salt	*and/or Gruyère cheese*
freshly ground black pepper	*4 tablespoons butter*

Beat the eggs in a bowl, with a fork, for 20 seconds or so, until just mixed. Beat the salt, pepper, and cheese into the eggs. Melt the butter in a large frying pan, at least 10 inches in diameter. When the butter starts to froth, tip in the eggs. Turn down the heat, as low as it will go. Leave the eggs to cook gently for 15 minutes, or until the underside is set. The top should still be runny.

Have the broiler preheated. Remove the eggs from the heat and put under the broiler for 1 minute to set, but not brown, the surface. Slide a metal spatula under the *frittata* to free it from the pan. Slide it onto a warm plate, cut into wedges, and serve.

CARAMELIZED ONION AND PARSLEY *FRITTATA*

A deeply savory dish, this. Let the onions cook for as long as possible, and do not worry when they blacken around the edges— it's just the natural sugar in the onions caramelizing with the heat. Suitable for lunch or supper, this dish is good warm or at room temperature.

FOR 4 AS A PRINCIPAL DISH WITH SALAD

1 pound onions, finely sliced

4 tablespoons olive oil

5 extra large eggs

*a large handful of fresh parsley,
   coarsely chopped*

½ cup grated Parmesan cheese

salt

freshly ground black pepper

1½ tablespoons butter

Put the onions in a shallow pan with the olive oil and cook over a medium to high heat, stirring occasionally, until the onions are golden and tinged with dark brown and almost blackened at the edges. This will take about 15 minutes.

Break the eggs into a bowl and beat them thoroughly with a fork. Remove the onions from their pan with a slotted spoon and stir them into the eggs. Season with the parsley, Parmesan cheese, salt, and pepper.

Heat the butter in a shallow, heavy-based pan, about 10 inches across, that does not stick. Tip in the egg, onion, and parsley mixture. Turn the heat to the lowest setting and cook until the *frittata* has set on the base but the surface is still runny, about 15 minutes.

Flash the pan under a preheated broiler to set the surface. Loosen with a metal spatula, then slide onto a warm plate. Cut into wedges and serve.

Good Things to Add to a *Frittata*

A *frittata* is cooked more slowly than other eggy things like omelets and scrambled eggs. This means that any additions to the basic mixture can be in slightly larger pieces, giving this substantial dish a certain rusticity. Fry all of the following ingredients in a little olive oil before pouring the egg mixture over them:

► Small eggplants, sliced as thick as silver dollars, seasoned with minced garlic

► Red pimientoes from a can or jar, cut into strips, sautéed until they smell sweet and have crisped slightly along their cut edges

► Zucchini, sliced, fried with a diced onion and sprinkled with chopped fresh parsley

► Diced or grated potatoes seasoned with fennel seeds

► Freshly ground curry spices or your favorite curry powder cooked in a little clarified butter till fragrant, then tossed with leftover cooked new potatoes, cut in half if large

A Plain Poached Egg

Poached eggs take about 3 minutes to cook. Use the freshest eggs to ensure that the whites hug the yolks rather than waft around in the cooking water like ghosts. Bring two eggs' depth of water to a boil in a shallow pan. Remove from the heat and gently break the eggs into the water. Cover tightly with a lid and leave for 3 minutes. Lift the lid: if the eggs are shrouded by an opaque white then they are ready. Lift out each egg gently with a perforated spatula (called the "holy spoon" in my house), then drain carefully for a second or two on a paper towel to get rid of any water. Serve while hot, on buttered toast.

Spinach with Poached Eggs and Bacon

A rather substantial salad. Use any green leaves, such as curly endive or *frisée* or soft, floppy lettuce leaves, instead of the spinach if you like. You can substitute slices of garlic sausage for the bacon, if you have some.

FOR 2

2 large handfuls of small spinach leaves, carefully washed
2 eggs
4 thick slices of bacon, cut into 1-inch long pieces
2 slices of white bread, cut into large dice

4 tablespoons virgin olive oil
4 teaspoons red wine vinegar
2 teaspoons grain mustard
salt
freshly ground black pepper

Divide the spinach leaves between two plates. Poach the eggs for 3 minutes, drain, and then put them into cold water to stop them cooking.

Fry the bacon till crisp, lift it out with a slotted spoon, and scatter it over the spinach leaves. Fry the bread cubes in the bacon fat, adding a little oil if there is not enough fat, till golden and crisp. Scatter them over the spinach.

Mix the oil, vinegar, mustard, and some salt and pepper in a small bowl. Remove the eggs from the cold water—they will still be slightly warm—and place one in the center of each plate. Pour the dressing into the hot pan (it will sizzle and spit), then drizzle it quickly over the eggs and spinach.

POACHED EGGS WITH HERBS

A lovely idea from Elizabeth David, this first appeared in her book *French Country Cooking* in 1951. Tarragon has a magical affinity with eggs, but chives are good too; snip them into ½-inch lengths.

FOR 2

4 tablespoons butter   *lemon juice*
4 poached eggs, drained
2 tablespoons chopped fresh herbs,
*   such as parsley and tarragon*

Melt the butter in a shallow pan such as an omelet or small frying pan. When the butter starts to bubble, slide in the eggs and sauté them without letting the butter burn.

Sprinkle in the herbs and squeeze over a few drops of lemon juice. Serve immediately.

FRIED EGGS

Olive oil, and the richer the better, is the only thing in which to fry eggs. Try one of the Spanish oils, which will impart some of its characteristic spiciness to the egg.

olive oil
2 extra large eggs per person

Pour a finger's depth of olive oil into a skillet and heat until you see a little smoke rise. Break each egg into a cup. Tilt the pan and slide the eggs, one at a time and no more than two in the pan together, into the hot oil.

Splash some of the hot oil over the egg with a spoon and fry it quickly until the white is set and the yolk runny. Remove carefully with a slotted spatula and eat with brown bread.

Stir-Fried Eggs

In her *Classic Chinese Cookbook,* Yan Kit So tells us that the idea of stir-frying eggs originates from Whampoa, a port near Canton. A stir-fried egg's consistency should be soft and only just set, rather like a cross between a scrambled egg and an omelet. Use a frying pan if you do not have a wok.

FOR 2 AS A SNACK OR QUICK BREAKFAST

Beat 4 eggs with a pinch of salt and a tablespoon peanut or vegetable oil until well mixed.

Heat a wok or frying pan until it starts to smoke. Add a finger's depth of peanut oil and carefully tip the pan to cover the sides of the pan with oil. Pour all but a couple of tablespoons of the oil into a heatproof container (that is, not back into the bottle).

Heat the oil until it starts to smoke. Slowly pour in the beaten egg while stirring it with a metal spatula. Drizzle over a tablespoon more of the oil, stirring and folding the egg over on itself at the same time. After 1 minute the egg will start to set in pieces. Slide the egg onto warm plates and eat while hot.

Stir-Fried Eggs with Scallions

FOR 2

4 eggs	*2 bunches of scallions, trimmed*
2 teaspoons sesame oil	*2 tablespoons vegetable oil*

Beat the eggs in a small bowl and add the sesame oil. Cut the scallions on the diagonal into small pieces. Heat a wok or frying pan until it is hot; before the pan starts to smoke, add the vegetable oil and the scallions. Cook, stirring the scallions and tossing the pan, till the green shoots start to wilt—about 30 seconds to 1 minute.

Pour in the eggs and stir-fry, moving the contents of the pan around quickly, until they start to set, about 1 minute. The texture is similar to that of a runny omelet. Slide onto a warm dish and serve immediately.

BUTTERED EGGS

A very quick dish, cooked in a matter of minutes. Use any good vinegar to sharpen the butter: ordinary red wine vinegar would be good enough, mellow sherry vinegar even better.

FOR 1

Melt 4 tablespoons butter in an omelet pan (or use a small frying pan). Break 2 eggs and slide them, without breaking the yolks, into the bubbling butter.

As soon as the whites are set, scoop the eggs out of the butter with a slotted spatula and slide onto a warm plate. Return the pan to the heat and cook over a slightly higher heat until the butter starts to brown and smell nutty. Sprinkle a few drops of vinegar into the butter and pour quickly over the eggs.

OEUFS EN COCOTTE

The simplest form of this dish uses nothing more than fresh eggs and a little butter.

Brush the inside of a china ramekin with butter. Do this with generosity. Break open a fresh, extra large egg and let the yolk and white delicately slide into the ramekin. Grind over a little black pepper and sprinkle with a very small pinch of salt.

Set the dish inside a larger one, say a gratin dish, and pour enough hot water into the large dish to come two-thirds of the way up the sides of the ramekin. Place a large pat of butter on top of the yolk and bake in a preheated 375 °F oven for 7–10 minutes. The egg is cooked when a thin, opaque film has appeared over the yolk. The texture must be soft and wobbly. Eat at once, with toast.

OEUFS EN COCOTTE—A DIFFERENT WAY

A grander version of *Oeufs en Cocotte* can be made by adding cream, asparagus, sliced mushrooms, or even truffles. Cream and Parmesan cheese are probably the best way to gild this lily.

FOR 4

½ cup heavy cream
salt
freshly ground black pepper

2 tablespoons freshly grated
Parmesan cheese
4 fresh, extra large eggs

Pour the cream into a small saucepan and warm it with a little salt and pepper. Stir in the cheese, and pour the mixture into 4 buttered china ramekins. Break an egg into each one. Set the dishes in a gratin dish and pour around enough hot water to come two-thirds of the way up the sides of the ramekins. Bake in a preheated 375 °F oven for 7–10 minutes, until the eggs are just set. Eat right away.

EGGS BAKED WITH MEAT JUICES

Now is the time to use up that container of gravy or meat juices that is lurking in the refrigerator.

FOR 2

butter, for greasing
4 extra large eggs
salt
freshly ground black pepper

¼ cup gravy or meat
cooking juices
½ cup grated well-flavored cheese

Butter 4 heatproof thick china cups. Use little ramekin dishes if you have them. Be generous with the butter.

Break an egg into each cup. Grind the peppermill over each one and sprinkle a little salt over each egg. Spoon a tablespoon of the meat juices into each cup, dribbling it over the egg yolk. Divide the grated cheese among the cups.

Set the cups in a gratin dish or roasting pan. Pour around enough boiling water to come halfway up the cups or ramekins. Place the whole thing carefully in a preheated 400 °F oven. Bake for 10–12 minutes, until the eggs are set.

CHAKCHOUKA

A classic North-African egg dish, quite substantial enough to serve for supper. This is my adaptation of Meg Jump's recipe from *Cooking with Chillies*.

FOR 2 AS A MAIN DISH

2 tablespoons olive oil
1 onion, finely sliced
4 tomatoes, chopped
1 large or 2 medium red bell peppers,
*   seeded and chopped*

1 small fresh hot green chili,
*   seeded and minced*
salt
freshly ground black pepper
4 eggs

Heat the oil in a medium frying pan, add the onion, and fry for 3 or 4 minutes, until the onion has softened. Add the tomatoes, peppers, and hot chili and season with salt and pepper. Let simmer, covered, until they soften.

After 15 minutes or so, taste the mixture and add more salt and pepper if necessary; also add a drop of water if it is sticking to the pan. When the vegetables are slushy, make 4 little hollows in which to cook the eggs. Break the eggs and slide them carefully into the hollows. Cook over a gentle heat until the eggs are just set, about 3 or 4 minutes.

I first cooked this simplified version of *Chakchouka* when I had even less time in the kitchen than usual.

FOR 2 AS A LIGHT SUPPER

Chop 6 medium tomatoes into rough pieces about as big as shelled walnuts. Cover the bottom of a small frying or omelet pan with olive oil and color a minced clove of garlic in it for a minute or so.

Before the garlic turns too brown and bitter, add the chopped tomatoes and cook for a couple of minutes. Turn up the heat to evaporate some of the liquid and concentrate the flavors, then smooth them out evenly in the pan.

Break 4 eggs carefully into the pan, in order not to break the yolks. Cook until the eggs are set, about 3 or 4 minutes. Scatter over some fresh herbs if you have them (parsley or cilantro would be nice, basil even better). Season with some coarse black pepper, and serve.

BAKED EGGS WITH TARRAGON AND GARLIC

FOR 4 AS A SNACK

⅔ *cup heavy cream*
2 *cloves of garlic, squashed flat*
   with the blade of a knife

3 *sprigs of fresh tarragon*
4 *eggs*

Pour the cream into a small pan, drop in the garlic cloves and the tarragon, and bring slowly to boiling point. Remove the pan from the heat, cover with a plate, and leave in a warm place for 10 minutes so the garlic and herbs can perfume the cream.

Butter 4 cocotte dishes or heatproof cups, break an egg into each one, and bake them for 8 minutes in a preheated 325 °F oven. Strain the cream and pour over each egg. Return to the oven to bake for 2 minutes. Eat right away.

STRACCIATELLA

Although I have eaten this simple soup in Tuscany, it is more often found in Rome. It is most important that the stock is a good one, preferably homemade.

FOR 4

4 *eggs*
¼ *cup grated Parmesan cheese*
1 *tablespoon fine semolina*

5 *cups homemade*
   chicken stock

Beat the eggs and, using a fork, whisk in the Parmesan and semolina. Pour in a teacupful of the stock and mix to a cream.

Bring the rest of the stock to a boil. When small bubbles are rising quickly to the surface, lower the heat and pour in the egg and cheese mixture. Whisk for 2 or 3 minutes, without letting the water actually boil. When the mixture starts to form little flakes in the stock—a further minute or so—it is ready. Serve immediately, with more Parmesan.

AN EGG SANDWICH

MAKES 1

2 eggs, hard-boiled but soft in the
   center
2 slices of soft white sandwich
   loaf

soft butter
salt
freshly ground black pepper

Slice the eggs thinly, using one of those steel egg slicers if you have one. Butter the bread and lay the egg slices on one slice. Sprinkle over some salt and pepper and place the second slice of bread on top. Cut in half diagonally.

A BETTER EGG SANDWICH

MAKES 1

2 eggs, hard-boiled but soft in the
   center
2 tablespoons homemade or good
   bought mayonnaise
2 slices of brown bread

a bunch of watercress, washed and
   tough stems discarded
salt
freshly ground black pepper
cayenne

Slice the eggs thinly. Spread the mayonnaise on the bread. Lay some small sprigs of watercress on one piece of the bread. Put the egg slices on top and season with salt, pepper, and a little cayenne pepper. Place the second slice of bread on top and cut in half.

Good Things to Team up with Eggs in a Sandwich

► Lettuce, the soft-leaf variety

► Spinach, small tender leaves, left whole

► Grated Cheshire or Cheddar cheese

► Mango chutney

► Lime pickle

► Chopped black olives or tapenade

► Scallions

► Cold Béarnaise sauce from a jar

► Anchovy fillets, drained, rinsed, and dried

CHAPTER THREE

FISH

F ish is the finest of all fast foods. The less time it cooks the better, the flesh having only to set rather than, like meat, to tenderize. Flatfish, such as sole and flounder, can be cooked whole or in fillets. They cook in minutes, either dusted with seasoned flour and laid in a pan of sizzling butter, or brushed with oil and broiled. For a sublime supper, serve with a salad of soft green leaves, or with green beans cooked for 4 or 5 minutes in boiling water.

Use your fish merchant. He is not there just for selling fish—part of his work is to prepare your fish for you. He will do all the horrid bits, ridding your chosen fish of the inedible, the uninteresting, and the downright disgusting. An extra three minutes in the market can save a good ten at home. If you prefer to buy your fish from the supermarket, packed in neat packages and wearing little sprigs of parsley, then do so. It is good fresh fish, but you are unlikely to be offered a great choice.

With this in mind I have stuck to a fairly catholic selection of fish here. This may seem unfair to the enterprising and passionate fish merchants who stock unusual fish and shellfish. But not really. Almost any fish you may choose can be cooked in the ways mentioned; for example, the cod recipes are perfectly suitable for hake, haddock, pollock, or tilefish. If your fancy turns to a flatfish, then flounder or turbot are covered by the sole recipes.

I have included several ideas for rather anonymous "fish steaks." There is a reason for this, which is that most cuts from the middle of common white fish cook similarly. The finished result will have a wonderfully different flavor, but the basic method remains the same. The choice is yours.

You know how to buy fish, but I will remind you. Go for bright vivid colors, sparkling eyes, and a smell that is of the sea rather than fishy. Avoid, at all costs, any specimen that is dry, limp, and sad-looking. If your fish merchant doesn't display his fish on ice, then go elsewhere, especially in summer. And remember, the biggest sin you can commit against a fish is to overcook it.

Shellfish are perhaps the highest order of fresh ingredients on the fast foodie's shopping list. I have deliberately included some and not others. Shrimp are here because they cook in seconds and are relatively easy to find, while fresh crab is not because it takes an age to prepare (not to mention the need for a hammer and a set of pliers) and the canned stuff often tastes horrid. Scallops and oysters are covered because they are genuine fast feasts, and mussels because they are such fun to cook and eat. (Accept nothing from your fish market that is not positively quivering with freshness.) Lobsters are excluded on the grounds that to be really succulent they must be bought alive and kicking and cooked at home. Most of us are too squeamish to kill one. And that includes me.

FRESH FISH

COD WITH PARSLEY SAUCE

Thick, lumpy parsley sauce was one of the many horrors that helped to put me off cod (the combination is a traditional one in the U.K.). Forget the flour and make a thinner sauce with the cooking juices from the fish, lots of vivid green parsley, and a little cream. Sharpen the sauce with a squeeze of lemon juice at the end, if you wish.

FOR 4 AS A MAIN DISH

a little butter
4 cod steaks, about 1 inch
  thick
1 cup fish or vegetable stock
a small bunch of fresh parsley

½ cup heavy cream
salt
freshly ground black pepper
squeeze of lemon juice (optional)

Rub the inside of a shallow baking dish with the butter. Put the cod steaks in the dish and pour over the stock. Bake for 8–10 minutes in a preheated 425 °F oven. Chop the parsley. Pour the stock from the fish into a shallow pan and return the fish, covered by a plate, to the switched-off oven to keep warm.

Reduce the stock over high heat to about half of its original volume. Pour in the cream, tip in the parsley, and leave to bubble over a high heat till slightly thickened, about 2 minutes.

Taste the sauce, adding salt and pepper and a squeeze of lemon juice if you want. Pour the sauce over and around the fish, and serve.

Breaded Cod

FOR 2

1½ pounds cod fillet, cut from the head end of the fish	*fresh bread crumbs*
flour	*peanut or sunflower oil and butter*
2 eggs, beaten	*lime or lemon halves*

Cut the fish into 1½–2-inch cubes. Roll them in flour, dip them in the beaten egg, and then coat them in bread crumbs.

Shallow-fry the fish in hot oil and butter till golden, turning carefully, for 10 minutes at the most. Serve with halves of lime or lemon and a few salad leaves.

Warm Cod, Parsley, and Potato Salad

Cod, potatoes, and parsley—the most basic of fish, vegetables, and herbs—make a fine *menage à trois,* this time as a warm salad. Two important points: don't overcook the potatoes, and mix the salad gently so as not to crush the juicy pieces of fish.

FOR 2 AS A MAIN COURSE

2 large or 4 medium potatoes	*freshly ground black pepper*
¾ pound cod fillet or steaks, 1 inch thick	*4 bushy stems of fresh parsley, chopped*
6 tablespoons olive oil	*1 medium yellow onion, thinly sliced*
2 tablespoons lemon juice	

Cut the potatoes into quarters or halves and cook in boiling salted water till tender to the point of a knife, about 10 minutes.

Meanwhile, put the fish in a small, shallow pan, cover it with water, and poach gently until the flesh is opaque and firm, about 5–7 minutes. Remove from the heat.

Mix the olive oil and lemon juice with the black pepper in a large serving bowl. Drain the potatoes thoroughly. Slice them into pieces as thick as silver dollars and put them in the serving bowl. The warm potatoes will soak up the dressing.

Drain the cod, peel off the skin, and break the flesh into bite-sized chunks. Toss the dressed potatoes with the chopped parsley and onion, and gently mix in the pieces of cod. Serve warm.

Baked Cod with Butter Sauce

The chemistry of white fish, butter, and wine is hard to beat, even when it is as simple as this. New potatoes, or the Waxy Potato, Anchovy, and Parsley Salad on page 176, and a leafy salad afterwards would be the best accompaniments.

SERVES 2

4 tablespoons cold butter, plus 2 tablespoons to finish
2 pieces of cod fillet, cut from the thick end, 1½ inches thick
1 wineglass of dry white wine

4 large sprigs of fresh parsley, chopped (or 6 of tarragon, or 7–8 of chervil)
salt
freshly ground black pepper

Spread a little of the butter on the inside of a shallow baking dish. Place the cod fillets in the dish and pour over the wine. Dot the rest of the butter over the fish and bake in a preheated 425 °F oven until firm and opaque, about 10–15 minutes. Baste the fish once or twice with the juices.

Remove the fish from the oven. Pour the liquid into a small shallow pan and return the fish to the switched-off oven. Reduce the cooking liquid over a high heat till it is one-third of its original quantity, about ½ cup. Whisk in the remaining butter with the fresh herbs. Whisk hard, until the sauce has slightly thickened, about 1 minute. Taste and add salt and pepper if you wish.

Remove the fish from the oven and lift onto plates with a slotted spatula. Spoon the sauce over the fish and serve.

Broiled Sole

The simplest treatment for the finest of fish.

Heat the broiler. Lay the whole sole (preferably a Dover sole) in the broiler pan and bathe it with butter—no, not oil—butter. Place it under the broiler and cook for 4 minutes per side (a minute less if you have lemon sole or other flounder), basting twice with butter from the pan. Season on each side with a little salt and pepper from the mill before and after you turn the fish.

Lift carefully using a slotted spatula, or even two, from the pan to a large, warm plate. Spoon over the buttery cooking juices, and serve with half a lemon.

Pan-Fried Sole

Ask your fish merchant to fillet a nice large fish, or buy prepacked fillets from the supermarket. Dust the fillets lightly with flour. You can season the flour with salt and pepper if you wish. Heat some butter to a depth of ¼ inch in a frying pan till hot, but not so hot that it smokes or colors. Fry the fish for 4 minutes per side (a minute less on each side if you have lemon sole or other flounder).

Remove the fillets to a warm plate. Throw some freshly chopped parsley into the pan and squeeze in the juice from half a lemon. Tip the butter mixture over the fillets, and eat while hot.

Skate with Black Butter

A quick classic.

FOR 2 AS A MAIN DISH

1 onion
salt
bay leaves
6 black peppercorns
2 medium skate wings, about
  1 pound in weight

1 teaspoon capers, rinsed of their
  brine or salt
6 tablespoons butter
1 tablespoon red wine vinegar
a little chopped fresh parsley

Put 1 quart of water on to boil in a saucepan. Slice the onion into very fine rings and toss them into the water with 1 teaspoon salt, a couple of bay leaves, and the peppercorns. When the water comes to a boil, turn down to a simmer and leave to cook for 10 minutes.

Slide the skate wings into the simmering water. Cook gently for 10 minutes, or a little longer if the fish is more than 1 inch at its thickest part. Drain the wings, keeping the cooking liquid for stock, and put them on warm plates. Scatter the capers over the fish.

Melt the butter in a small frying pan, and let it foam and darken to a nutty brown. Add the vinegar to the pan, followed by the parsley, then immediately pour the whole lot over the fish.

Sautéed Halibut Steaks

Halibut is not essential for this dish. Use any white fish steak that is about 1 or 1½ inches thick; cod, hake, or haddock will all be fine. As this dish is so quick, you have time to prepare a salad, say arugula leaves with a dribble of extra virgin oil and a grinding of black pepper.

FOR 2

flour
2 halibut steaks, about 1
   inch thick

juice of 1 lemon
oil for frying—olive would be good
lemon wedges, for serving

Put a thin layer of flour on a plate. Dip the halibut steaks into the lemon juice, then into the flour. Don't forget the other side.

Fry the fish until firm and cooked right through, about 5 minutes on each side. Serve hot with large pieces of lemon.

Fish Steaks with Lemon, Cilantro, and Cream

A rather luxurious dish, its richness cut only slightly by the cilantro and lemon. Bulb fennel, either finely shredded in mild vinaigrette or stir-fried until just tender but still crisp, works well as an accompaniment.

FOR 2

2 fish steaks, cod or halibut, about
   1 inch thick
½ cup heavy cream
juice of ½ lemon

2 tablespoons fresh cilantro
   leaves, loosely packed
salt
freshly ground black pepper

Place the fish steaks in a shallow baking dish. Mix the cream with the lemon juice and cilantro leaves, and grind over a little salt and black pepper. Pour the lemon cream over the fish steaks and cook in a preheated 400 °F oven for 12 minutes. Serve with the fennel salad described above.

FISH FILLETS WITH PARSLEY AND GARLIC

This bright-flavored sauce is slightly adapted from a chicken recipe in *Cook's Garden* by Lynda Brown. I have tried the recipe with large pieces of cod and mackerel fillets, and both worked extremely well. I prefer not to thicken the sauce, so suggest you serve it in deep-rimmed plates to hold the juices.

FOR 4, WITH TINY STEAMED POTATOES

5 large sprigs of fresh parsley
3 plump cloves of garlic, peeled
4 steaks or large fillets of white fish, about 6 ounces each

3 tablespoons grain mustard
1 wineglass of dry white wine
¼ cup heavy cream
1 teaspoon wine vinegar

Pull the leaves off the parsley, keeping the stems for stock. Mince the parsley leaves and the garlic together. Brush the fish fillets with the mustard and roll them in the parsley and garlic.

Lay the fillets in a gratin dish. Pour the wine around, but not over, them and cover with a butter wrapper, or piece of buttered foil. Bake in a preheated 400 °F oven till firm, about 10–12 minutes. Carefully remove the fish with a slotted spatula and keep warm. Boil the wine over a direct heat for 2 or 3 minutes till it has reduced by half. Pour in the cream and vinegar, boil for a minute or two, and then serve under, rather than over, the fish.

BAKED FISH STEAKS WITH TOMATO AND BREAD CRUMBS

I think this idea works best when the bread crumbs are kept coarse, almost like diminutive croûtons. If you have some fish in the freezer and a bunch of fresh parsley, this makes a quite reasonable emergency supper.

FOR 2, AS A MAIN DISH WITH SALAD

4 tablespoons butter
1 clove of garlic, chopped
1 cup chopped canned plum tomatoes
salt
freshly ground black pepper

2 fish steaks, about 6 ounces each, and 1 inch thick
2 tablespoons stale, coarse bread crumbs
2 tablespoons chopped fresh parsley

Melt the butter in a frying pan. Add the garlic and cook for 2 or 3 minutes over a medium heat until it has softened, taking care that it does not scorch. Stir in the chopped tomatoes and their juice and simmer for 5 or 6 minutes, until most of the liquid has evaporated.

Add salt and pepper. Put most of the tomato mixture in a gratin dish, lay the fish steaks on top, and cover with the bread crumbs. Bake in a preheated 400°F oven for 10 minutes. Sprinkle with the parsley and serve.

BROILED SPICED FISH STEAKS

A dish born while trying to recreate a similar dish I had eaten in India. If "fish steaks" sound a little anonymous, it is quite deliberate. Use whatever fish you have at hand; cod, tuna, swordfish, and halibut are all fine, and frozen will do. Serve with a side dish of sliced sweet tomatoes.

FOR 4

1 slightly heaped tablespoon garam
    masala
1 onion, roughly chopped
3 large cloves of garlic
1-inch piece of fresh ginger,
    peeled and grated
½ teaspoon hot chili powder
juice of 1 lime or ½ lemon

1¼ cups plain yogurt
salt
freshly ground black pepper
4 fish steaks, about ½ pound each,
    and 1 inch thick
2 tablespoons chopped fresh
    cilantro

Put the *garam masala,* onion, garlic, and ginger in the bowl of a food processor. Whizz. Add the chili powder, lime or lemon juice, and yogurt and mix slowly, on a low setting or with a spoon or spatula. Add salt and pepper to taste.

Place the fish steaks in a shallow dish and smother them with the marinade. Set aside for as long as you can, but 20 minutes will do.

Heat the broiler. Transfer the fish steaks to the broiler pan and cook for about 8 minutes, 4 inches away from the heat. Pull a little of the fish away from the bone, which is the test for doneness; if the fish resists it will need a couple of minutes longer. Eat hot, with a sprinkling of cilantro.

BROILED SALMON

Salmon is a fish rich in oil. When cooked, it needs something piquant to offset this, particularly if broiled, but less so if poached. Lively partners include salty olives, sharp sorrel, tiny green-tinged tomatoes, and peppery basil.

Your salmon steaks for broiling should be no more than 1 inch thick. They need little lubrication, having enough of their own oil. Brush each steak with a small amount of oil, olive for preference, just enough to glisten but hardly enough to be seen. Put them under a very hot, and I mean very hot, broiler. Set the broiler pan about 4 inches away from the heat.

Cook the steaks until the flesh is firm but springy. At 1 inch thick this will take barely 4 minutes a side, but test them after 3. Transfer them to a warm plate. Don't forget to scoop up the pan juices.

Good Things to Serve with Broiled Salmon

Basil Butter
Cream ½ cup (1 stick) of butter in a bowl. This is easier if the butter is at room temperature first. Chop up a little shallot and stir it into the butter. The shallot is not essential, so don't worry if you don't have one. Shred a small handful of basil leaves. Stir them into the butter with a pinch of salt and a good squeeze of lemon. Refrigerate until you need it. Drop a spoonful onto the hot salmon as you serve it.

Black Olive Butter
There are two ways to make a good olive butter. Either whizz a handful of pitted black olives, an anchovy fillet or two, and a clove of garlic in the blender till smooth, then mix in about 4 tablespoons of softened butter. Alternatively, if time or temper forbid even that, stir a spoonful of black olive paste, from a jar, into an equal amount of softened butter. Either way, serve a dollop of it, as chilled as you can get it, on the hot salmon as you serve.

Quick Cherry Tomato Sauce
Cut ½ pound cherry tomatoes in half. Scoop out the seeds and discard them, or add to a vegetable stock later. This won't take as

long as you think it will. Chop the tomato flesh and scoop it into a small bowl. Add 2 tablespoons fruity, extra virgin olive oil and a splash of white wine vinegar. If you have any fresh herbs—tarragon, basil, or cilantro—now is the time to throw a tablespoon of the chopped leaves in too. Taste the purée and add salt and white pepper if you wish, then spoon over the salmon.

Sorrel Sauce
The sharp lemon notes of sorrel are just what is needed with the salmon. Melt some butter in a small frying pan and drop in a handful of washed sorrel leaves. Stew them in the butter for 4 or 5 minutes. Stir. They will have melted into the butter. You have a sauce.

BROILED SALMON WITH WATERCRESS-CREAM SAUCE

Watercress has a pleasing peppery bitterness, which works magically with oily-fleshed fish like salmon. A green salad, perhaps of iceberg lettuce with a mustard-seed dressing, would go well with this.

FOR 4 AS A MAIN DISH

2 tablespoons butter	*2 teaspoons lemon juice*
4 salmon steaks, about 4 ounces each	*2 bunches (approximately 4 ounces) of watercress leaves and*
½ cup heavy cream	*tender stems, chopped*

Heat the broiler. Set the pan 4 inches from the heat. Put the butter in a rectangular dish large enough to hold the fish. Let it melt under the broiler. Remove the dish from the heat and place the fish in the butter, turning to coat. Broil until firm and lightly golden on top, about 4 minutes. Turn the steaks over, baste with the butter, and broil for 4 minutes. Remove and test the fish; if it comes away from the bone easily it is done.

Pour the butter into a small pan and set over a high heat. Keep the fish warm. Stir the cream, lemon juice, and chopped watercress into the butter. Let it bubble for 2 minutes. Taste it—you may like to add salt and pepper. Pour the sauce, scraping up any crusty bits from the dish, over the fish.

SALMON STEAKS WITH DILL BUTTER

As an apprentice in a restaurant kitchen I prepared this dish almost daily. In those days I had to clean and scale the fish, then cut it into steaks (everything, in fact, except actually go fishing for the thing). Nowadays, a prepacked salmon steak from the supermarket or a prepared piece of fish from the fish merchant is more my style. Beautifully moist in its foil wrapping, it is particularly suitable for those who prefer their fish without a rich sauce.

FOR 2

*2 salmon steaks, about
   1 inch at their thickest part
2 tablespoons chopped fresh dill
   fronds*

*4 tablespoons softened butter
salt
freshly ground black pepper
¼ cup dry white wine*

Lay each salmon steak on a piece of foil or parchment paper large enough to wrap up the fish. Mix together the herbs and butter and spread over the pieces of fish. Season with salt and pepper. Tip the wine over the fish and quickly close the foil to make a package. Bake in a preheated 425 °F oven for 12–15 minutes. Serve with boiled unpeeled potatoes and a green vegetable.

BAKED SALMON WITH SOUR CREAM

Sharp creams such as *crème fraîche* or sour cream enhance and lift the flavor of salmon.

FOR 2 AS A MAIN DISH

*2 salmon steaks, about 4 ounces
   each
1 small onion, minced
½ cup sour cream or
   crème fraîche*

*1 tablespoon lemon juice
2 tablespoons chopped fresh dill*

Place the salmon steaks in a small baking dish. Mix together the remaining ingredients, retaining half of the dill. Spoon the sauce over the salmon steaks. Bake in a preheated 425 °F oven for 15–18 minutes. Sprinkle with the remaining dill, and serve with a cucumber salad or sautéed zucchini.

Pan-Fried Salmon with Capers and Vinegar

Capers are the buds of the Mediterranean caper plant, picked just before they burst into flower. Whether they come packed in salt from old-fashioned Italian grocers, or in jars of brine from the supermarket, they need rinsing. An ideal accompaniment would be a mound of fresh spinach that has been cooked quickly in a pan with a little water and no butter.

FOR 2 AS A MAIN DISH

6 tablespoons butter
2 pieces of salmon fillet, about 5 ounces each

2 tablespoons capers, rinsed
1 tablespoon red or white wine vinegar

Melt half the butter in a frying pan over a medium heat. When the butter starts to froth, add the salmon pieces and fry until the fish is firm and gold-tinged, about 3 minutes on each side. Cook for 2 minutes longer if you like your fish cooked right through.

Remove the fish to a warm dish. Melt the remaining butter and add the capers. Pour in the vinegar and let it bubble away for a couple of minutes, scraping at any crusty bits on the bottom of the pan with a wooden spatula. Pour the sauce over the fish.

A Way with Raw Salmon

FOR 2 AS A SUMMER MAIN DISH

Chop ½ pound salmon fillet very finely. Do not reduce it to a pulp, though. Drop it into a bowl and pour over the juice from 2 limes. Chop a bunch of watercress, and stir it in with 2 tablespoons thick plain yogurt. It is important that the watercress, and the salmon, are very, very fresh. Serve in little mounds with a cucumber salad.

Poached Salmon

Many people make a *court bouillon* in which to cook their piece of salmon; I am not sure that poaching it in a broth of wine, cloves, herbs, and vegetables is altogether necessary. Water, with a little sea salt, is fine.

For two people you will need two pieces of salmon weighing about 6 ounces each. Bring enough water to cover the fish to a boil and salt it generously. Turn it down to a simmer—shudder would be more accurate. Slide in the fish, and cook for 3 minutes. Press the salmon with your finger; it should be firm rather than squashy and should be opaque. If not, cook it for another minute and test again. Remove the fillets with a slotted spatula and drain, briefly, on a dish towel or paper towel. Place on warm plates and serve with tiny new potatoes and whatever takes your fancy.

Good Things to Serve with Poached Salmon

► Spoonfuls of thick plain yogurt, with chopped fresh tarragon and a splash of wine vinegar stirred in

► Black olive paste from a jar

► Parsley and lemon butter: stir a generous amount of chopped fresh parsley into softened butter and sharpen with a good squeeze of lemon juice

► A verdant mustardy sauce: throw a handful of chopped fresh parsley in the blender with a small onion, minced, a teaspoonful chopped fresh tarragon, a garlic clove, 6 tablespoons olive oil, 2 tablespoons wine vinegar, and a tablespoon grain mustard. Whizz

► Bulb fennel, grated coarsely, pan-fried in a little butter and moistened with a glug from the Pernod bottle

TROUT

To cook a trout to perfection you need nothing more than some butter, half a lemon, and 10 minutes.

For two trout, which depending on their size may feed one or two people, melt enough butter in a frying pan to come ½ inch up the sides of the pan. Dust the cleaned fish with flour, though this is not essential, and when the butter has started to foam pop the trout in the pan. The heat should be medium, the butter bubbling.

Cook for about 4 minutes on each side. You cannot see the flesh, so trust your judgment and remove the fishes when each side of the skin is deep, shiny brown. Eat as it is, with lemon, or:

► Discard the cooking butter. Drop a new pat of butter, a generous one, in the pan and let it melt. It will foam. When the foam subsides, pour in the juice from the lemon. It will spit. When the butter has turned slightly brown, and smells rich and nutty, pour it over the trout and serve

► Add a large and juicy clove of garlic, flattened but not peeled, to the butter in the pan and cook it over a medium heat for a minute or two till soft, making sure it does not burn. Its purpose is to scent the butter sauce subtly. Tip in about ½ cup of heavy cream and stir while it bubbles till thick, about 2–3 minutes. Throw in some chopped fresh parsley or chervil if you have some, then pour it over the fish

► Use that expensive jar of fancy mushrooms sitting on the shelf. *Cèpes, shiitake, chanterelle,* and all manner of exotic mushrooms are sold in jars in expensive food stores, where they sit on the shelves for months on end. If you have ever bought one, or have been given one, and don't know what to do with it, then let me tell you.

Remove the trout from the pan. Add a clove or two of chopped garlic. The amount will depend on the size of the cloves. Cook them over a medium heat until soft. Drain the bottle of mushrooms, discarding the brine. It is important to rinse the fungi well in a strainer under running water. Shake them dry. Tip the mushrooms into the butter and stir around for a couple of minutes till hot and buttery. Throw in a small handful of chopped bright green, fresh parsley. Taste and add black pepper, and perhaps salt. Eat hot, with the trout

TROUT IN A FRESH HERB AND LIME CRUST

The fresh herbs and citrus juice here work together to lift the slightly dull flavor of farmed trout. Use lemons if you don't have limes, and any suitably delicate herbs.

FOR 2 AS A MAIN COURSE

4 large trout fillets, skin removed
3 limes
⅓ cup mixed chopped fresh
  herbs: parsley, tarragon, dill

2 tablespoons fresh bread crumbs
salt
2 tablespoons butter

Check that all the bones have been removed from the fish by running your fingers over the flesh, and remove any stubborn ones. Finely grate the zest from two of the limes and add to the herbs and bread crumbs. Add a little salt.

Melt the butter in a small pan and add the juice from the two grated limes. Put the herb mixture on a flat plate and press the fillets down firmly on one side. The herbs will stick to the fish. Place the fillets on a baking sheet and spoon over the lime butter.

Bake in a preheated 400 °F oven for 6 minutes. Serve with crisp green beans and the remaining lime, cut in half.

RED MULLET

The red mullet, beloved of the Romans and popular all over Europe today, is not a mullet at all, but a member of the goatfish family (goatfish are available in the U.S. only on the East Coast and Florida). Red mullet has a sweet, rich flesh and beautiful pink color. A saltwater fish, it is rarely more than 1 pound in weight.

When the fish is cleaned, the liver should be left intact (it is a delectable little morsel) and it should be left in during cooking. As red mullet is not a big fish, cook it whole, on the bone. Natural partners are olive oil, tomatoes, olives, and bulb fennel, all from the Mediterranean, though the fish is often caught during the summer months off the coast of Cornwall, in England.

Red mullet has a high ratio of bone to flesh, so if you hate struggling with fish bones, you can have the fish filleted, and reduce the cooking time by half.

RED MULLET WITH FENNEL AND PERNOD

A wonderfully light dish for a summer evening, where the fish is perfumed with bulb fennel and some Pernod. A chilled rosé, perhaps one from Provence, and some olive bread would complete the picture.

FOR 2 AS A MAIN DISH

2 red mullet, cleaned, livers intact
salt
freshly ground black pepper
2 bulbs of fennel, about 4 ounces each, trimmed

1 small onion, sliced
1 tablespoon olive oil
Pernod

Season the fish inside and out with salt and pepper. Shred the fennel finely, and sweat it with the onion in the oil in a shallow pan until it starts to soften, about 5–7 minutes. Try not to let it color as this would coarsen the flavor of the dish. Put the sweated mixture in a gratin dish to form a bed for the fish. Lay the fishes on the fennel and add a good glug from the Pernod bottle (or use Ricard if that is what you have). Bake in a preheated 350 °F oven for 20 minutes, until the fish is firm and tender.

RED MULLET WITH TOMATOES AND THYME

FOR 2 AS A MAIN DISH

2 red mullet, cleaned, livers intact
salt
freshly ground black pepper
2 bay leaves
2 sprigs of fresh thyme

olive oil
½ lemon
4 tomatoes
1 wineglass of dry white wine

Rub the fish inside and out with salt and pepper. Put a bay leaf and a sprig of thyme inside each fish, then put them in a gratin dish. Dribble over a little olive oil, remembering that this is a rich fish, and squeeze half a lemon over both fish. Bake for 7 minutes (10 for a fish weighing over ¾ pound) in a preheated 425 °F oven. Remove the dish from the oven, and add the tomatoes cut in half and the wine. Cook for a further 7 (10) minutes. Test the fish for doneness; it should be firm to the touch, and a small piece should slide easily from the bone. Spoon the pan juices over the fish as you serve. Eat with a salad of thinly sliced bulb fennel dressed with oil and lemon juice.

BROILED MACKEREL

Of all broiled fish, it is the mackerel that undergoes the most magical transformation. A small whole one takes barely 10 minutes to cook, its flesh becoming rich and sweet, taking on a smoky note from the skin as it chars. I find an earthy accompaniment, such as a plate of bulgur wheat salad or skirlie (hot fried oatmeal, see pages 192 or 198), better here than the more traditional sharp fruit sauces such as gooseberry.

FOR 1

1 mackerel, fine and plump, about
  8 inches long, cleaned

1 lemon, cut in half

Heat the broiler. Squeeze half the lemon over the fish and put it under the broiler. What you are trying to do is to cook the skin to a golden crisp while keeping the flesh sweet and juicy. Cook for about 4 minutes—5 if the fish is very plump—per side. Serve, with more lemon juice, plus the juices that have escaped into the broiler pan.

FRIED MACKEREL WITH MUSTARD AND CORIANDER SAUCE

The coriander seeds add a fruity spiciness to the mackerel, the mustard a deep warmth. Eat the fish with a plate of bitter leaves and citrus fruits: watercress and orange, Belgian endive and grapefruit, or arugula leaves with lime juice and black pepper.

FOR 2 AS A MAIN DISH

2 mackerel, cleaned
flour
butter and oil for frying
1 tablespoon coriander seeds

2 tablespoons butter
½ cup heavy cream
½ lemon
2 teaspoons mustard: Dijon or whatever

Dust the mackerel with flour. Heat a little oil and a pat of butter in a frying pan, no more than ¼ inch depth of fat. Fry the fish till it is cooked right through to the bone, about 5 minutes on each side. Remove the fish to warm plates, and keep warm.

Crush the seeds with a pestle and mortar, or in a small bowl with the end of a rolling pin. Pour off most of the fishy oil and melt the butter in the pan. Throw in the crushed coriander seeds. After a minute or maybe less they will fill the kitchen with a spicy, orangey aroma. Take care that they do not burn. When the spiced butter starts to foam lift the pan off the heat, pour in the cream, and return to the heat. When it foams again, lift the pan up from the flame, swoosh the sauce around in the pan, and put it back down again.

Let the sauce bubble for a couple of minutes, then squeeze in the juice from the lemon. Stir in the mustard. Stop cooking now or you will lose the aroma of the mustard. Spoon the sauce around the fish and serve.

MUSTARD MACKEREL

This quick and deliciously savory way with mackerel is one of my favorite recipes. It takes barely 15 minutes from start to finish. Serve with a watercress and blood orange salad.

FOR 2

2 tablespoons grain mustard
juice of ½ lemon

1 tablespoon olive oil
4 mackerel fillets (2 mackerel)

Lightly oil a shallow baking pan. Mix the mustard with the lemon juice and olive oil and spread it over the mackerel fillets. Cook in a preheated 425 °F oven until tender enough to cut with a fork, about 8–10 minutes.

Lift the sizzling fish from its pan, and serve with the aforementioned salad and whole wheat bread.

MACKEREL TERIYAKI

I was inspired to cook this particularly savory dish after a light lunch at Wakaba, a beautifully minimalist designer Japanese restaurant in London. The recipe is based on one in Joan and Peter Martin's *Japanese Cooking*. I have used the same idea, with differing degrees of success, for herring (jolly good) and salmon (less so). A few beansprouts and mushrooms, quickly stir-fried with garlic in oil over a high heat, make an interesting bed for the fish. Spoon a little of the fish marinade over the vegetables just as they finish cooking.

FOR 2 AS A MAIN DISH

4 mackerel fillets (2 mackerel)
2 tablespoons mirin (sweet rice wine) or pale, dry sherry
2 tablespoons sake (rice wine)

1 clove of garlic, minced
3 tablespoons soy sauce, shoyu for preference

Lay the mackerel in a shallow dish. Mix together all the remaining ingredients in a small saucepan and bring to a boil. Pour the hot marinade over the fish and leave for 15 minutes.

Heat the broiler. Lay the marinated fish fillets in the broiler pan and cook for barely 5 minutes on each side. Brush with some of the marinade as they cook. The fish are done when they are coated with a shiny brown glaze.

FISH STICK SANDWICH

A fish stick is a piece of fresh fish, frozen at sea, then coated in batter or crumbs. Most people seem to like them but will rarely admit to it. I suspect they think fish sticks are rather common. You may be interested to know that these useful freezer standbys were originally marketed in Britain as "crispy cod-pieces."

FOR EACH PERSON

*2 breaded fish sticks—a reputable
  brand*
*1 small baguette or ⅓ of a French
  stick*
*ready-made tartare sauce, tomato
  ketchup, or mayonnaise*

1 small dill pickle
lettuce, the soft-leaved variety
½ lemon

Broil or bake the fish sticks till crisp, turning once, taking care not to overcook them to dryness. Split the little baguette and spread with the lubricant of your choice (I suggest the tartare sauce). Chop the pickle and scatter over. Pile on a few small lettuce leaves, which you have rinsed and shaken dry. Lay the fish sticks on top of the lettuce, squirt with lemon juice, and add the other half of the bread.

SHELLFISH

MUSSELS

Mussels make surprisingly fast food. Cleaning them need not be a tedious chore if you are cooking for no more than two or three people. Choose small mussels, which have no barnacles to remove; they are usually cleaner than larger mussels. Soak them for a few minutes in cold water, scrupulously discarding any that float (miss any at your peril), and pull away their coarse beards with a little knife. A good rinse and they are ready to cook.

A mussel is cooked when its shell opens. This will take from 30 seconds to 4 minutes over a fierce flame. Obstinate mussels that refuse to open should be thrown away. One of the best seafood suppers imaginable can be made in just 10 minutes, with a bag of mussels, some dry white wine, a clove of garlic, and a few sprigs of fresh parsley. Add heavy cream and lemon juice, and you have a warming meal for eating on cold winter nights.

More adventurous quick-cooks may want to test the 30-minute time limit on the recipes by removing the mussels from the shells, frying them till crisp, and stuffing them into rolls slathered with garlicky mayonnaise, see page 88. Friends of the mussel, apart from white wine and garlic, are hard cider, tarragon, and, perhaps surprisingly, bacon.

Allow 2½ pounds of mussels between 2 diners, plus copious amounts of crusty white bread and chilled Muscadet.

MUSSELS WITH CREAM AND HERBS

Fill the sink with cold water. Tip in the mussels and leave for a couple of minutes. Scoop up any mussels that are floating on the surface, or bobbing up and down questionably. Throw them away. Pluck each mussel from the water, and pull off its fibrous beard with the help of a small knife. Scrub the shells if they are dirty (this is unlikely) and drop them into a bowl of clean cold water. Do not feed them with oats or whatever else you have been told to do with clams; mussels do not eat porridge.

FOR 2 AS A MAIN DISH, WITH PERHAPS A SALAD TO FOLLOW

2 wineglasses of dry white wine
1 fat clove of garlic, or 2 smaller
*   ones, minced*
5 or 6 black peppercorns
2½ pounds scrubbed mussels
½ cup fromage blanc

1½ tablespoons butter
2 tablespoons chopped fresh herbs:
*   parsley and tarragon or chervil*
freshly ground black pepper
an optional squeeze of lemon juice

Bring the wine to a fierce boil in a deep saucepan—one to which you can find a lid. Throw in the garlic and the peppercorns. Tip in the washed mussels. Clap on the lid and cook the mussels till they start to open—about 4 minutes at the most. Shake the pan now and again. Scoop out the mussels with a slotted spoon as they open and put them in a large bowl. Keep warm. Strain the cooking liquid back into the pan.

Boil until it is reduced by half, a matter of 2 minutes on a high heat. Add the *fromage blanc* and the butter and throw in the herbs. Check for seasoning; it may need pepper and lemon juice but salt is unlikely. Ladle into warm bowls and serve with the mussels and lots of bread, the crustier the better. Eat the mussels with your fingers, scooping up the sauce with the shells. You will need napkins, or at least paper towels.

HOT MUSSELS IN CURRY CREAM

Mussels in jars suffer from the horrid liquid in which they are bottled. The offending liquid permeates the mussel and renders it useless for almost any recipe. Except, I think, this one.

FOR 1

½ teaspoon mild curry powder
⅔ cup heavy cream
a dozen mussels from a jar,
*   drained*

1 teaspoon lemon juice
1 slice of hot toast, lightly
*   buttered*

Stir the curry powder into the cream. You may need a little whisk to do this. Simmer till it is reduced by about half. Rinse the mussels thoroughly under running water. Tip them into the curry cream sauce and warm through for a minute or two. Sharpen the flavor with the lemon juice, and serve on hot toast.

Other good things to do with Mussels

► Use hard cider, a dry one, instead of wine in the recipe on page 86

► Cut 4 thick slices of bacon, smoked or unsmoked, it matters not, into small dice. Cook in a frying pan, with a little extra fat if necessary, until crisp and golden. Cook cleaned mussels with a little white wine and garlic, as in the recipe on page 86, but without the herbs. Keep the mussels warm. Add a wineglassful of white wine and the strained cooking liquid from the mussels to the bacon and boil to reduce, then pour in ½ cup of heavy cream. Bubble till thickened, then serve with the mussels, and plenty of bread

► If you have the time and patience (a good friend will also do), cook the mussels briefly with a little white wine, then quickly remove from the heat, and remove the mussels from their shells. This is easy: just push the fat little mollusks out with your thumb. The most important point here is not to overcook the mussels, which must be removed from the heat as soon as they open. Toss the mussels in flour, which you have seasoned with salt and pepper, and shallow-fry them in very hot peanut oil till golden, plump, and crisp, a minute or so. Eat them as they are, with lemon, or stuff them into crisp rolls that you have spread with garlic mayonnaise. A feast

Scallops

Whether you buy them fresh or lift a bag from the freezer, scallops are expensive. They have a fine, delicate flavor that can easily be spoiled by overcooking. The wobbly flesh needs only to set, which takes just a couple of minutes.

Scallops are a luxurious ingredient for those short of time. The inherent richness allows you to get away with a pound among three people. If their price really is a problem, but scallops it must be, then slice them thinly and toss them with boiling potatoes for a substantial salad. Buy scallops fresh if you can, because they are often cheaper this way than frozen. Ask for the shells, if available. You will find untold uses for them, few of which will have anything to do with a scallop recipe.

Perfect partners for scallops include mundane pantry staples such as butter, bread crumbs, and lemons. Basil and garlic, and fresh cilantro and cream, are welcome too, though scallops need little to make them memorable. If you come across the tiny bay scallops, pick some up; they are wonderful when steamed for 2 minutes (no longer) and served with melted butter and lemon.

Broiled Scallops with Garlic Butter

This is cheating, I suppose, but it smells and tastes too good to matter. It is my interpretation of a dish mentioned by Alan Davidson in his book *North Atlantic Seafood,* from an idea he picked up on the pier in Boston.

Brush the broiler pan with butter, and be generous about it. Sprinkle lightly, and I mean lightly, with garlic powder. Put cleaned sea scallops on the buttered and seasoned pan and cook under the broiler for 5–6 minutes, till firm and lightly golden. Serve with all their buttery juices.

BREADED AND PAN-FRIED SCALLOPS WITH PARSLEY AND LEMON

The rich person's answer to fish sticks. A lemon and garlic butter, flecked with parsley, is as near as we get to tomato ketchup. But a tomato salad, scattered with olive oil and black pepper, would make a quick accompaniment.

FOR 2, AS A MAIN DISH WITH A SALAD OR VEGETABLES

1 clove of garlic, minced
finely grated zest of ½ lemon
3 tablespoons chopped fresh flat-leaf
  parsley
6 tablespoons butter, at room
  temperature
freshly ground black pepper

8 large, juicy sea scallops, cleaned
1 egg, beaten
fresh bread crumbs
butter and peanut oil, for
  frying
2 handfuls of mixed salad leaves

Mix the garlic, lemon zest, and parsley into the butter. Season with the black pepper. Dip the scallops in the beaten egg, then roll them in the bread crumbs.

Heat enough oil and butter to measure one finger's depth in a shallow pan. When hot, slide in the scallops and fry till the crumbs are golden and crisp, about 3 minutes on each side. Place the salad leaves on 2 plates and put the hot scallops on top. Throw the oil and butter out of the pan, add the lemon and parsley butter, and warm for 30 seconds. Spoon over the scallops and serve.

SCALLOPS AND POTATO SALAD

Cut into thin slices, scallops marinate to perfection in minutes. Orange or lemon juice will alter their texture, sometimes almost jellylike, to firm tender morsels. Served with warm new potatoes, they make a good main-course salad for a special occasion. The parsley, in this instance, plays an important part.

FOR 2 AS A MAIN-COURSE SALAD

6 large sea scallops, cleaned
6 tablespoons light oil, such as
  peanut
2 tablespoons olive or nut oil
  (hazelnut for preference)
2 tablespoons each orange and
  lemon juice, or 4 of lemon

salt
freshly ground black pepper
¾ pound waxy new potatoes
a small fistful of shelled hazelnuts
2 handfuls of assorted salad leaves
chopped fresh parsley, for garnish

Slice the scallops into large disks; you should get 4 from each scallop. Lay them in a shallow glass or china dish. Pour over them half the oils and citrus juice, seasoned with a little salt and pepper. Refrigerate for at least 25 minutes.

Boil the potatoes, scrubbed but not peeled, till tender to the point of a knife, about 15 minutes. Toast the nuts under a preheated broiler. Rub them in a cloth while still hot, to remove some of their skins. Chop them coarsely. Drain the potatoes and slice into rounds ½ inch thick. Toss them in the remaining citrus juice and oils. Taste and season. Remove the scallops from the marinade and place them, prettily if you wish, on 2 large plates. Spoon a pile of dressed potatoes in the center and spoon their dressing over the lot. Sprinkle some chopped bright green parsley and the hazelnuts over the dish and serve.

BROILED SCALLOPS WITH CILANTRO AND LIME BUTTER

Peppery cilantro and fresh lime juice lift a fresh scallop to even greater heights, if that is possible. Use plenty of butter, sweet and unsalted; it is not the time for olive oil.

FOR 2 AS A LIGHT MAIN DISH

*2 tablespoons chopped fresh
  cilantro
6 tablespoons butter, at room
  temperature*

*juice of 1 lime
10 large sea scallops, cleaned*

Mix the cilantro with the butter and the lime juice and use a third of it to spread over the broiler pan. Put the scallops about 2 inches apart in the pan. Dot with the rest of the butter and cook under the preheated broiler for 4–5 minutes, till firm. Test regularly as they easily overcook. Spoon over the buttery, herby juices from the pan and serve with a crisp *frisée* salad or bread, tiny new potatoes, or Jerusalem artichokes.

OYSTERS

You cannot have a much faster meal than a plate of freshly opened oysters. If you are a dab hand at opening them, then fine, go ahead; if not, then ask your fish merchant to do the honors. But remember that you will inevitably lose some of the precious juices in the back of the car on the way home.

You will need at least 6 oysters per person. This is not the time to practice the "less is more" philosophy. Ignore everything you have been told (and certainly what I was told at Hotel School) about hot pepper sauce, horseradish, or God forbid, tomato ketchup and chili concoctions.

You need lemon, and nothing more, to accompany your fine, and probably quite expensive, oysters. Eat them all by yourself, with some brown bread and butter, cut thin, and a glass or two of chilled dry white wine.

OYSTER PO' BOYS

Ask the fish merchant to shuck and clean the oysters for you. Persuade him to save the juices, which he may expect you to carry home in a plastic bag. The garlic mayonnaise here will raise a few purist eyebrows, but to my mind is far more suitable than the usual tartare.

FOR 1

6 oysters, the larger and fatter the better, shucked and cleaned, plus their juice
1 small baguette, or 2 crusty rolls
1 egg, beaten
fine cornmeal or fresh bread crumbs

4 tablespoons butter
1 tablespoon olive oil
good-quality garlic mayonnaise from a jar
a handful of salad leaves
¼ lemon

Strain the oyster liquid meticulously to remove any grit and shell. Split the baguette or rolls in two lengthwise and scrape out enough bread to make a hollow. Warm the bread slightly in the oven if you like. Put the egg in a shallow bowl and the cornmeal or bread crumbs on a deep plate.

Melt the butter with the oil in a shallow pan—an omelet pan is fine. Drop the oysters into the egg, and next into the cornmeal. When the butter is sizzling, slide in the oysters. They need 1 minute per side, no more.

Slather mayonnaise into the bottom of the hollowed baguette. Be generous in the extreme. Cover with a layer of salad. Fish the oysters from the hot butter with a slotted spoon and slide them on top of the leaves. Pour half of the butter out of the pan, tip in the oyster juice, and bring quickly to a boil. Squeeze lemon juice over the oysters, then pour on the bubbling buttery juices from the pan. Put on the top half of the baguette, press gently together, and eat immediately with a bottle of very cold beer.

Three more good things to do with Oysters

► Broil them: put the opened oysters, on their half shells, in a broiler pan on top of a thick layer of ceramic baking beans or rock salt, to stop them rolling over and spilling their juice. Pour enough heavy cream into the shells to come to the top, grind over a little pepper, and sprinkle with finely grated Parmesan cheese. Place under a pre-heated broiler until the edges of the oyster curl, about 2 or 3 minutes

► Sauté them: dredge the shucked oysters in seasoned flour. (You might like to add the merest touch of paprika with the salt and pepper.) Fry them in hot, sizzling butter for 2 minutes till golden. (Any longer and you might as well not bother.) Serve them as a snack with crisp baguette and lemon wedges. They are, incidentally, quite sublime in a crisp roll with lots of garlic mayonnaise

► Bake them: set the oysters, on their half shells, in lots of rock salt in an ovenproof dish. Place a piece of butter, the size of a walnut half, on each oyster and sprinkle over a tablespoon fresh white bread crumbs. Bake them in a 425 °F oven for 4 or 5 minutes, till the butter and juices are bubbling

SHRIMP

Most shrimp offered for sale in this country are frozen. Even when sold thawed they are almost certain to have been frozen. No doubt this is because they spoil within hours unless they are cooked or frozen (and even then they should not hang around). More than anything with shrimp, it is a case of you get what you pay for. Large cold-water shrimp will cost you more than smaller warm-water shrimp, but they are probably worth it, though I can think of more than a few uses for the latter. It may be worth remembering that despite the fact shrimp are rich, they are hardly filling and will need bolstering with something substantial if they are to be truly satisfying. A warm potato salad or some such starchy offering usually works well.

BROILED SHRIMP

You will need about 1½ pounds large raw shrimp for 4 people. If you are lucky enough to have a supply of these then you will know that they are best cooked simply. Flashing under a hot broiler is, I think, far superior to all the fancy sauces and preparations that abound elsewhere. I often cook them whole, as the shrimp tends to stay juicier that way.

Lay the shrimp flat on a broiler pan and cook under a preheated broiler till pink, sizzling, and opaque, about 3–4 minutes. Eat while hot, peeling back the shells with your fingers and dipping the shrimp in melted butter mixed with a generous amount of coarse salt and ground black pepper.

A dozen ways to cheer up Shrimp

Peeled raw or cooked shrimp are a very convenient standby to keep in the freezer.

► Marinate cooked peeled shrimp in plenty of lemon juice for at least 20 minutes; an hour will perk them up even more

► Leave shrimp in a mixture of olive oil, crushed garlic, salt, and pepper for 25 minutes before cooking them under a hot broiler

► Sprinkle shrimp with Pernod just before you serve them. Pernod-laced shrimp are particularly good tossed with a little olive oil and lemon juice, finely shredded bulb fennel, and thinly sliced mushrooms

► Serve them dressed with thick plain yogurt and minced watercress and tarragon

► Soak them in a marinade of peanut oil, finely grated fresh ginger, lime juice, and garlic. Drain and cook them in a hot frying pan

► Scramble them with eggs and chopped fresh cilantro

► Marinate thawed shrimp in lemon juice, a little ground turmeric, and minced garlic. Toss them in a hot pan, or bread them and deep-fry till golden, about 3–4 minutes

► Serve the shrimp with a warm dressing of crisply fried bacon and its cooking fat and balls of chilled melon. Sprinkle with fresh chives

► Marinate cooked shrimp in a mustardy vinaigrette (5 parts olive oil and 2 parts white wine vinegar, generously seasoned with smooth French mustard, minced garlic, and salt). After half an hour stir them into good-quality mayonnaise with a drop of hot pepper sauce. Serve them with bitter salad leaves and lemon

► Cook a chopped onion in butter for about 5–7 minutes, till soft and golden. Stir in a teaspoonful mild curry powder and fry for 1 minute, then slowly pour in enough water to make a thick sauce. Simmer for 10–12 minutes, until it has thickened. Stir in ⅓ cup chopped tomatoes (these can be canned and drained) and 2 handfuls of shrimp. Simmer for a further 5 minutes, then taste and correct the seasoning with salt and pepper. Serve very hot, on toast or with rice

► Put cooked shrimp, well seasoned with salt and freshly ground black pepper, between slices of hot toast spread with butter and mango chutney, and add some crisp, hot bacon

► Get out the Pernod bottle again. This time cook the shrimp in a little butter in a frying pan for 2 minutes. Add a good slug of Pernod. Stir. Lift out the shrimp with a slotted spoon and pour in about ½ cup of heavy cream. Let it bubble for 1 minute, then return the shrimp to the pan. Taste and correct the seasoning. Serve while bubbling, with rice or on toast

SMOKED FISH

When buying smoked fish choose the ones with the moistest flesh. Fish merchants who smoke their own are often the best source, as well as mail-order smokers. The workaday supermarket frequently stocks the vacuum-packed variety, whose apparent juiciness may be oil brushed on before packing.

All manner of fish are smoked: trout, kippers (which are, in fact, herrings before they are "kippered"), and, of course, salmon. But I would rather have a lightly smoked mackerel any day than some of the bright orange, shiny salmon I have eaten recently.

Look out also for smoked fish that are supple and pale in color; a kipper as stiff as a board and as brown as a coffin will be far from the juicy and subtly smoky supper you are probably hoping for. Mackerel should be silvery-blue when smoked; the visually tempting golden ones have probably been dyed.

A smoked trout or mackerel is a fine supper with little more than some bread and salad, perhaps tomato and onion, or a green salad with mustardy dressing. Kippers likewise. But a piece of lightly smoked haddock (finnan haddie) cooked in milk can be soothing after a busy day, especially when it shares a plate with a pile of smooth, mashed potatoes. Smoked salmon can sometimes fit the bill, too, but only when there is plenty of it and it is cut in thick enough slices.

BROILED KIPPERS

To keep kippers moist I use the method that Jane Grigson mentions in her book *Good Things,* and then broil them for a shorter time than usual.

FOR 2

Put the whole kippers, 1 for each person, head down, into a large pitcher and pour over enough boiling water to cover them. Leave them for 2 minutes, then remove and discard the water.

Place the kippers on the broiler pan and cook—under a preheated broiler—for 2 minutes on each side. Serve with a little butter and lots of brown bread.

KIPPER AND CUCUMBER PÂTÉ

I use the word pâté loosely here—it is actually more of a paste.

SERVES 2

2 kippers
½ small English hothouse cucumber
(about 4 ounces)
squeeze of lemon juice

1 scallion, trimmed and minced
freshly ground black pepper

Put the kippers in a large bowl. Pour over boiling water and leave for 3–4 minutes. Lift out the kippers, drain, and throw away the water.

Remove all the bones from the kippers, dropping the flesh into a bowl. Grate the unpeeled cucumber into a small bowl, squeeze it to remove some of the water, and stir it into the kipper, mashing thoroughly with a fork.

Add a squeeze or two of lemon juice and the scallion. Season with the pepper, and chill if you have time. Serve with whole wheat bread or a salad of mixed sprouted seeds.

BROILED BREADED KIPPERS

With a small bowl of salad, perhaps watercress and tomato, this makes an elegant supper for two.

FOR 2

4 kipper fillets
1 tablespoon olive oil

½ cup fresh bread crumbs
lemon, for serving

Brush the kipper fillets with the oil. Spread the bread crumbs on a plate and gently press the kipper fillets into them.

Place the breaded fillets on a broiler pan and cook under a preheated broiler for 7 minutes on each side. Serve with buttered brown bread and lemon wedges.

HOT KIPPER TOASTS

FOR 2 AS A SNACK

2 slices of hot brown toast
butter
Worcestershire sauce
2 kipper fillets, cooked and
  mashed

½ cup grated sharp cheese
2 tablespoons heavy cream

Spread the hot toast quite generously with butter and shake over a few drops of Worcestershire sauce.

Stir the kipper fillets with the cheese and the cream. Add more cream if necessary. Spoon onto the buttered toast and flash under a preheated broiler till bubbling.

SMOKED HADDOCK BROILED IN MILK

FOR 2 AS A MAIN DISH WITH MASHED POTATOES

butter   *1 cup milk*
2 large, plump smoked haddock
  fillets (finnan haddie)

Heat the broiler. Butter a dish that will withstand the heat from the broiler. Lay the fillets of smoked haddock in the buttered dish. Place it in the broiler pan, and pour in enough milk almost to cover the fish. It should just lap the edges of the haddock. Dot over a little butter.

Broil, about 4 inches from the heat, until the fish is firm and a flake will come out easily when pulled, about 6–7 minutes.

SMOKED HADDOCK WITH CREAM

Cream and smoked fish make a smashing combination. Think of smoked salmon and sour cream, or smoked trout and horse-radish cream. A light lunch or supper dish this, with perhaps a couple of large tomatoes, broiled whole in their skins, at the side.

FOR 2

¾ pound smoked haddock fillets (finnan   *freshly ground black pepper*
  haddie)   *⅓ cup fresh bread crumbs*
butter
¾ cup heavy cream

Poach the haddock for 5 minutes, just covered with barely simmering water. Drain, remove the skin, and flake the fish, removing any fine bones. Place the flaked fish in a buttered ovenproof dish. Pour over the cream, season with black pepper, and scatter over the bread crumbs. Bake in a preheated 400 °F oven for 20 minutes or so, till bubbling.

SMOKED SALMON

There is only one way to eat the best smoked salmon and that is in generous slices with buttered brown bread.

Serve it with a little lemon if you like, but ignore those who say the salmon should be carved thinly; it is at its most glorious only when served in slices as thick as a quarter, and not, I repeat not, drowned in lemon juice.

SMOKED SALMON TRIMMINGS

These can be useful for the snacker, and are often sold cheaply in delicatessens and supermarkets. Take care, though, that they are fresh; too often they are hard and of little use to anyone other than the cat.

When they are good—that is, a soft orangey-pink color and moist but not shiny—then take advantage of their cheapness and throw them into salads and plates of creamy pasta, or, best of all, into softly scrambled eggs.

FOR 1

2 pieces of butter, each the size of a walnut
2 extra large eggs, beaten with a fork
salt

freshly ground black pepper
⅓ cup shredded smoked salmon trimmings

Melt a piece of the butter in a small solid saucepan. When the butter starts to foam, add the eggs all at once, with some salt and pepper. Stir the egg with a wooden spoon, making sure to get right into the edges of the pan, otherwise the egg will stick.

While there is still a good amount of liquid egg remaining, take the pan off the heat, stir in the second piece of butter and the smoked salmon, and serve immediately.

Smoked Salmon with Warm Pasta

Heat does nothing for smoked salmon, but gentle warming with hot pasta and cold, sharp *fromage blanc* seems to bring out the flavor.

FOR 2 AS A MAIN DISH

*dried shell or tubular pasta for
  two*
1 tablespoon olive oil
*leaves from 2 sprigs of fresh
  tarragon, chopped*

4 ounces smoked salmon
1 cup fromage blanc *or sour cream*
salt
freshly ground black pepper

Put the pasta on to cook in plenty of boiling salted water, until it is tender but still *al dente*.

Place the oil in a warmed large serving bowl. Toss the chopped tarragon in the oil. Cut the smoked salmon into wide ribbons.

Remove the pasta from the heat and drain. Tip it into the serving bowl with the olive oil. Add the shredded smoked salmon and stir in the *fromage blanc* or sour cream. Season lightly with salt and pepper.

Smoked Salmon Pâté

You can make a quick pâté with salmon trimmings by mixing equal quantities of smoked salmon pieces and ricotta cheese in the food processor, squeezing in a generous amount of lemon juice, and seasoning with freshly ground black pepper. Allow 2 ounces salmon and cheese per person. Serve with fingers of hot brown toast.

SMOKED MACKEREL, HOT POTATOES, AND BITTER LEAVES

Radicchio, the deep red and white chicory, the fashionable arugula, or just plain watercress are all good leaves to use in this substantial warm salad. I think the mustard in the dressing quite important.

FOR 4

1 pound new potatoes, scrubbed
2 heads of radicchio, about the size
  of tennis balls
½ pound smoked mackerel,
  skinned and filleted

a wineglassful of salad dressing,
  preferably one made with a
  milder olive oil and a good dollop
  of seed mustard

Boil the potatoes until tender, about 15–20 minutes. Peel the leaves of the radicchio away from each other, wash them if you think it important (I do not), and shred them into manageable-sized pieces.

Break the mackerel into large chunks, though probably no larger than you would like to put into your mouth, and put it into the dressing.

Drain the potatoes and cut each one in half so that the dressing can soak into the flesh. Warm the dressing and mackerel in a shallow pan over a gentle heat (don't let it boil), then add the potatoes while they are still warm. Throw in the radicchio leaves and move everything gently around the pan for about 2 minutes, without breaking up the fish or the potatoes. Divide among 4 warm plates and eat with some good bread.

CANNED FISH

A can of sardines has saved my life many times when I've come home without having shopped, or in need of something savory and comforting and very, very fast. Sardines can almost better than anything. They are, in fact, one of the few foods that actually improve in the can. Posh sardine shippers even declare vintages, like those in wine.

I have no doubt that French sardines, canned in fruity golden oil, have the best flavor. They also rarely crumble when you lift them from their oil. The more popular, and a darned sight cheaper, Portuguese numbers are a different "k of f" altogether. But they are not to be despised just because they are cheap and the oil is less than interesting; they can still provide a perfectly decent supper when broiled or jazzed up with a little mustard. The French ones are good enough to eat alone for supper with hunks of bread and perhaps a glass of wine.

Tuna, smoked oysters, and mussels can be useful pantry hoards, too. First, they must be rid of their packing liquid, which is almost invariably horrid. Drain tuna gently of its brine, but put mussels and oysters in a strainer and rinse under running water. They will need a bit of help if they are to be really good to eat, such as a dressing of some sort, and perhaps a little lemon juice or mustard.

ANCHOVIES ON BREAD

A very good picnic snack, this open sandwich tastes better eaten outdoors—but, then, doesn't almost everything? It is worth remembering that something like this stands or falls by the crustiness of the bread and the flavor of the tomato.

FOR 2

2 slices from a fresh brown or
   white loaf
your best olive oil
wine vinegar
freshly ground black pepper

a 2-ounce can anchovy fillets,
   drained of their oil
2 tomatoes
16 black olives, pitted

Place the slices of bread flat on the bread board. Drizzle over a little olive oil and a few drops of vinegar; the bread should be juicy rather than drenched.

Season with a little black pepper. Divide the anchovy fillets among the bread, laying a few on each slice. Slice the tomatoes, lay them on the bread, and scatter over the olives.

ANCHOÏADE

A classic garlicky, fishy paste made in minutes from pantry ingredients. If you have a few capers and some black olives, scatter them over the toasts as they emerge from the broiler.

FOR 2

a 2-ounce can anchovy fillets,
   drained of their oil
2 cloves of garlic, chopped

2 tablespoons olive oil
1 teaspoon white wine vinegar
10 thin slices of French bread

Rinse the anchovies, pat them dry, and pound them in a mortar or bowl with the end of a rolling pin till reduced to a thick paste. Blend in the garlic. Add the oil, gradually, pounding all the time. Stir in the vinegar.

Toast the bread lightly on one side under the broiler. Spread the *anchoïade* on the untoasted side and broil for 2 or 3 minutes. Serve immediately.

See also Scrambled Eggs, page 46.

ANCHOVY MAYONNAISE

Mash 4 rinsed and dried anchovies with the blade of a knife; it will take a matter of seconds. Stir them into 1 cup homemade or good-quality bought mayonnaise. Add a hefty squeeze of lemon juice and a grinding of pepper, white if you have it.

Use this as an instant dressing for vegetables that have been cooked briefly in boiling salted water, such as green beans, broccoli, or tiny new potatoes.

ANCHOVY IDEA

Fry slices of white bread in olive oil till crisp. Lay 3 rinsed and dried anchovy fillets on each one and put on hot plates. Spoon a dollop of thick, cold, plain yogurt on top and serve.

SARDINE AND SMOKED OYSTER SAVORY

Another snack made almost entirely with things from the pantry.

FOR 2

a 3½-ounce can smoked oysters	*1½ tablespoons butter*
a 4-ounce can sardines in olive oil, drained	*lemon juice*
	cayenne pepper
	2 slices of whole wheat toast

Drain the smoked oysters of their nasty oil. Rinse, pat dry, and put them in a small bowl. Roughly flake the sardines. Add the butter, a drop of lemon juice, and a generous pinch of cayenne pepper. Spread the mixture on toast and cook under a preheated broiler till bubbling, a couple of minutes.

SARDINE BUTTER

Drain the oil from a can of sardines and tip the sardines into a small bowl. Mash them, using a fork, with an equal quantity of butter, preferably at room temperature. Squeeze in a little lemon juice and season with salt and freshly ground black pepper.

Good things to do with Sardine Butter

► Spread the sardine butter on hot toast

► Spoon it into a split baked potato

► Spread the butter on toast and scatter over a handful of grated Cheddar cheese

► Stir a double portion of it into a dish of cooked, drained pasta for two

► Eat in a sandwich, spread generously, with slices of peeled cucumber dressed with lemon juice, white pepper, and chopped fresh tarragon

Sardine Sandwiches

► Mash up a large can of drained sardines and add a teaspoon lemon juice. Mince half a small English hothouse cucumber and add to the sardines

► Make a sardine butter by mashing a large can of drained sardines with 1½–2 tablespoons butter. Add some chopped fresh parsley if you have some. Use this mixture to spread on the bread, preferably wholegrain, and fill the sandwiches with watercress and thin slices of tomato

► Mash the contents of a large can of sardines, drained, with a fork. Mix it with roughly an equal quantity of sour cream and spread it on dark bread

► Sardine-paste sandwiches are terribly good. Mash a large can of drained sardines, removing any large bones, to a paste. Add a drop of anchovy paste if you have some, and 2 tablespoons butter. Squeeze in the juice of ½ lemon and add a minced scallion. Stir the mixture well, and spread it on crusty French bread

SARDINES WITH BUTTER SAUCE

An idea inspired by Ambrose Heath, one of the most prolific British food writers of the 1940s and 1950s. He produced practical little books with titles such as *Good Food from Tinned Food* and *What's Left in the Larder.*

FOR 2

4 slices of bread, cut into fingers
6 tablespoons butter
2 4-ounce cans sardines in
  olive oil
2 egg yolks

½ teaspoon English mustard
1 teaspoon tarragon vinegar
salt
freshly ground black pepper

Fry the fingers of bread in 4 tablespoons of the butter until golden. Drain the sardines and place them on the fingers of fried bread in an ovenproof dish.

Place them in a preheated 425°F oven. While they are heating through, mix together the egg yolks, mustard, remaining butter, and vinegar. Add a little salt and pepper and heat through in a small saucepan until the mixture starts to thicken. Coat the sardines with the sauce and serve hot.

MUSTARD SARDINES

A pantry snack if ever there was one.

FOR 1 AS A SNACK

a 4-ounce can sardines in
  olive oil
2 tablespoons grain mustard

lemon wedges, for serving

Drain the sardines of their oil, pat them dry with a paper towel, and put them in a shallow heatproof dish. Brush them with the mustard and cook them under the broiler for 1–2 minutes, until they sizzle. Serve them with lemon wedges and thick pieces of brown bread, and eat them while they are still very hot.

Curried Sardines with Mango Chutney

I know this sounds distinctly dodgy, but it is an interesting way of approaching yet another can of sardines. I first came across the idea in Goa, where, of course, they used fresh fish.

FOR 2 AS A SNACK

a 4-ounce can sardines in
  olive oil
1 teaspoon curry powder

1 tablespoon lemon juice
mango chutney

Carefully lift the sardines from the can with the help of a flexible knife. Discard the oil. Slide the fishes onto a broiler pan, preferably lined with foil to cut down on the dish washing.

Stir the curry powder into the lemon juice. Spoon it all over the sardines, then flash them under a preheated broiler until they start to sizzle, barely 1 minute. If you overcook them they will taste horrid. Serve them with brown bread and a dollop of mango chutney.

Herring Roe on Toast

Nancy Shaw's slim volume *Food for the Greedy,* has given me many ideas in hungry moments. This is my version of her lovely dish, to which I always add some chopped fresh parsley if I have some, but only if it is very fresh and green and has lots of flavor.

FOR 2

4 tablespoons butter
a 4-ounce can herring roe,
  drained
salt

freshly ground black pepper
¼ cup heavy cream
1 tablespoon chopped fresh parsley
4 slices of hot buttered toast

Melt the butter in a small saucepan. Put in the herring roe and stir around with some salt and pepper, mashing them against the side of the pan, for 3 or 4 minutes.

Stir in the cream and the parsley, and spoon the mixture over the hot buttered toast. Serve immediately.

PASTA WITH TUNA, CAPERS, AND CREAM

Use whichever pasta you happen to have around for this. Serve some freshly grated Parmesan cheese separately.

FOR 4

*4 ounces dried shell or tubular
   pasta*
2 cloves of garlic, minced
*a small handful of fresh parsley,
   chopped*
1 tablespoon capers, rinsed

½ cup heavy cream
*a 7-ounce can line-caught
   tuna, drained*
salt
freshly ground black pepper

Cook the pasta in boiling salted water until it is tender but still has some bite to it.

Put all the remaining ingredients in a serving bowl and mash roughly with a fork. Drain the pasta and tip it into the other ingredients. Stir it around and serve.

CANNED SALMON BAKE

Canned bears little resemblance to fresh. That said, it has its uses. It is quite good here, baked with tomato juice and bread crumbs.

FOR 2 AS A MAIN DISH

*a 13-ounce can salmon,
   drained, or cooked flaked
   salmon*
½ lemon
*whites of 4 scallions, trimmed
   and minced*
salt

freshly ground black pepper
*½ cup tomato juice from a
   can or bottle*
⅓ cup coarse fresh bread crumbs
*2 tablespoons cold butter, cut into tiny
   dice*

Put the salmon into a small gratin dish. Flake the salmon a little with a fork, but don't mash it. Squeeze the lemon juice over and stir in the scallions and some salt and pepper. Spoon the tomato juice over the top.

Mix the bread crumbs and the butter and scatter over the salmon. Bake in a preheated 400 °F oven for 25 minutes. It is ready when the crumbs are golden brown and the fish is bubbling.

SALADE NIÇOISE

Salade Niçoise is one of those wretched dishes that never seems to taste quite the same as it does in the South of France, when eaten at lunchtime on the beach. I think this has more to do with sea air than the ingredients, though it may be true to say that the tomatoes will have had more sunshine, and that makes a great deal of difference. Some green beans, blanched for a couple of minutes in boiling water, then cooled under running water and drained, make a rather good addition to this substantial snack.

FOR 4

a handful of leaves from the heart of a crisp lettuce
6 ripe tomatoes
3 hard-boiled eggs, cut into quarters

2 7-ounce cans line-caught tuna, drained and roughly flaked
6 anchovy fillets, drained of their oil
16 black olives

FOR THE DRESSING:

4 tablespoons virgin olive oil
1 tablespoon wine vinegar
1 clove of garlic, minced
2 tablespoons chopped fresh parsley

1 teaspoon capers, rinsed
salt
freshly ground black pepper

Divide the lettuce leaves among 4 bowls. Cut the tomatoes into quarters and add them to the lettuce. Add the eggs and the roughly flaked tuna. Mix together the dressing ingredients and pour over the salad, tossing the ingredients gently in the dressing. Lay the anchovy fillets over the top of each salad and scatter over the olives.

CANNED TUNA FOR SUPPER

Tuna from a can can make a fine supper. Open a small can and remove the fish to a bowl. Scatter over a few capers, rinsed of their nasty vinegar, and a couple of chopped anchovies if you have them. Stir. Pile the fish onto lumps of crisp French bread to which you have generously applied some thick bought or homemade mayonnaise.

TUNA WITH CANNELLINI BEANS, TOMATO, AND CHILI

There are times when recipes like this, made entirely from pantry items, are a godsend. It is quite good as it stands, but will benefit from any fresh herbs you may have around, especially parsley or oregano. It is particularly useful as a sauce for pasta, and can also be topped with cheese and baked till melted and golden.

ENOUGH FOR 4 AS A MAIN DISH

2 tablespoons olive oil
1 medium onion, sliced
2 large cloves of garlic
1 fresh medium-hot chili, halved, seeds removed, and minced
a 16-ounce can plum tomatoes, chopped

a 16-ounce can cannellini beans, drained and well rinsed
a 7-ounce can line-caught tuna, drained and coarsely flaked
2 tablespoons chopped fresh herbs, such as parsley and oregano
salt
freshly ground black pepper

Heat the oil in a saucepan. Add the onion and let it soften over a medium heat, about 5 minutes.

Add the garlic and the chili and stir into the onion. Cook for a further 5 minutes, or until the onion is quite translucent and the chili is soft. Tip in the tomatoes and their juice, the beans, tuna, and herbs. Cook until the beans are heated through. Season generously with black pepper and salt. Serve hot.

TUNA SANDWICH

I love this sandwich. Even in the depths of winter it can remind me of summer. The ingredients are based on the classic *Pan Bagna,* or bathed bread, where the bread is stuffed with a *salade niçoise* mixture and then pressed by a weight so that the olive oil dressing soaks into the bread. We don't have time for all that, so here is a speeded-up version, and hardly the worse for it.

FOR 2 AS A RATHER SUBSTANTIAL SNACK

a round, flat loaf or French
    baguette
½ cup virgin olive oil
4 tablespoons wine vinegar
salt
freshly ground black pepper
1 clove of garlic, minced
2 large tomatoes, thinly sliced

1 medium sweet onion, thinly sliced
1 red bell pepper, cored, seeded, and cut
    into strips
12 anchovy fillets, washed and
    patted dry
12 black olives, pitted
½ 7-ounce can line-caught tuna,
    drained and roughly crumbled

Slice the loaf in half horizontally. Sprinkle the oil, vinegar, salt, pepper, and garlic on the cut sides.

Arrange the tomatoes, onion, bell pepper, anchovies, olives, and tuna on one half of the loaf. Place the other half on top. Wrap the bread well in plastic wrap and press gently but firmly with your hands. This will spread the dressing through the bread. Unwrap and enjoy.

A PIQUANT SAUCE FOR CANNED TUNA

FOR 2 AS A MAIN DISH

2 tablespoons smooth French
    mustard
1¼ cups olive oil
4 tablespoons wine or tarragon
    vinegar
2 tablespoons minced fresh
    parsley
2 tablespoons minced fresh
    chives
2 tablespoons minced fresh
    tarragon or chervil

1 small pickled gherkin or cornichon,
    minced
⅓ cup heavy cream
½ small English hothouse cucumber, cut into
    small dice
½ small head iceberg lettuce
a 7-ounce can line-caught tuna,
    drained and coarsely flaked

Whizz the first 8 ingredients in a food processor or blender for a few seconds. Stir in the diced cucumber. On a large plate make a bed of the lettuce and tip the tuna in the center. Cover with the sauce.

PASTA

The British have finally embraced pasta. Its soft, comforting form fits in with our love of bland, warming food, like oatmeal, bread sauce, and rice pudding. Pasta's cheapness and convenience appeals to our rumored disapproval of spending money or time on food.

Good-quality dried pasta, made with durum wheat flour, cooks in about 9–11 minutes. Fresh pasta cooks in 2 or 3, depending on its thickness. The best sauces will cook in the time it takes the pasta to cook. What could be better news to those who long for sustaining food—fast? It is worth remembering that different shapes take different times to cook. Noodles are about the quickest, while some of the complicated shapes, especially those made from whole wheat flour, can take up to 20 minutes.

You need lots of water to cook pasta. And a generous amount of salt. Allow 4½ quarts of water to a pound of pasta and ½ teaspoon salt per quart.

Cook the pasta in a covered pan to bring it back to a boil quickly. Pasta is cooked when it is *al dente,* that is, tender but with a bite to it. The only real way to tell is to test it; the pasta should be firm to the bite without any taste of flour. Ignore those who tell you to put oil in the water to stop the pasta sticking together. It certainly works, but it also stops any sauce sticking to it as well.

I eat pasta several times a week. Rarely spaghetti, which I am convinced is the Italians' idea of a practical joke, or those little butterflies, *farfalle,* which go floppy at the tips by the time the knot in the middle is cooked. I find the most useful shapes are those that have good sauce-holding properties. *Conchiglie* holds sauces well in its shell shape as does the nib-shaped *penne.*

Whole wheat noodles are deeply satisfying. Matched with earthy ingredients, like parsley, spicy sausage, garlic, mustard, or mushrooms, they take on a robustness that I find pleasing during cold weather. In summer I need little excuse to make fresh pesto with basil leaves and pine nuts; simple it may be, but what can beat lightly cooked *fettuccine* with warm pesto sauce? Cold pasta is rarely good. I prefer to toss warm noodles in cold sauces, such as an impromptu one of cottage cheese and any fresh herbs, perhaps marjoram, that I have on hand.

► Many delicatessens and markets keep a supply of homemade sauces and pastes. Black olive paste, subtle and addictive artichoke paste, and tomato and garlic rich *Napoletana* sauce can be brought home with a bundle of fresh pasta. You have a meal in 5 minutes

► Parmesan cheese is the accepted accompaniment for most pastas. Forget the ready-grated stuff in cartons. You might as well scatter sawdust instead. Go for a block and grate it as you need it. If you are desperate for time or a decent grater, then ask the grocer to do it for you in his machine. Really fresh Parmesan and a little butter is all you need to make good pasta sing

► Commercial soft cheeses, the ones sold in pleated foil packages and which reek of garlic, make a wonderfully fragrant sauce when cut into chunks and thrown into hot pasta

► A great favorite of mine are the stuffed pastas sold in Italian grocers: pumpkin, available in the autumn and winter, and ricotta and spinach are the best buys. The meat filling of *tortellini* can sometimes resemble cat food. Butter, softened rather than melted, is a straightforward lubricant, while grated cheese can be added for those who like it rich

PASTA WITH YOGURT AND HERBS

A dish for summer eating with a sauce that can be made in the time it takes to cook the pasta. Use as few or as many herbs as you like, and alter the combination to suit what you have. Fresh chervil, parsley, and tarragon are good together, as are parsley and basil or mint and watercress.

Tip a tub of thick plain yogurt into a heatproof bowl. Set the bowl over a pan of simmering water. Stir in a loosely packed cup of chopped fresh herbs. Season with 4 or 5 twists of the peppermill and heat until the yogurt is just warmed through.

Cook enough pasta for two in boiling salted water till *al dente*. Any shape of pasta will do. Drain and return it to the pan, off the heat. Stir in the warm yogurt and herb sauce, scooping out the dish with a rubber spatula.

PASTA WITH WHOLE GARLIC, GOAT CHEESE, AND THYME

When garlic is cooked whole, the cloves lightly crushed, at a low temperature for a long time, it takes on a deep, sweet flavor. Its fragrance is warm and soft and makes this a dish truly for all the senses.

You will need fresh thyme too; no, not dried, fresh. A little bunch from the supermarket or garden will be enough. The garlic takes about 25 minutes to cook, so don't attempt it if you have only 10.

FOR 2 AS A MAIN DISH

a large head of garlic, the cloves
  plump and pink
4 tablespoons extra virgin olive oil
about 6 healthy sprigs of thyme

6 ounces dried pasta
6 ounces crumbly white goat
  cheese

Separate the garlic cloves. Crush each one lightly by pressing down hard with the flat of a knife blade or the heel of your hand, which will loosen the skins. Pop the cloves out of their papery skins.

Pour the oil into a small pan and add the garlic. Cook over a gentle heat for 20–25 minutes, until the cloves are tender, golden, and sweet. They must not burn or they will turn horribly bitter.

Strip the thyme leaves from their branches and add them to the garlic, 15 minutes after it has started cooking. Cook the pasta in boiling salted water until it is *al dente,* drain, and toss gently with the olive oil, garlic cloves, and thyme. Crumble the goat cheese and stir in.

PASTA WITH BROILED TOMATOES AND ONIONS

Broiling the tomatoes and onions gives the sauce a wonderful, caramelized flavor. But there is nothing subtle about this dish. It is one I value on cold autumn evenings when I am in search of sweet, robust flavors and something that will stand up to a bottle of cheap red wine.

SERVES 2

5 large tomatoes, very ripe
1 tablespoon fresh thyme leaves, chopped
salt
freshly ground black pepper
olive oil
10 ounces dried pasta

2 medium onions, sliced into rounds about ¼ inch thick
2 cloves of garlic, minced
Parmesan cheese, for serving

Slice the tomatoes in half and scoop out the seeds. Put them, skin-side up, in an ovenproof dish in the broiler pan. Sprinkle them with half the thyme and a little black pepper and drizzle over some olive oil. Put under a preheated broiler and cook until the skins blacken and smell sweet—about 4–6 minutes.

Cook the pasta in boiling salted water until it is *al dente*. Remove the tomatoes from the ovenproof dish and place the onion slices, drizzled with olive oil and the rest of the thyme, under the broiler. Turn them once as they cook. They should be soft and browned at the edges—about 6–7 minutes. Chop the tomatoes roughly, charred skins and all, and throw them in a pan with the broiled onions, their oil, and the garlic. The easiest way to chop the tomatoes is to use a knife and fork or to whizz them briefly in the blender. Simmer for 2 minutes.

Season with salt and some more black pepper. Drain the pasta and stir in the tomato, onion, and oil. Be generous with the Parmesan.

FUSILLI WITH OLIVES, ANCHOVIES, AND CAPERS

A pantry supper with a Mediterranean flavor, as good cold as it is hot. If you don't have any corkscrew-shaped *fusilli,* then quill-like *penne* or almost any tubular pasta is just as good.

FOR 2

⅓ cup pitted black olives
4 anchovy fillets, rinsed and dried
1 tablespoon capers, rinsed
3 tablespoons olive oil
2 sun-dried tomatoes packed in oil,
    finely sliced
1 pound fresh or 4 ounces dried
    pasta
freshly grated Parmesan cheese

Chop the olives and anchovies, but not to a purée, then add the capers. Warm the oil in a shallow pan and stir in all the ingredients except the pasta and Parmesan. Let the ingredients warm through gently, but do not let them bubble (if the capers become too hot they tend to overpower everything else).

Cook the pasta in boiling salted water until it is *al dente.* Drain and tip into a warm serving bowl. Pour over the heated olive sauce. Stir gently and serve, with Parmesan.

WHOLE WHEAT PASTA WITH SAUSAGES, MUSTARD, AND CARAMELIZED ONIONS

A marvelously robust dish to come home to on a winter's night. Any whole wheat (or any other for that matter) pasta is fine, though *fettuccine* is my favorite. It is very good with a glass of beer.

FOR 2

6 ounces fresh spicy link sausage
3 tablespoons olive oil
2 large onions, cut into thin rings
½ pound whole wheat pasta
⅔ cup chicken or vegetable
   stock

2 tablespoons chopped fresh
   parsley
1 tablespoon grain mustard
salt
freshly ground black pepper

Slice the sausage into thick rounds. Fry it in the oil for 4 minutes, then add the onion rings. Continue cooking, covered, until the onions start to soften, adding a drop more oil if necessary.

Bring a large pan of water to a boil, add a little salt, and throw in the pasta. Cook until it is firm but tender.

After about 15–20 minutes, when the onions are golden and caramelized and are ever-so-slightly burned at the edges, add the stock. Bring to a boil, scrape up the good things stuck to the pan with a wooden spatula, and stir in the chopped parsley and the grain mustard. Add the cooked, drained pasta and season with salt and pepper. Serve hot.

COLD PASTA WITH TOMATOES AND SCALLIONS

The sharp vinaigrette and cherry tomatoes, of the fork-dodging variety, lift cold leftover pasta into a bright-tasting, quickly-put-together snack. Be generous with the herbs—basil is not essential but the parsley certainly is. No matter if your leftover pasta has a little of last night's sauce clinging to it; just put it in a colander and rinse it under lots of cold running water.

FOR 2

1 pound leftover cooked pasta	*4 tablespoons olive oil*
6 scallions, trimmed and	*salt*
chopped	*freshly ground black pepper*
¾ pound cherry tomatoes	*fresh parsley and basil*
2 tablespoons wine vinegar	

Rinse the pasta in cold running water to separate the pieces and remove any remaining sauce.

Chop the scallions and place them in a serving dish with the cherry tomatoes. Mix together the wine vinegar, olive oil, and some salt and pepper with a fork and pour this dressing over the tomatoes and scallions.

Drain the pasta thoroughly and tip into the serving dish. Chop as much parsley and shred as many basil leaves as you can spare and add to the pasta. Toss together the ingredients, and eat cold.

NOODLES WITH BUTTER AND GREEN PEPPERCORNS

For this you will need a small jar of those soft, green Madagascan peppercorns that you can buy in smart specialty food stores. Incidentally, the brine they are stored in takes up enough of their flavor to render it a spicy addition to salad dressings and sauces. Just remember to go easy on the salt. Serve as an accompaniment to broiled poultry or meat.

FOR 4 AS AN ACCOMPANIMENT

½ pound thin noodles	*2 tablespoons bottled green*
4 tablespoons butter	*peppercorns*

Cook the noodles in boiling salted water until firm but tender. This will probably take 2 or 3 minutes once the water has returned to a boil.

Soften the butter in a small pan over a medium heat until it has almost melted. Chop the peppercorns roughly and add to the butter. You can leave them whole, but they are the devil to get onto your fork.

Drain the noodles and add to the butter, tossing them so that the noodles are coated in butter and peppercorns.

FRIED NOODLES WITH BEANSPROUTS AND BROCCOLI

I like the contrasting textures of the soft noodles and crisp broccoli in this dish. Sometimes I use sugar-snap peas, or even asparagus, instead.

FOR 2

4 ounces Chinese or Japanese noodles
4 tablespoons vegetable oil
1 medium onion, diced
a small piece of fresh ginger, peeled and chopped
4 cloves of garlic, minced
6 ounces broccoli, broken into large florets (about 2 cups)

2 handfuls of beansprouts (about 5 ounces)
4 scallions, trimmed and sliced
3 tablespoons dark soy sauce, plus more for serving

Cook the noodles in boiling salted water (for about 2 or 3 minutes) until they are just tender. Drain and toss them in half the vegetable oil. In the remaining oil, fry the onion, ginger, and garlic for about 2–3 minutes, until they start to soften. Add the broccoli and stir-fry for a couple of minutes, then tip in the noodles. Toss in the beansprouts and stir-fry, keeping the ingredients in the pan moving, for 3 minutes. Add the scallions, soy sauce, and some salt and pepper and stir-fry for another minute. Serve hot.

A Spicy Sauce in which to Toss Noodles

I once shared a kitchen briefly with a young Chinese cook. When it was discovered that he was working illegally, he disappeared into thin air. His legacy was this instant and exceptionally garlicky sauce, for which I never had the chance to thank him.

FOR 4 AS A MAIN DISH

⅓ cup sesame paste
5 tablespoons light soy sauce
2 tablespoons dry sherry
1 tablespoon wine vinegar

1½ tablespoons sesame oil
4 cloves of garlic, minced
hot noodles for 4, cooked and
  drained

Put all the ingredients except the noodles in a food processor or blender with 4 tablespoons water. Whizz. Pour into a pan and bring slowly to a boil. Pour into a large serving bowl. Add the drained noodles and toss. Serve with a crisp salad, perhaps beansprout, bell pepper, and banana dressed with lots of lemon juice.

Blue Cheese Pasta

Any dried pasta is suitable for this dish. I use a soft blue cheese, such as Gorgonzola, Dolcelatte, or that rather delicious hybrid with layers of Dolcelatte and Mascarpone, sold in specialty cheese stores.

FOR 2

½ pound dried pasta
6 ounces soft blue cheese, such as
  Gorgonzola

4 tablespoons butter, cut into small
  pieces
freshly ground black pepper

Cook the pasta in boiling salted water until it is *al dente*. Meanwhile, mash together the cheese and butter in a large warm serving bowl.

When the pasta is cooked, drain it and toss with the cheese and butter in the bowl. Give the pasta one or two grinds of the peppermill, and serve.

FETTUCCINE WITH CREAM AND PARMESAN

FOR 2

10 ounces fettuccine
1 cup heavy cream
4 tablespoons butter

¾ cup freshly grated Parmesan
  cheese
freshly ground black pepper

Cook the *fettuccine* in boiling salted water until it is *al dente*.

Pour the cream into a saucepan, add the butter, and bring slowly to a boil. Reduce the heat and leave the sauce to simmer gently for 2 minutes. Stir in the Parmesan and several grinds of black pepper. Pour the sauce over the *fettuccine* and toss to coat.

PAPPARDELLE WITH OLIVE PASTE AND GRUYÈRE

Pappardelle is my favorite of the flat noodles. It is wider than *fettuccine* or *tagliatelle,* and sadly more difficult to find. You can, of course, use any ribbon pasta for this, and any cheese.

FOR 2 AS A MAIN DISH

½ pound dried pappardelle
1 tablespoon olive oil
⅓ cup black olive paste

1 tablespoon pine nuts
¾ cup finely grated cheese

Cook the *pappardelle* for 6 minutes in boiling salted water. Drain. Pour the oil into a medium gratin dish and add the drained noodles. Toss the noodles in the olive oil and the olive paste. Cover with the pine nuts and the grated cheese. Bake in a preheated 400 °F oven for 15–20 minutes, until the cheese has turned crispy, the dish is singing, and the pasta on top is slightly crisp with the underneath moist and fragrant.

DOLCELATTE *GNOCCHI*

I think *gnocchi* from a vacuum pack is rather good. It isn't as light as homemade, but on a cold winter's night I am often thankful for a plate of rib-sticking creamy, cheesy dumplings. Buy the pasta and the cheese from the deli counter and serve with a refreshing salad, such as watercress and grapefruit.

FOR 2, GENEROUSLY, AS A MAIN DISH

1 pound vacuum-packed
  gnocchi
7 ounces Dolcelatte cheese

⅔ cup heavy cream
salt
freshly ground black pepper

Cook the *gnocchi* in boiling salted water. It is done when the dumplings rise to the surface. Scoop them out with a slotted spoon and put them into a shallow gratin dish.

Cut the cheese into chunks and add, with the cream, to the *gnocchi*. Season with black pepper. Bake in a preheated 400 °F oven for 15 minutes, or until bubbling.

WHOLE WHEAT SPAGHETTI WITH ANCHOVY AND GARLIC

I love whole wheat pasta. It is so comforting, earthy, and rich. I use it with other robust ingredients that it will stand up to, such as the anchovies, garlic, and parsley here.

FOR 4

4 anchovy fillets, rinsed and dried
10 ounces whole wheat spaghetti
6 tablespoons olive oil
3 cloves of garlic, chopped

6 large sprigs of fresh flat-leaf
  parsley, chopped
freshly ground black pepper

Mince the anchovies. Put the pasta into a large pan of boiling salted water and cook until firm but tender. Pour the oil into a saucepan, add the garlic, and heat very gently for about 1 or 2 minutes, until the garlic sizzles. If the garlic becomes black and burned the dish will be ruined. When the garlic starts to turn golden and has softened, add the anchovies and the parsley. Immediately remove the pan from the heat. Drain the pasta and add it to the anchovy and parsley mixture. Season with a little black pepper, toss thoroughly, and serve hot.

SPAGHETTI WITH HERBS AND TOASTED CRUMBS

I often snip tender herbs, such as chervil and tarragon, over a bowl of cooked pasta. I include toasted bread crumbs if there is some bread that needs using up.

FOR 4

*2 large handfuls of fresh
  bread crumbs*
3 tablespoons olive oil
*¾ cup snipped
  fresh herbs: parsley, chervil,
  tarragon, and basil*

*4 scallions, trimmed and
  chopped, or 2 small shallots,
  chopped*
½ pound dried spaghetti
freshly ground black pepper

In a shallow pan fry the crumbs in 1 tablespoon of the olive oil until golden and crisp, stirring regularly so that they do not burn. Put to one side.

In a warm serving bowl, combine the chopped herbs, the scallions or shallots, and the remaining olive oil.

Cook the pasta in boiling salted water until it is *al dente,* then drain it and mix it with the herbs and olive oil. Mix well and grind some black pepper, quite coarsely, over the pasta. Scatter over the bread crumbs and serve warm.

PASTA WITH HOT BUTTER AND HERBS

A lovely buttery sauce for pasta. Most fresh herbs work well, including dill, flat-leaf parsley, tarragon, and chervil. If you fancy cilantro pasta, you will only need 1 tablespoonful.

FOR 2

½ pound dried pasta
1 cup (2 sticks) unsalted butter
1 small onion, minced

2 tablespoons chopped fresh herbs
2 tablespoons chopped parsley
juice of ½ lemon

Cook the pasta in boiling salted water. Melt the butter in a saucepan. Add the onion and your chosen fresh herbs, but not the parsley, and cook over a gentle heat for about 5–7 minutes, until the onion has softened. When the pasta is tender but still firm, drain and tip it into a large warm serving dish. Throw the parsley into the butter sauce, squeeze in the lemon juice, and pour over the cooked pasta.

EVEN FASTER PASTA

These sauces, although that is too grand a word for them, are instant additions for pasta that you have brought home from the market. Fresh pasta cooked for 3 or 4 minutes and a spoonful or two from the list below is literally a meal in minutes.

Crème d'olive, Black Olive Paste

Kalamata olives from Greece are very finely chopped and mixed with olive oil to make a savory paste. It is available from specialty food stores and some supermarkets. Warm it gently in a small pan and toss it with cooked, drained pasta.

Carciofini sott'olio, Artichokes in Oil

Of all the good things that come in jars, baby globe artichokes must be among my favorites. So tiny and tender, they can be eaten whole, choke and all. Preserved in olive oil, they are often sold loose in Italian grocers. Cut each one in half and add them to hot spinach or egg pasta.

Some specialty food stores carry jars of artichoke paste. A wonderful addition to the pantry, this soft green paste has a gently addictive flavor. Stir it straight from the jar into cooked pasta. Throw in an olive or two if you have some.

Frozen Spinach

Although I find frozen spinach useful, I avoid buying it in blocks. Those dark green bricks take ages to thaw, and if you try to speed up the process, by leaving it in a saucepan over a low heat, the outside overcooks while the middle remains frozen. Far better are the bags of loose frozen leaves.

Thaw them in seconds in a shallow pan over a gentle heat. Add a chopped anchovy fillet or two and some thick plain yogurt and warm, without boiling, for a couple of minutes. Stir in the drained pasta.

Pomodori Secchi, Sun-Dried Tomatoes in Oil

Tomatoes that have been dried in the sun, usually in Italy, have a deep, concentrated tomato flavor, with salty and smoky overtones. They come in three forms: dried, bottled in olive oil, and as a purée or cream. Whichever way you buy them, they are far from cheap, but to my mind worth every penny.

Those with little time will find the oil-preserved ones a better bet than the loose, slightly cheaper dried ones. A couple of oil-packed tomatoes, thinly sliced, will brighten up a bowl of whole wheat macaroni like nothing else. Don't throw the oil away. It is full of flavor. Drizzle some over the pasta as you toss it, throwing in a few fresh basil leaves if you have some.

Creamed dried-tomato is an expensive little delicacy. Made from crushed dried tomatoes and olive oil, it needs nothing more than a pan of steaming, *al dente* tubular pasta to show its worth.

Cottage Cheese

Don't heat cottage cheese for pasta. Cold, straight from the refrigerator, it makes a nice contrast to ribbons of hot pasta. Add a handful of chopped fresh herbs or a blob of crunchy grain mustard. The one with tarragon in it is good.

Olive Oil

I often lubricate pasta with nothing more than a glug or two from a bottle of olive oil. But if supper is going to be that simple, then both the pasta and the oil must be very, very good. Wide ribbons of, say, *pappardelle,* from a good pasta-maker, and thick, deep green, extra virgin olive oil, preferably estate-bottled at that, is the minimum.

Nut Oils

The deep flavor of walnut and hazelnut oil is achieved by pressing the nuts after they have been roasted. Pour any nut oil over hot pasta and toss gently to release the wonderful rich fragrance as the pasta warms the oil. Scatter over a handful of nuts, preferably toasted quickly first.

Sesame Oil

A bowl of hot noodles, a drop or two of toasted sesame oil, and a pinch of dried hot pepper flakes make a supper hard to beat.

Butter, Ice-Cold

I find paper-thin slices of butter, cold and hard from the refrigerator, rather fine with hot pasta ribbons. To be really good the butter must be extremely fresh, very sweet, and *unsalted*.

Butter, Melted and Nut Brown

By melted I mean softened. Leave unsalted butter in a warm place, such as at the back of the stove, for a few minutes and it will become soft but not liquid.

Best of all, I think, is to cook butter until the solids in it start to turn brown. This gives the butter a fragrant, nutty quality. Slowly melt the butter in a heavy-based pan over a low heat. Foam will rise to the surface. Skim this off with a spoon. Pour the golden liquid off the white milky sediment. Discard the sediment and return the liquid to the pan. Heat gently until it turns a light golden brown. When it smells nutty and sweet, pour it over the cooked pasta.

Chili Paste

A hot and spicy paste from southern Italy. Most commercial chili purées also have garlic, tomatoes, and bell peppers added to them. Try stirring chili paste into a carton of heavy cream, a spoonful at a time—keep tasting—then warming it over a low heat before tossing it with steaming noodles.

Bottled Pimientos

Turn on the broiler. Drain the pimientos of their bottling juice and lay them flat on a chopping board. Slice them into long, thin strips. Put on the broiler pan and drizzle over the merest amount of olive oil. When they start to sizzle and have browned appetizingly at the edges, lending a wonderful sweetness, tip them, with their juices, into a bowl of cooked pasta. Add a little more olive oil, and a few shredded fresh basil leaves. Toss in a handful of black olives if you have them. Sublime.

VEGETABLES
and SALADS

O f all my food shopping, it is poking around the vegetable stalls that I enjoy most. My diet contains a vast amount of vegetables, and there is almost none I do not enjoy—although, for the record, I am not very fond of yams, snow peas, or cooked carrots.

Crisp white fennel, huge flat mushrooms, and rude green asparagus I find hard to resist, knowing that they need little or no time in which to cook in order to taste wonderful. Fat purple eggplants and bright red bell peppers need only olive oil and heat to change miraculously from the bland and hard to the sweet and tender. Potatoes, too, fascinate me, with their earthy smell and comforting, homey quality.

The vegetable and salads chapter of this book is particularly large, though far from comprehensive. Peppers are broiled, eggplants are fried, and avocados come dressed with bacon and seedy mustard. Potatoes are sautéed with olive oil, mashed with butter and herbs, or served, nutty and new, with spoonfuls of *crème fraîche*. Given all the quick ways of preparing the vegetable family, it is not difficult to eat the recommended 14 ounces per day in order to keep us healthy.

There is probably more choice in our greengrocers and supermarkets than ever before. The major chains work hard at bringing us year-round summer vegetables, and up to a point I am grateful to them, but what can match the excitement of finding the first local asparagus or the first green peas of the season, and rushing them home for a quick feast? But it is difficult to resist the year-round green beans and lush spinach imported from hotter climates, though their flavor rarely reaches the heights of freshly picked local produce. And, what beats grabbing a clutch of greens from the grocers on the way home for an instant stir-fry supper?

There has been much talk about organically grown vegetables lately, that is, vegetables produced without the excessive use of chemicals. I am lucky enough to have a reasonably good supply of organically grown vegetables locally, and big cities now have thriving organic markets, but supplies elsewhere are hardly abundant. Even so, there is usually a fair selection at the wholefood markets and many farmers' markets, though the message is proving more difficult to get through to the supermarkets. When vegetable shopping, the organic section is my first stop, though short supply inevitably means a further rummage through the rest of the display.

I find the best way to store salad stuffs and green vegetables is in damp newspaper in the refrigerator, not necessarily in the euphemistically named "salad crisper." A little and often seems the best way to buy if freshness is your aim, and I am sure that it is. Generally speaking, the softer the leaf then the shorter time it will stay in peak condition. Corn salad, or *mâche,* and baby spinach leaves are notoriously difficult to store. My favorite leaf, arugula or *roquette,* with its pungent aromatic bitterness, is all fine and dandy when I know I can devour it right away, but there is much to be said for having a crunchy cut-and-come-again iceberg lettuce in the refrigerator, too.

EGGPLANTS

The eggplant is more evident nowadays in our cooking. This is no doubt due to our embracing of the food, if sadly not the way of life, of the Mediterranean. No longer do I have to trek to Indian or Cypriot shops for the versatile vegetable; it is here in my local market, in all its shining purple glory.

I think of the eggplant as the beefsteak of the vegetable world. Sliced and brushed with oil it grills or broils aromatically, and tastes even better. For all its connections with Middle-Eastern cooking, *imam bayildi*—stuffed eggplants—and mousaka, it is actually from Asia proper, the fat purple-black variety being just one of many. The reason for its name was made obvious once I had seen the white, almost oval varieties now imported.

I am not convinced of the need to put eggplants through the ritual salting that many cooks say is obligatory to rid them of bitterness. It is rare I come across a bitter one. Perhaps it is necessary with the enormous examples, which, like monster squash, I never buy.

Eggplants are heavy drinkers. Allow a generous amount of oil, which must be of the best quality, when you are grilling them. They will soak up extra virgin olive oil greedily, and store it in their tender flesh, so that they taste even better.

GRILLED EGGPLANT WITH CHICK PEA PURÉE AND *HARISSA*

FOR 2 AS A LIGHT LUNCH OR SUPPER WITH SALAD

a 16-ounce can chick peas,
   drained
a sprig of fresh thyme, plus 1
   tablespoon chopped leaves
1 large potato (about ½ pound),
   peeled and diced
3 large cloves of garlic, halved
salt

1 large eggplant, weighing about
   10 ounces
⅔ cup virgin olive oil
4 tablespoons butter
2 tablespoons plain yogurt
harissa *sauce*
1 lemon

Tip the chick peas into a pan and cover them with water or vegetable stock. Throw in the thyme sprig and bring to a boil. Add the diced potato, 2 of the garlic cloves, and salt and simmer for 15 minutes.

Meanwhile, slice the eggplant into 12 rounds about ½ inch thick. Chop the 2 remaining garlic cloves and add to the oil with the thyme leaves. Brush the eggplant with the thyme and garlic oil and cook on a hot ridged grill pan or under the broiler for 7–8 minutes, brushing with more oil as necessary and turning once. They are ready when tender and golden brown. Remove the thyme sprig from the chick peas, drain them, and mash with a potato masher. Stir in the butter and yogurt. Season with salt.

Put 6 of the hot grilled eggplant slices on a warm serving dish and place a generous spoonful of chick pea purée on each. Spread the remaining slices with a thin layer of *harissa,* then place on top of the others to form 6 eggplant and chick pea sandwiches. Serve 3 to each person, with an extra dollop of chick pea purée in the center. Cut the lemon in half and squeeze the juice over as you eat.

BROILED EGGPLANT WITH LEMON, BASIL, AND CRACKED CORIANDER

Whole coriander seed, lightly crushed as you need it, is quite different from the ready-ground spice. Release the ribbed spice's subtle orange scent by cracking the seeds with the end of a rolling pin in a small bowl, or by grinding briefly with a pestle and mortar. The idea is to crack the spice, rather than to pulverize it. It is rare to come across an eggplant dish without garlic, but this recipe brings out the full flavor of the eggplant.

FOR 2 AS A SIDE DISH

*1 large eggplant, weighing about
  ½ pound*
extra virgin olive oil, about ¼ cup
*½ teaspoon coriander seeds, lightly
  crushed*

2 teaspoons lemon juice
*1 tablespoon shredded fresh basil
  leaves*
salt

Slice the eggplant lengthwise about ¼ inch thick. You will get about 6 slices. Brush each slice generously with olive oil. Scatter over half the cracked coriander seeds and cook under a preheated broiler, turning once. They will need approximately 6 minutes on the first side and 4 on the second. Scatter over the remaining coriander seeds as you turn the slices. The object is to get the outside crisp while keeping the inside meltingly tender and slightly charred at the edges.

Mix the lemon juice and basil with a little salt, drizzle over the eggplant slices, and serve warm.

PESTO EGGPLANT

This is my approximation of a dish cooked by Simon Hopkinson at his London restaurant, Bibendum. Set in the magnificent Michelin Building, it is one of my favorite places for lunch, with food that I would describe as a professional version of Mother's cooking.

FOR 2 AS A MAIN DISH

2 large eggplants, not too plump, weighing about ½ pound
3 cloves of garlic, peeled
2 handfuls of fresh basil leaves, about ½ ounce

2 tablespoons pine nuts
2 tablespoons freshly grated Parmesan cheese
4 tablespoons olive oil, plus about ½ cup for frying

Cut the eggplants in half lengthwise. Cut slits into the eggplant flesh in a lattice fashion, without piercing the skin. This will allow the eggplant to cook right through quite quickly. Heat a finger's depth of olive oil in a shallow pan, slide in the eggplant halves, skin-side up, and cook till golden and tender, about 10 minutes. Turn the eggplants over and cook for 2 minutes more.

Meanwhile, whizz the garlic, basil, pine nuts, Parmesan, and 4 tablespoons of olive oil in the food processor or blender.

Lift out the eggplants. Put them flesh-side up in a broiler pan. Spread with the pesto and cook under the broiler, about 3 inches from the heat, until the pesto just starts to bubble. Overcooking will turn it bitter. Serve with a lightly dressed salad of corn salad (*mâche*) or spinach.

AVOCADOS

The less you do to an avocado the better. Ignore anyone who tells you that it tastes good when puréed and set with gelatin into a dinky little mousse. Avocados demand gentle treatment: perhaps a dash of lemon juice, some crisp bacon, or a dribble of olive, or better still walnut, oil. Or at a push they can be broiled with a covering of nutty cheese.

There are several varieties of this pear-shaped fruit. My favorite is the small Hass avocado, recognizable by its dark knobbly skin, hence its other name, the alligator pear. I find its greeny-yellow flesh has the richest flavor. I also find it the easiest to peel.

To test an avocado for ripeness squeeze the stem end very gently; if it yields slightly then it is ready. It is unusual to find an avocado ripe, and still in good condition, in the store. I buy them unripe and put them in a brown paper bag to ripen. Once sliced they should be eaten as soon as possible, though a squeeze of lemon or lime will hold off the inevitable discoloration for an hour or two.

SPROUTED SALAD WITH AVOCADO DRESSING

FOR 2 AS A SNACK

1 ripe avocado	*1 cup sprouted wheat*
1 cup thick plain yogurt	*½ pound Caerphilly or Monterey Jack*
freshly ground black pepper	*cheese*
1 cup sprouted mung beans	*a bunch of watercress*

Mash the peeled avocado with a fork in a small bowl until it is smooth. Stir in the yogurt, then grind over a little black pepper and mix thoroughly. In a salad bowl toss together the sprouts. Crumble the cheese into rough pieces and add to the bowl. Spoon over the avocado dressing and fold in gently.

Wash the watercress, cutting off any coarse stems. Scatter the watercress on 2 plates and spoon the cheese and sprout salad on top. Serve with whole wheat bread.

AVOCADO SANDWICH

Avocados are rich and filling, and make a much more satisfying snack than you might imagine. This is the sort of sandwich I make for myself at lunchtime when I am working at home. I usually use whole wheat bread, though on the occasion when there was some walnut bread in the house this particular sandwich scaled new heights.

FOR 1 AS A SNACK

2 slices of whole wheat bread
1 ripe avocado, preferably Hass
1 tablespoon wine vinegar
2 tablespoons olive oil or 1 each
  olive and nut oil

salt
1 small onion, sliced into thin
  rings

Toast the bread. Cut the avocado in half, peel it, and remove the pit. Cut the flesh into thick slices. Mix the wine vinegar with the oil or oils and add the salt.

Place the slices of avocado on the bread and add the onion rings. Spoon over the dressing.

AVOCADO WITH WARM BACON VINAIGRETTE

Small, hard-skinned Hass avocados are perfect for this. The bacon is not essential to the dish, but I find its affinity with avocado quite irresistible.

FOR 2 AS A SNACK OR FIRST COURSE

2 thick slices of bacon
2 tomatoes, peeled, if you have
  time, and diced
3 tablespoons red wine vinegar

4 tablespoons olive oil
2 tablespoons Dijon mustard
2 ripe avocados, preferably Hass

Cut the bacon into 1-inch pieces and fry in a shallow pan till crisp. Pour off excess fat. Throw in the tomatoes, the vinegar, and the olive oil. Stir in the mustard and leave to bubble for 1 minute.

Halve, pit, and peel the avocados. Place two halves on each plate and slice into thick wedges. Pour over the bubbling dressing, and serve hot.

GUACAMOLE

This is a basic *guacamole*. Try adding chopped scallions, fresh cilantro leaves, a peeled chopped tomato, and a minced clove of garlic. I often eat it with bread rather than the traditional tortilla chips, but it is also good when scooped up in generous quantities by hot and crisp pita.

MAKES 1¼ CUPS

2 large ripe avocados
½ small onion, minced
1 or 2 small fresh hot green chilies,
   minced

juice of 1 lime
salt

Halve the avocados, remove the pits, and peel away the skins. In a bowl, mash the green flesh with a fork. Stir in the onion, chilies, and lime juice and season with a little salt.

ANOTHER GUACAMOLE

Great debate exists over whether this avocado dip should be smooth and creamy or roughly diced. I think they are both excellent. I use this one if my avocado is on the firm side. It is particularly good with sweet red onions.

FOR 2

1 ripe avocado
2 medium tomatoes
1 clove of garlic, minced
2 fresh hot chilies, seeds
   removed, finely diced

juice of ½ lemon
1 tablespoon olive oil
1 tablespoon chopped fresh cilantro
salt
freshly ground black pepper

Halve and pit the avocado and peel away the skin. Place the avocado on a board and chop it into small dice, then scrape it into a bowl.

Put the tomatoes in boiling water, count to 20, remove them, and peel away the skins. (Depending on the ripeness of the tomatoes it may take another try.) Cut in half, remove the seeds with your fingers, then dice the flesh and add to the bowl.

Mix in the garlic, chilies, lemon juice, and olive oil and season with the cilantro, salt, and pepper. Chill for a few minutes, longer if you can, for the flavors to amalgamate.

BEANS AND PEAS

I could not have had a more convincing introduction to green beans. As a child I was sent to pick string beans from the local farm. Weaving my way in and out of the lush leaves and scarlet flowers is probably my happiest memory, together with the smell of the broken raw beans. Boiled when truly fresh, just till they lose their opaqueness, and eaten hot and crisp without their usual smothering of butter, is my favorite way with this green bean.

Fava beans stir some sort of passion in most people, with the majority firmly shunning them. Perhaps those who dislike them so positively have never eaten them peeled of their papery skins. I have great affection for their flavor and smell and their fat fur-lined pods. I like them every way, but never fail to enjoy the flat fetus-shaped pulse with piquant goat cheese or peeled and beaten to a buttery mush. Great things can come of their pairing with ham.

I prefer green peas before they meet hot water or the freezer. Try them freshly shelled with a sharp sheep cheese (try them on the same fork as Harbourne or Beenleigh Blue cheese), tossed with a green salad, or cooked in olive oil and stirred into warm green lentils. Sugar-snaps, the peas where the pod and peas are both edible, can be fun, but nothing can persuade me to eat snow peas. Like the miniature ears of corn with which they too often share a plate, they have no flavor. I have a theory that they are popular only because they are as convenient as frozen peas and as sweet as sugar.

Green Beans, Poached Eggs, and Fancy Leaves

Perhaps my dislike of the tiny green bean, sometimes called French or *haricot* beans, comes from working in restaurants in the late 1970s, when it was *the* ubiquitous vegetable, and having to trim hundreds of the things each night. That said, I do still pick up a handful of them occasionally for a crisp addition to a plate of salad.

Cook some green beans, trimmed, in boiling water for 3 or 4 minutes. Fish one out to see if it is ready: it should be bright green and very crisp but must be cooked through. If not, leave them for another minute or two. Drain in a colander and rinse under the tap for a few seconds, not to cool them but just to arrest their cooking.

Toss a few handfuls of fancy salad leaves, such as one of those mixtures from the supermarket, in a little olive oil and lemon juice. Divide among individual plates. Place a handful of the crisp, blanched green beans over them and top with a nice, soft, poached egg.

Fava Beans with Bacon

This is fast food, but should you have some time on your hands then I suggest that removing the papery skins from the fava beans is time well spent. A dish to eat with a bottle of beer.

FOR 2 AS A MAIN DISH

1 pound shelled fresh fava beans or frozen lima beans (about 3 cups)	4 ounces Canadian bacon, diced salt
1 tablespoon olive oil	freshly ground black pepper

Drop the beans into a pan of boiling salted water and blanch for no more than 3 minutes if frozen, 10 if fresh.

Warm the olive oil in a frying pan and fry the diced bacon until it starts to crisp at the edges. Drain the beans and add them to the bacon with a light grinding of pepper. Stir well and then cover with a lid. Taste the beans with some of the bacon to see if you need to add salt; you probably will not. Cook for 5 minutes, until the beans are absolutely tender.

FAVA BEANS AND GOAT CHEESE

Fava beans and goat cheese are an extraordinarily good combination. It was Claudia Roden who first brought them to my attention in her book, *The Food of Italy.* Ms. Roden adds the shelled beans to chopped onion fried in olive oil, then simmers the two with water until very tender. Finally, they are drained and served with goat cheese warmed under the broiler.

I have also cooked the beans in boiling water till tender, then drained and placed them in a shallow gratin dish. Then I covered them thoroughly with slices of cheese cut from a goat-cheese log and popped them under the broiler until the cheese had just melted. Eaten with crisp French bread it made a delightful lunch.

Very soft goat cheese can be stirred into a bowl of freshly cooked and still hot fava or lima beans as a side dish for a plate of thinly sliced ham, such as Italian Parma, Spanish *serrano,* or Westphalian.

Possibly best of all is a simple lunch dish for eating outside in the early summer sunshine. Catch the beans when they are very young and tender. Place them on the table, in their furry pods, alongside a small whole goat cheese in perfect condition. Let everybody shell their own beans, eating them as they go, with slices from the cheese washed down with a bottle of cold, dry white wine.

Good ways to cook Green Beans

► Green beans can be boiled or steamed and tossed with hot new potatoes, butter, and lots of chopped fresh parsley. A fine accompaniment to a plate of cold roast beef or a broiled sole

► If your green beans are past their best, try cooking them in vegetable stock spiked with fresh hot chilies. Trim the beans. Cook a chopped scallion in vegetable oil till it wilts, then add the beans and a chopped small hot chili. Pour in enough vegetable stock, from powder or cube if necessary, just to cover the beans. Simmer uncovered for 6 or 7 minutes, then drain and serve

▶ Green beans make a good substitute for the yard-long beans found in Asian greengrocers. If you have a few basic Chinese ingredients in the house you can make this savory salad very quickly.

For 1 pound beans, rinse a tablespoon Chinese black beans thoroughly, then pat dry. Chop them roughly with a large knife, then fry in 2 tablespoons bland-tasting oil such as peanut or vegetable for about a minute. Add a small piece of peeled fresh ginger, grated or finely shredded, and stir-fry for a further minute, taking care not to burn the beans. Remove from the heat and stir well with a tablespoon vegetable oil, a tablespoon vinegar (wine or rice if you have it), and half a tablespoon sesame oil. Blanch the trimmed green beans in boiling salted water, then drain and dress with the black bean and ginger dressing. Enough for 4 as a side dish

PEAS WITH *FETTUCCINE,* BASIL, AND PUMPKIN SEEDS

Pumpkin seeds are not essential here; sunflower seeds or pine nuts are just as good. I have a jar of pumpkin seeds in the kitchen that I constantly pick at, and they often get added to food that will benefit from something nutty and crunchy, such as pasta. Use mint instead of the basil if you like, and use another shaped pasta if you have no *fettuccine.* Be resourceful.

FOR 2 AS A MAIN DISH

⅓ cup pumpkin seeds
fresh fettuccine *for two*
1½ cups shelled green peas, fresh or
  frozen
4 tablespoons olive oil

1 clove of garlic, minced
8–10 fresh basil leaves, torn to
  shreds
salt
freshly ground black pepper

Scatter the pumpkin seeds on a baking sheet and cook under a preheated broiler until lightly brown and fragrant. Cook the pasta, uncovered, in boiling salted water till tender.

Put the green peas and oil in a small pan, add the garlic and the basil, season with a little salt and pepper, and cook over a gentle heat for 10 minutes, or 7 if using frozen peas.

Drain the pasta and toss in a large bowl with the hot peas and their olive oil, and the toasted pumpkin seeds.

PEAS COOKED IN BUTTER WITH FRESH GARLIC

New season's garlic, which is fresh and mild with a soft fragrance, is perfect with peas. Use older cloves if that is what you have, although the dish will lose some of its subtlety.

FOR 4 AS AN ACCOMPANIMENT

3 cloves of garlic, the fresher the better
6 tablespoons butter
1 pound shelled green peas, fresh or frozen (3 cups)

a small bunch of fresh parsley, chopped
6 tablespoons vegetable stock or water
salt

Peel the garlic and slice each clove very thinly. Melt the butter in a medium saucepan and tip in the garlic. Cook over a gentle heat until the garlic has perfumed the butter, about 5–7 minutes. On no account should the garlic color.

Add the peas, a drop or two of water, and the parsley. Pour in the stock or water, add a little salt, and cover with a lid. Simmer fresh peas for 15 minutes and frozen for 6 or 7. Serve alongside broiled fish or meat, with rice or pasta, or, best of all, with mashed potato to soak up the buttery, garlicky juices.

ARTICHOKE HEARTS AND PEAS

A hot vegetable dish for serving as an accompaniment or perhaps as a first course. A fresh herb, such as tarragon, basil, or mint, would be an interesting addition, but it is quite good as it is.

FOR 4 AS A SIDE DISH OR FIRST COURSE

2 tablespoons olive oil
4 ounces button mushrooms, the smaller the better
1½ cups shelled green peas, fresh or frozen

juice of 1 lemon
salt
freshly ground black pepper
8 artichoke hearts, canned, bottled, or frozen, drained

Put the oil into a medium saucepan and warm slowly over a medium heat. Add the mushrooms, the peas, and the lemon juice. Season with salt and pepper. Simmer for 10 minutes (6 or 7 if the peas are frozen), covered with a lid.

Cut the artichokes into quarters. Add them to the pan and cook for 3 or 4 minutes, until the artichokes are heated through.

WARM PEA AND LENTIL SALAD

The marvelous thing about this light, warm salad is the sharp contrast of flavors and textures: the nutty lentils with the fresh green peas, the earthy pulses, and the sharpness of the lime. Small lentils, such as the French *de Puy*, need no soaking and cook surprisingly quickly.

FOR 4 AS AN ACCOMPANIMENT, OR 2 AS A LIGHT LUNCH WITH CHEESE AND FRUIT TO FOLLOW

1 cup small lentils, green or brown
1 heaped cup shelled green peas, fresh or frozen
4 tablespoons olive or sunflower oil
4 fresh chives, snipped into short lengths
juice of 1 lime or lemon
salt
freshly ground black pepper

Rinse the lentils in a strainer under running water. There is no need to soak them. Place them in a saucepan, cover with water, add a little salt, and bring to a boil. Turn the heat down to a simmer and cook for 12 minutes. They should be cooked through but still have bite to them.

Tip the peas into a small saucepan with the oil and chives. Cook over a gentle heat for 8–12 minutes, or 5–6 if you are using frozen peas.

Drain the lentils and place them in a serving dish. Tip the hot peas together with their cooking juices on top. Squeeze the lime or lemon juice over the peas and lentils, grind over a little pepper and salt, and serve hot.

PEAS WITH OLIVE OIL AND MINT

Gentle cooking, in olive oil rather than water, with salt, fresh mint, and an onion, gives a much more interesting result than just throwing peas into a pan of water. Use them as an accompaniment or toss with cooked pasta.

FOR 2 AS AN ACCOMPANIMENT

4 tablespoons olive oil
1½ cups shelled green peas, fresh or frozen
1 small onion, sliced into paper-thin rings
2 sprigs of fresh mint
salt

Pour the oil into a medium saucepan and tip in the peas, onion, and mint. Add the salt and 1 tablespoon water and cover with a lid. Bring to a boil, then turn down the heat and simmer over a gentle heat for 10 minutes if the peas are fresh, or 6 or 7 if frozen. Shake the pan occasionally. Serve hot.

GREENS

The Cabbage Family

Once the most dreaded word in a child's vocabulary, "greens" has a new hopeful ring to it. Perhaps the buzzword of the 1990s will have the side effect of inducing more of us to eat them up. Cabbage has been beneficially linked to reducing risk of cancer. Broccoli is particularly well blessed with minerals and vitamins. Spinach is a splendid source of iron, though best assimilated when eaten with a partner rich in vitamin C, such as a squeeze of orange.

Brussels sprouts, cabbage, broccoli, and cauliflower are all brassicas, a group of vegetables linked by their color and strident, sometimes coarse, flavor. Textures vary from the glass-like hard white or pale green cabbage to tough and frilly kale; colors from the deep purple of red cabbage to the soft pastels of the bizarre Romanesco, which resembles a fairy-tale castle.

Hard, round white or pale green cabbage provides a welcome crunch in winter salads. Shred it finely and match it with something fruity, like huge juicy raisins, black grapes, or slices of tangerine or grapefruit. White cabbage keeps for several days in the bottom of the refrigerator, but, like any vegetable, will leach vitamins and minerals during storage. Avoid buying cabbage with a yellow tinge, which indicates age and bitterness.

Pork, in the form of bacon or sausage, is a happy match with all of the cabbage family. A stir-fry of shredded dark green Savoy cabbage with garlic and smoked bacon is frugal and comforting. Anchovies work well with both broccoli and collard greens, especially when chopped into a garlicky dressing. Mustard, either in a creamy binding for shredded Brussels sprouts or whisked into a vinaigrette dressing for coleslaw, has an affinity with both the greens and their porky partners.

Spinach

Interest in leafy green vegetables such as spinach has blossomed since we learned how to cook it (briefly), and Popeye with his pipe and muscles was exposed as the antithesis of the modern man. Spinach needs virtually no water at all. Wash the leaves, even if you have bought them ready-washed, but do not shake them dry. Drop them into a pan, slam on the lid, and cook over a medium heat till they wilt. They will be ready in 2 or 3 minutes, maybe less if the leaves are young. Boil the tenderest spinach leaves in water and you will end up with slime.

Many dislike the effect spinach has on the teeth, as if a layer of it has dissolved on your enamel; you can limit this by cooking large leaves as above, then draining and tossing them in butter or oil. When buying spinach check the leaves carefully for any sign of sliminess, as they rot easily. Avoid very large leaves, which are inclined to be tough. Tiny gentle-flavored leaves are perfect for a salad.

Exotics

If you have ready access to Asian greens, such as tiny-leaved Chinese water spinach, yellow-blossomed flowering cabbage, and stubby crisp-stemmed *bok choy,* use them in much the same way as spinach. They are tender and need brief cooking only, especially the mildly hot, floppy-leaved mustard cabbage. The crisp and refreshing pale green and white Napa cabbage stores well, and can be sliced in much the same way as an iceberg lettuce for stuffing pitas and sandwiches.

White Cabbage with Orange and Sesame

An idea inspired by the late British food writer, Jeremy Round.

FOR 4 AS AN ACCOMPANIMENT

3 tablespoons vegetable oil
a 2-pound head crisp white cabbage,
  finely shredded as if for coleslaw

freshly grated nutmeg
finely grated zest of 1 orange
1 tablespoon sesame oil

Heat the vegetable oil in a large saucepan until it starts to shimmer. Tip in the cabbage and cook in the hot oil, stirring and tossing to move it around the pan, for 4 or 5 minutes, until it has started to turn golden in parts but is still crunchy.

Grate a little nutmeg over the cabbage, then stir in the orange zest. Tip into a warm serving dish and drizzle over the oil.

Rumbledethumps

The Scottish name for this traditional British dish of mashed potatoes and cabbage was what first tempted me to try it (it's called Colcannon in Ireland). In her book, *Scottish Cookery,* Catherine Brown tells us that the name is derived from rumble, meaning to mix, and thump, to bash together. Whatever, this is good food of the first order.

FOR 4 AS A PRINCIPAL DISH

1 pound green cabbage
4 tablespoons butter
1 medium onion, minced
1 pound cooked potatoes, mashed
  (about 2 cups)

salt
freshly ground black pepper
extra butter

Wash the cabbage and shred it finely. Throw it in a pan with a little water and cook it, covered, for a couple of minutes till tender.

Melt the butter in a large saucepan and cook the onion until soft, about 5–7 minutes. Add the cooked mashed potatoes, the cabbage, drained of any water, and some salt and pepper and mix well. Put into a warm serving dish and stir in a few cubes of extra butter. Eat hot.

CABBAGE WITH BLACK-EYED PEAS

Arriving home one cold February evening, I scanned the previous week's papers for something interesting to cook. Michael Bateman, who writes the food column in the *Independent on Sunday*, had given a recipe for spinach with black-eyed peas. Rummaging in the refrigerator I failed to come up with the required spinach, but did find half a head of dark green cabbage. Here is my version of his good idea.

FOR 1 AS A COMFORTING, SOLITARY SUPPER

⅓ cup dried black-eyed peas
4 tablespoons olive oil
1 bay leaf (optional)
1 small onion, quite finely shredded

½ pound dark cabbage, such as
*   Savoy, shredded (about 2 cups)*
salt
freshly ground black pepper

Throw the beans in a pot with water to cover, a tablespoon of the oil, and a bay leaf if you have one. Salt, and cook the beans at a steady boil for half an hour. If you cannot wait that long, open a can of black-eyed peas, drain, and rinse them well. Heat them up in a spoonful of the olive oil.

Cook the onion slowly for about 10–15 minutes in the remaining oil; it should caramelize slightly. Throw in the cabbage, cook for a minute or two, then drain the beans and add them to the cabbage and onion. Season with a little salt and pepper.

BUBBLE AND SQUEAK

This dish, where cabbage greens are mashed with potatoes and then fried, is not fast food. But if it is made with yesterday's left-over cooked potatoes and cabbage, then it is. I have eaten this delightfully buttery and frugal food made from freshly prepared ingredients but, more often, made from leftovers. They both taste just as good.

The potatoes, whether mashed or not, have probably hardened. You will need to soften them, and you might as well do it in butter. Melt plenty of butter in a pan over a low to medium heat, say about 4 tablespoons to 2½–3 cups of potato. Add the potato and let it warm in the butter. Mash it, and not too finely, with a potato masher or fork. Chop the cooked cabbage into pieces roughly 1 inch square.

There should be, I think, always more cabbage than potato, but in any case at least an equal amount.

Stir the cabbage, which can also be kale or even spinach, into the potato. Season it well with plenty of salt and pepper. Melt enough butter, or better still, drippings, to cover the bottom of a frying pan. Pile in the cabbage mixture and squash it down flat with a metal spatula. Turn the heat to low and cook until the bottom has crisped and browned in the butter. If you wish, turn the whole thing over in the pan to brown the other side. I often don't bother, and instead just tip it out onto a warm serving plate.

Traditionally, Bubble and Squeak was served as an accompaniment to sliced cold beef. I think it deserves to be eaten as a main dish in its own right. It is, I concede, improved immeasurably by being surrounded with a pool of hot gravy.

STIR-FRIED CABBAGE

FOR 2 AS A PRINCIPAL DISH

1 pound green cabbage
2 tablespoons oil: vegetable or
  peanut

2 cloves of garlic, finely sliced
½ teaspoon salt

Remove any tough stems from the cabbage. Roll the cabbage leaves into tight rolls, then shred them finely with a large knife.

Heat a large frying pan or wok over a high heat until very hot, then add the oil and the garlic. Fry, stirring constantly, for no longer than 30 seconds. Add the salt and the shredded cabbage and cook, stirring and tossing the cabbage in the hot oil, for 3 minutes, until the cabbage is wilted but still crisp and with a bright color. Tip onto a warm serving dish.

SAVOY CABBAGE AND BACON

Cabbage and smoked meat are a wonderful combination and, of course, all cabbages and greens (collard, turnip, etc.) will work here, too. The carrots are a sweet addition and not essential, but their bright color adds a bit of life to this otherwise dark dish. I will happily eat this as a main dish, though it makes a good side dish, too. Make sure to drizzle any bacon fat and cooking juices from the pan over the cabbage as you serve it. If there is more than one of you eating, then you'll need a very large pan or a wok.

FOR 1 AS A MAIN DISH OR 2 AS AN ACCOMPANIMENT

2 cloves of garlic, peeled	*1 teaspoon caraway seeds*
2 medium carrots, scrubbed	*salt*
4 ounces smoked bacon:	*freshly ground black pepper*
thick slices or slab	
1 pound Savoy cabbage leaves,	
washed	

Slice the garlic finely, and cut the carrots into matchstick-size strips. Cut the bacon into dice about ½ inch square. Shred the cabbage leaves finely with a large knife.

Cook the bacon in a large frying pan until it starts to brown. Add the garlic, carrots, and cabbage to the bacon and toss the vegetables in the bacon fat over a medium heat. Cook until the carrots are tender but still have some crunch to them, about 5 minutes. Sprinkle over a few caraway seeds, about a teaspoonful, then season with salt and pepper.

RECYCLED GREENS

Many a mini feast has been made from the pathetic leftovers lurking in the refrigerator. Next time you open the refrigerator door to be greeted by little more than some leftover greens and a cup of juices from yesterday's roast, consider this:

▶ Heat up the juices in a wide pan, adding a few glugs of wine or some stock or water if they are very concentrated. As they come to a boil, stir in a teaspoon arrowroot mixed with a tablespoon water. When the mixture starts to thicken, put in the leftover greens, roughly chopped, and toss them in the meat juices. Eat as soon as the greens are warmed through. Soak up any of the juices that remain on your plate with bread

► Shred half a small, tight head of cabbage. Chop an apple, without bothering to peel it, into rough cubes, discarding the core. Melt some butter in a shallow pan, put in the shredded cabbage, chopped apple, and some salt and freshly ground pepper, and cook over a medium heat, covered with a lid, until the cabbage has softened (about 10 or 12 minutes depending on how finely you shredded the cabbage). When the cabbage is tender but still crisp, stir in ½ cup of thick plain yogurt or some sour cream. Grind over a little nutmeg if you have some around, then serve with good pork link sausages or, better still, blood sausage

COLLARD GREENS AND ANCHOVIES ON GARLIC TOAST

FOR 2 AS A HEARTY SNACK

1 pound collard greens or broccoli raab	12 anchovy fillets, rinsed and patted dry
½ cup extra virgin olive oil	salt
2 plump cloves of garlic, thinly sliced	freshly ground black pepper

FOR THE TOAST:

4 slices from a crusty, chewy white loaf	1 clove of garlic

Remove and discard any tough stems from the greens and then cook for 2 minutes in a large pot of boiling salted water. Drain.

Pour half the olive oil into a large frying pan and, over a medium heat, cook the thin slices of garlic and 4 of the anchovy fillets for 2 minutes. Add the greens and some salt and pepper. Be enthusiastic with the pepper.

Toss the greens around in the oil until they are warmed through. Meanwhile, toast the bread under the broiler or, preferably, in the oven if it is on. Cut the garlic clove in half and rub the toast with the cut side.

Put the toast, which should now really be called *bruschetta,* on plates and divide the greens and anchovies among them. Dribble over the remaining olive oil and add the rest of the anchovy fillets.

SPINACH WITH BLUE CHEESE AND PASTA

Any soft blue-veined cheese will be right for this. There is little point in using a great cheese, such as Gorgonzola or Irish Cashel Blue, unless you have some to use up. A Dolcelatte or blue Brie is quite adequate. I like to follow this rich and almost instant dish with a plate of salad leaves to mop up the cheesy sauce, corn salad (*mâche*) if I happen to have some, or just some floppy-leaved lettuce.

ENOUGH FOR 2 AS A MAIN DISH WITH SALAD TO FOLLOW

10 ounces fresh pasta, any curled
   or ribbon shape
2 double handfuls of spinach leaves,
   washed and torn up
6 ounces soft blue cheese, cut into
   cubes

1¼ cups light cream
salt
freshly ground black pepper

Cook the pasta, uncovered, in boiling salted water till *al dente*. Put the spinach, still wet from washing, in a pan over a medium heat. Cover with a lid and cook till it starts to wilt, a matter of 2 minutes or so. Add the blue cheese and the cream. Cook over a gentle heat until the cheese melts into the cream. Taste it and then season accordingly, remembering that some blue cheeses are a little salty.

When the cheese has melted and the spinach is still bright green, drain the pasta and fold it into the sauce. Eat hot.

Other ways to cook Spinach

► Spinach can be hot and ready to eat in 2 minutes. Dunk the leaves into deep cold water. Lift out the spinach and, without shaking off any water, drop it into a large pan set over a medium heat. Cook, covered with a lid, for a couple of minutes, shaking the pan now and again. The wrinkly, deep green leaves will cook in their own steam. Pour over some good olive oil and perhaps a hefty squeeze of lemon juice, or smother with butter

► Spinach salad is one of the most satisfying leaf-based salads I know. The young and tender, pale green leaves are fine enough eaten whole, thin stems included. The larger, older ones should not be dismissed, and should be just torn or shredded finely.

Try a simple dressing of plain yogurt beaten with a minced garlic clove and a fairly generous addition of salt and freshly ground pepper. Lemon juice with walnut oil is a splendid dressing too, particularly if you can throw in a handful of shelled walnuts, toasted under the broiler till fragrant, and a few halved black grapes.

Bacon, cooked till crisp and then crumbled, can be zapped over a bowl of shredded dark-leaved spinach. Turn it into a complete meal by tossing with cannellini beans or black-eyed peas, either freshly cooked, or canned ones that have been warmed through in the bacon fat.

Brussels Sprouts

Brussels sprouts have never grabbed me. I find their flavor coarse and difficult to marry with other ingredients. Retrieved from boiling water 1 minute too soon and they are hard as bullets, 1 minute too late and they are little balls of pungent yellow slush. They also smell disgusting.

But Brussels sprouts *can* be good. The trick is to keep them well away from boiling water. Try them stir-fried with bacon or in a salad with a mustard dressing. I have also enjoyed them shredded finely and deep-fried—sprinkled with salt and a little sugar, they distinctly resemble the so-called seaweed of Chinese restaurant fame.

Choose the smallest sprouts you can find, preferably no bigger than large marbles. Real whoppers are most likely to be bitter. Romanticism it may be, but I really cannot look at a sprout until the first frosts have appeared—year-round Brussels I can live without.

BRUSSELS SPROUTS IN A CREAMY MUSTARD DRESSING

Small sprouts, when they are nutty and new, can be shredded and dressed with a mixture of nut oil and lemon juice. Or you can turn them into a more substantial affair with some sour cream spiked with mustard. They then make a nice lunch with a lump of Stilton or sharp Cheddar and a glass of apple cider.

FOR 4 AS A SIDE SALAD

Choose ½ pound young, tight little sprouts. Shred them with a large sharp knife, or push them through the food processor armed with the shredding disk.

Make a mustardy, creamy dressing by stirring together 1 table-spoon white wine vinegar, a large pinch of salt, 2 tablespoons Dijon mustard, and 4 heaped tablespoons sour cream in a bowl. With a fork or a small whisk, beat in at least 3 tablespoons oil. This can be olive or a mixture of olive and a nut oil. Toss the shredded sprouts in the dressing and serve.

BRUSSELS SPROUTS AND BACON

This is the best way of cooking sprouts I know.

FOR 2, OR 4 AS A SIDE DISH WITH SAUSAGES OR FRIED EGGS

Heat 1 tablespoon drippings or butter in a large, shallow pan. When it is warm add ½ cup lean bacon (pancetta, the Italian bacon, has a deeper flavor than most), cut into small dice.

Shred 1 pound Brussels sprouts. This can be done in minutes with a sharp knife or in seconds with the slicing disk of the food processor.

When the bacon has crisped throw in the shredded sprouts. Salt and pepper them. Fry the shredded sprouts till slightly golden in parts, about 3 or 4 minutes.

The sprouts are ready to eat when they have turned slightly golden brown here and there and are thoroughly coated with the bacon juices and drippings or butter. Eat with a glass or two of cold beer.

Broccoli with *Bagna Cauda*

Anchovies, those salty little fillets, and olive oil, a light and fruity one, seem to have an affinity with broccoli. A simple lunch can be made from little more than a can of anchovies, a head of garlic, and some olive oil, simmered and served as a hot dipping sauce for broccoli. *Bagna Cauda* (hot bath), for that is what it is called, is a classic sauce from Piedmont, and as old as the hills. I tend to blanch the broccoli in boiling water, though many would eat it raw. Don't forget some crusty bread and a bottle of red wine, as rough as you like.

FOR 4 AS A LIGHT LUNCH

6 tablespoons butter
8 cloves of garlic, minced
12 anchovy fillets, rinsed and dried

1 cup olive oil
1 pound broccoli

Melt the butter in a small saucepan. Add the garlic and cook over a gentle heat for 2–3 minutes. It must not brown and turn bitter. Add the anchovies, which will virtually dissolve with a bit of stirring. Pour in the olive oil slowly, stirring all the time. Simmer, not boil, for 10 minutes. Blanch the broccoli in boiling water for a couple of minutes; keep it crisp. Serve the sauce hot, in a bowl, stirring it up with the drained sprigs of broccoli each time you dip them in. Soak up the remaining sauce with hunks of bread.

Good ways to cook Broccoli

▶ Cook stems and florets of broccoli in boiling salted water till tender but crisp, about 3 or 4 minutes. Drain and put on a serving dish. Drizzle with extra virgin olive oil while still warm. Serve with wedges of lemon to squeeze over and hot garlic bread

▶ Cook broccoli florets and stems in boiling water till tender. They will be ready in 3 or 4 minutes, maybe even less. At any rate, they must be removed while they are still bright and crisp. Quickly cool the broccoli in a colander held under the cold tap for a few minutes. Set a bowl of garlic mayonnaise from a jar in the center of a large plate. Surround the bowl with the blanched broccoli and leave in the middle of the table for everyone to help themselves

► Steam or boil some broccoli till tender, about 3 or 4 minutes. Keep it crisp and brilliant green. Heat a couple of tablespoons best olive oil in a shallow pan. Cut a few bottled or canned pimientos into long strips and toss them gently in the warm oil, with some sliced cloves of garlic, if you like. When they are warm and the garlic pale gold, add the broccoli and some salt and freshly ground pepper. Tip onto plates and scatter over a few rinsed capers—remember, though, what bullies they can be, and that many people don't like them anyway. Eat while warm, with crusty bread

MUSHROOMS

Mushrooms are perfect for the cook in a hurry. They cook quickly, especially when quartered or sliced, and have a satisfying meatiness about them.

There is virtually nothing I enjoy more than large flat mushrooms, brushed with olive oil and a squeeze of lemon, then broiled and served with the juices that have collected in the broiler pan. I find those huge flat mushrooms, the most mature of all cultivated fungi, as juicy and tender as a piece of steak. I am convinced that the flavor improves after a few days in a brown paper bag in the bottom of the refrigerator. The more earthy, woodsy, or, well, mushroomy, they smell and the blacker the gills then the deeper the flavor.

Open cup mushrooms are probably the most common. Although they are often sliced for cooking and salads, I invariably cut them into quarters so they appear as juicy nuggets. Immature white button mushrooms have little of the sweet earthiness of the larger fungi. They are best tossed with a squeeze of lemon and some chopped fresh parsley and eaten raw. They have the ability to absorb other flavors, such as garlic or herbs, in the way that beancurd (tofu) does.

I never peel mushrooms, believing that there is much flavor in the skin. If they are covered in little lumps of growing medium, then I wipe it off with a wet thumb. I do not, as some cooks insist, wash mushrooms. Even the freshest fungi soaks up water like a sponge.

Supermarkets have tried offering us all sorts, including the savory *shiitake* and the soft grey oyster mushroom. They all have a place in the quick cook's repertoire, either in stir-fries, omelets, or risotto. Each has its own characteristic smell and flavor and makes a change from the workaday little tan cups. Mushrooms will all keep for a few days in the refrigerator. I find the fancier the fungi the faster it rots, so if I have treated myself to something unusual then I eat it that day.

BROILED MUSHROOMS

Two ways to broil large flat mushrooms, the first with olive oil and garlic, the second purely with butter and lemon.

FOR 4

1 pound large flat mushrooms	*1 tablespoon chopped fresh parsley*
6 tablespoons olive oil	*salt*
1 clove of garlic, chopped	*freshly ground black pepper*

Wipe the mushrooms and cut any soil from their stems. Pull out the stems and cut them in half. Place the caps and stems on an oiled broiler pan and brush with some of the oil. Scatter over the garlic and parsley and season with the salt and pepper. Cook under the broiler for 5 or 6 minutes, occasionally spooning over a little more oil. Turn the caps and stems over and broil for a further 3 or 4 minutes. Serve hot.

FOR 2

6 large flat mushrooms	*freshly ground black pepper*
6 tablespoons butter	*½ lemon*
salt	

Wipe the mushrooms and brush away any soil. Place the mushrooms on a broiler pan. Put large lumps of butter all over the mushrooms and season each one with salt and pepper and a good squeeze of lemon. Cook under a preheated broiler for 10 minutes, spooning the butter and juices over them from time to time.

MUSHROOMS ON TOAST

Resisting the temptation to slice large flat mushrooms, I serve them whole, in all their glory, astride a piece of thick toast to soak up their juices.

FOR 2

2 very large, flat mushrooms
butter, softened
salt

freshly ground black pepper
2 thick slices of white bread

Brush the mushrooms generously with butter and broil or sauté them till soft and cooked all the way through, about 5–7 minutes. You can test this by removing the stem and piercing the flesh with the point of a knife; if the juices run out, it is cooked.

Toast the slices of bread and top each with a mushroom, spooning over the buttery juices.

MUSHROOM *CROSTINI*

A somewhat elegant version of mushrooms on toast, where the mushrooms are softened in garlic butter, then piled onto slices of French bread. Be generous with the parsley and pepper.

FOR 3

4 tablespoons butter
1 clove of garlic, lightly crushed
1 pound mushrooms, sliced
2 tablespoons chopped fresh
  parsley

salt
freshly ground black pepper
12 slices of French bread,
  ¼ inch thick

Melt the butter in a small pan. Add the crushed garlic and cook gently until the butter smells sweet and garlicky. Remove the garlic clove before it turns dark brown and bitter. Turn up the heat and toss in the mushrooms.

Cook for 4 or 5 minutes, stirring occasionally if the mushrooms stick to the pan, until they soften and soak up the garlic butter. Stir in the parsley and add a little salt and 2 or 3 twists from the peppermill.

While the mushrooms are cooking, toast the slices of bread. Spoon the mushrooms over the toasted bread and eat while hot.

BROILED HERBED MUSHROOMS

FOR 2 AS A FIRST COURSE OR LIGHT SUPPER WITH SALAD, BREAD, AND WINE

6 large mushrooms	*freshly ground black pepper*
a small fistful of parsley and mint,	*4 cloves of garlic, finely sliced*
chopped	*1 wineglass of olive oil*
salt	

Twist out the stems from the mushrooms and mince them. Wipe the mushroom caps and lay them, gill-side up, in a baking dish. Mix together the herbs and seasonings and stir in the chopped stems.

Press the thin slices of garlic here and there into the mushroom caps. Scatter over the herb mixture and then pour the olive oil over the top. Leave for 10 minutes while you heat the broiler.

Broil the mushrooms, spooning over the cooking juices, until they are cooked right through, about 5–7 minutes.

MUSHROOMS WITH POTATOES AND GARLIC

If I have some, I use new potatoes for this, though nothing as good as Jersey Royals. But large potatoes cut into small chunks work just as well. I serve it either as an accompaniment or as a substantial *salade tiède* on a pile of salad leaves.

FOR 2 AS A MAIN COURSE SALAD, 4 AS AN ACCOMPANIMENT

1 pound very small potatoes	*2 tablespoons chopped fresh*
2 thick slices of bacon, diced	*parsley*
¾ pound mushrooms, quartered	*salt*
2 fat cloves of garlic, minced	*freshly ground black pepper*

Scrub the potatoes and cut them in half. Fry the bacon in a frying pan till crisp. Tip in the potatoes and stir well. Cover and cook for 10 minutes on a gentle heat. Add the mushrooms, garlic, and 1 tablespoon of the parsley. Season with salt and pepper, then cook for 15 minutes, covered, until the potatoes are tender to the point of a knife. When they are ready, pour in 3 tablespoons boiling water, bring to a boil, and scrape up any crusty sediment in the pan. Boil for 1 minute. Toss in the remaining spoonful of parsley and serve hot or warm.

STIR-FRIED MUSHROOMS

I once went to a series of Chinese cooking demonstrations. Lots of good things came out of it, including the stir-fried zucchini recipe on which this dish is based. If your local supermarket or green-grocer stocks the meaty *shiitake* mushrooms, use them here; if not, use common button or open cup ones instead.

FOR 2 AS A MAIN DISH WITH RICE OR NOODLES

⅔ cup vegetable oil
1 pound small mushrooms
2 cloves of garlic, minced
   with 1 teaspoon salt

1 tablespoon soy sauce
2 tablespoons oyster sauce
2 tablespoons dry sherry
1 teaspoon sugar

Heat the oil in a frying pan or wok. Drop a tiny mushroom into it; when it starts to sizzle the oil is hot enough. Toss in the mushrooms and move them around with a slotted spoon for 2 minutes.

Drain away the hot oil. Sprinkle the garlic salt over the mushrooms and turn over a few times, then add the soy and oyster sauces, sherry, and sugar. Reduce the heat and leave the mushrooms to cook for 2 minutes.

BUTTERED MUSHROOMS

My interpretation of an idea from Eliza Acton.

FOR 2 AS A SNACK OR LIGHT SUPPER

½ cup (1 stick) butter
½ pound mushrooms, wiped
salt

cayenne pepper
ground mace

Melt the butter in a pan, tip in the mushrooms, and cook over a gentle heat, shaking the pan from time to time, until the mushrooms soften and give up some of their juices. Add a little salt and a fine sprinkling of both cayenne and mace. Serve hot with bread or, better still, some reheated mashed potato.

MUSHROOM BEIGNETS

Antonio Carluccio's delicious little Wild Mushroom Beignets are for those lucky enough to know where to gather wild fungi. For those who make this recipe, a good way is to use a mixed bag. Make sure the mushrooms are dry so that they do not exude too much water.

FOR 4

4 eggs
1½ cups flour
⅔ cup milk
salt
freshly ground black pepper

1¾ pounds mixed fresh wild
* mushrooms, cut into strips*
1 small onion, minced
plenty of peanut or sunflower
* oil for frying*

Beat the eggs in a bowl, then stir in the flour and the milk, followed by salt and pepper to taste, to form a thick batter. Now add the mushrooms and onion and mix together. Pour about ½ inch of oil into a frying pan and bring to frying temperature. Carefully add the mushroom batter, a tablespoon at a time. Fry the beignets gently until brown and crispy on one side, then turn, and cook the other side. Serve hot.

PAN-FRIED MUSHROOMS WITH ONION AND CREAM

A quick and creamy dish to be served on toast or with a little boiled brown rice.

FOR 2 WITH RICE OR ON TOAST

Peel a small onion, or a couple of shallots, and mince. Put into a frying pan with a tablespoon vegetable oil and 1–2 tablespoons butter and fry gently over a medium heat until the onion starts to turn golden.

Cut 1 pound wiped mushrooms, plump white cups if possible, into quarters. Turn up the heat and add the mushrooms to the pan. When the mushrooms have absorbed most of the butter and oil, turn down the heat, and season with salt and a few turns of the peppermill. Cook the mushrooms for 3 minutes, shaking the pan from time to time.

Pour in about ½ cup heavy cream and simmer for another couple of minutes before serving.

Mushrooms à La Crème

Another idea for those who like a little cream with their fungi, this time peppered with basil.

Cook 1 pound little mushrooms with a minced garlic clove in 2 tablespoons olive oil until they have absorbed most of the oil, about 7–10 minutes. Season with a shake or two of salt, add the leaves of a healthy branch of fresh basil, torn into small pieces, and stir in 1¼ cups light cream. Cook over a gentle flame for a couple of minutes, then serve very hot, with toast.

Funghi Ripieni

The Italian way of stuffing large mushroom caps, with their chopped stems and bread crumbs, is repeated here with the addition of anchovies and olives.

FOR 4

12 large mushrooms, wiped	*2 tablespoons chopped fresh parsley*
1 onion, chopped	*salt*
1 clove of garlic, minced	*freshly ground black pepper*
olive oil	*½ cup soft fresh bread crumbs*
3 anchovy fillets, drained and chopped	*1 egg, beaten*
1 tablespoon chopped green olives	

Remove the mushroom stems and chop. Cook the onion and garlic in 2 tablespoons olive oil until the onion softens, then add the chopped mushroom stems. Cook over a gentle heat for 5 minutes, and then add the chopped anchovies and the olives. Cook for 2 minutes more and stir in the parsley. Season to taste. Mix with half the bread crumbs and bind the mixture with the beaten egg.

Fill the mushrooms with the anchovy and olive stuffing and place them in a lightly oiled ovenproof dish. Scatter over the rest of the bread crumbs and a little olive oil. Cover with foil and bake in a preheated 400 °F oven for 10–15 minutes. Remove the foil and bake for a further 5 minutes to crisp the stuffing.

MUSHROOM ROLLS

Hollowed-out rolls, crisped in the oven and filled with a creamed mushroom mixture, are the idea of Elizabeth Raffald, and appear in her 1782 edition of *The Experienced English Housekeeper.* The lemon juice is an important addition, preventing the mixture from being too cloying.

FOR 2

4 bread rolls, white or brown	*1 cup heavy cream*
4 tablespoons butter	*a large squeeze of lemon juice*
1 small onion, chopped	*salt*
4 cups sliced mushrooms	*freshly ground black pepper*

Slice the tops from each of the rolls with a bread knife and hollow out half the bread. Melt the butter in a small pan and brush a little of it inside the rolls and on the cut side of the lids. Put them in a preheated 400 °F oven for about 7–10 minutes, until crisp.

Meanwhile, fry the onion in the rest of the butter in the pan for about 5 minutes until soft, then add the mushrooms and cook for 4–5 minutes, until they start to soften. Pour in the cream and allow to bubble for a couple of minutes; the mixture will start to thicken. Season with the lemon juice and some salt and pepper.

Remove the rolls from the oven and spoon in the creamed mushroom filling. Cover with the lids and serve immediately.

Mushroom Soup

The simplest of mushroom soups, this comforting autumnal dish is based on a recipe in Mrs. C. F. Leyel and Miss Olga Hartley's *The Gentle Art of Cookery* (1925). You can use it as a base to which you can add a glass of white wine, some chopped fresh parsley, or a grating of coriander. Serve with chunks of bread for dunking.

FOR 6

4 tablespoons butter
½ pound mushrooms, minced
1 small onion, minced
1 clove of garlic, chopped
2 tablespoons flour
1 quart chicken or
  vegetable stock

1 cup heavy cream
1 cup milk
freshly grated nutmeg
salt
freshly ground black pepper

Melt the butter in a saucepan and sweat the mushrooms, onion, and garlic. When the onion becomes translucent, stir in the flour and cook for 2 minutes to cook out the raw taste of the flour, which would show in a soup of this sort. Pour in the stock and simmer gently for 10 minutes.

Tip the soup into a food processor or blender, and whizz with the cream and milk and a grating of nutmeg until fairly smooth. Correct the seasoning and eat with crusty bread.

Dried Mushroom Broth

There have been times when I have had little more in the pantry than half a package of those expensive dried mushrooms, bought for a special occasion then carefully stored and forgotten. They make a richly scented and satisfying broth when cooked with some stock and a drop or two of sherry.

FOR 4

1 ounce dried cèpes (porcini) or other
  dried mushrooms
5 cups vegetable or
  chicken stock
bay leaf, thyme, parsley, and
  rosemary

3 tablespoons sherry or, better still,
  Madeira
salt
freshly ground black pepper

Rinse the mushrooms and place in a bowl. Warm the stock and pour over the mushrooms. Leave the mushrooms for 10 minutes to reconstitute and then pour the stock and mushrooms into a saucepan, making sure that none of the grit lurking at the bottom of the bowl gets in.

Simmer the broth with the herbs for 25 minutes. Strain the broth and discard the mushrooms. Tip in the sherry or Madeira, season carefully, and serve steaming hot.

Suggestions

► In her book *The Cook's Garden,* Lynda Brown fills mushroom caps with a purée of cooked parsnips and covers that with thin shavings of Cheddar or Gruyère. Brushed with olive oil and baked for 20 minutes in a hot oven, they make an earthy-tasting snack

► Edouard de Pomiane cooks canned *cèpes* by first softening 3 shallots and a minced clove of garlic in some olive oil in a frying pan. He heats the *cèpes* for 6–7 minutes, then sprinkles them with salt, pepper, and chopped fresh parsley

► Margaret Costa's Club Mushroom Breakfast:
4 thick bacon slices, ½ pound mushrooms, ½ pound fresh soft roes, about 2 tablespoons butter, 4 slices of toast, salt, and pepper. Fry the bacon and mushrooms in one pan. Fry the roes in the butter in another. When all are cooked, cover the slices of toast with bacon, then the roes, and, lastly, pile on the mushrooms. Season well

► Garlic purée, either homemade or from a bottle (check, though, that it contains no sugar), makes a good accompaniment for broiled or baked mushrooms

BELL PEPPERS

This indigestible vegetable has become a great favorite of mine since I discovered that it has rather more magic when roasted or broiled than it does sliced raw and tossed into a salad. The sweetness of a broiled pepper, peeled and anointed with rich sherry or balsamic vinegar, is a delicacy to remind one of sunny summer lunches in the garden. The following recipes work with red or yellow varieties; somehow the hard green bell pepper fails to exude the same rich juices when heated.

BROILED RED BELL PEPPERS AND BLACK OLIVE *CONCHIGLIE*

Conchiglie is shell-shaped pasta. I use it more than any other because its clever shape so neatly holds a good dollop of sauce, cream, or olive oil. You could, of course, blanch the peppers in boiling water instead of broiling them, but you would be missing the sweet smoky juices released by broiling.

FOR 2 AS A MAIN COURSE

2 large red bell peppers, halved, cored, and seeds and stem removed
6 tablespoons virgin olive oil
2 cloves of garlic, peeled
4 ounces dried pasta
4 tablespoons black olive paste
salt
freshly ground black pepper
3 tablespoons grated Parmesan cheese

Put the halved peppers in the broiler pan, skin-side up, and pour over 4 tablespoons of the oil. Throw in the garlic cloves. Cook under a preheated broiler till the skins blister and char, about 7–8 minutes.

Cook the pasta, uncovered, in a pan of boiling salted water till *al dente,* about 11 minutes. Drain. Stir in the olive paste.

Place the peppers carefully in an ovenproof dish. Pile the olive pasta into the broiled pepper shells. Pour the cooking juices with the broiled garlic into the food processor or blender and add the remaining oil. Whizz. Taste the garlic dressing, then add salt and pepper. Pour the dressing over the pasta and peppers, scatter with Parmesan cheese, and place under the broiler till it turns golden and crisp.

Broiled Bell Peppers with Balsamic Vinegar and Basil

There is an exciting mixture of flavors here. The whole point of broiling the peppers is to release their sweet, smoky juices and exploit them in the warm dressing with the deep sweet-sour richness of balsamic vinegar. The resulting sweetness is then balanced by the basil and lemon.

FOR 2

2 medium red bell peppers
1 eggplant, weighing about ½ pound
1 medium onion, peeled
4 bushy sprigs of fresh thyme
2 plump cloves of garlic, minced
¾ cup extra virgin olive oil
salt

freshly ground black pepper
2 large plum tomatoes, halved and
 cut into thick slices
1 tablespoon balsamic vinegar
juice ½ lemon
a small handful of fresh basil
 leaves, shredded

Cut the peppers in half through the stem, then pull out and discard anything that isn't red. Put the halves in a broiler pan, on the bottom rather than the rack, with their cut-sides down. Halve the eggplant lengthwise, cut each half into ¼ inch thick slices, and put in a bowl.

Cut the onion horizontally in slices no thicker than silver dollars. Separate the rings and add them to the eggplant. Strip the leaves from the thyme branches, add to the onion and eggplant with the garlic, and pour over the olive oil. Grind over a little black pepper and salt, then toss together the vegetables and thyme with a spoon, making sure they are all covered with oil.

Scatter them over the rest of the broiler pan and cook under a preheated broiler, about 3–4 inches from the heat. When the pepper skins start to blacken, turn them over. Stir the eggplant mixture around as it starts to brown. After 15 minutes cooking, add the tomatoes. Continue broiling until the eggplant and onion are tender, and the peppers have lightly charred skins and soft, but far from collapsing, flesh—about a further 10–12 minutes.

Remove the pan from the broiler and carefully spoon out the pan juices into the bowl in which you mixed the vegetables. Whisk in the balsamic vinegar, lemon juice, and shredded basil with a fork. Taste for seasoning; you may need a bit more salt and pepper. Place the peppers on warm plates and stuff with the broiled vegetables. Spoon over the warm dressing and eat right away, with crusty bread to mop up the juices.

POTATOES

Potatoes are one of our most loved foods. Almost everyone I have met seems to have a soft spot for them cooked in one way or another: fluffy baked potatoes oozing with butter, diminutive nutty new ones for dipping into sour cream, or thick fingers of fries, eaten from a cardboard container.

As a crop the potato produces more food per acre than almost anything else. As a food it is cheap and plentiful and immensely satisfying. I am always happy to come home to a baked potato smothered in butter or a warm salad of waxy new potatoes with onion, wine vinegar, and lots of fresh parsley.

The potato is far more nutritious than is often imagined. It is high in complex carbohydrate and fiber and is an important source of vitamin C and several minerals. When steamed, boiled, or baked it is low in calories, only becoming a worry to people who care about such things when it is fried. I rarely peel potatoes, so saving fiber, vitamins, and time. Most of the vitamins are stored just underneath the skin. New potatoes may have flaky skins that need nothing more than a gentle wipe; larger "old" potatoes usually need a good scrub.

There are ways to cook potatoes for the short-of-time. Tiny new potatoes can be as good as a feast when piled high and steaming and served with a bowl of thick *crème fraîche*. New potatoes can also be used as a substantial addition to a salad of arugula or spinach and Taleggio or Cantal cheeses.

Cubes of potato can be pan-fried with butter and garlic for an accompaniment to broiled chicken or fish. Or they can be made into French fries. Baked potatoes take a good hour to cook, but I still think of them as fast food. I find their ability to look after themselves while baking a boon. I scrub a couple of large potatoes, dump them in the oven, then forget about them till 10 minutes before they should be ready, when I make a filling.

To say I have a deep affection for mashed potatoes is something of an understatement. It is almost an addiction. Gloriously buttery mash fits into this book not just because it can be on the table within 20 minutes or so, but because it comes under the heading of comfort food along with oatmeal and risotto.

It is important to find the right potato for the job. A firm waxy-fleshed variety is perfect for a salad but will turn to glue if puréed for mash. Similarly, a mealy variety for baking will crumble to nothing if you try to toss it in a vinaigrette dressing. It is sad to relate that there are hundreds of different varieties of potato and yet only four or five normally in the markets. Fancy varieties, with blue, black, or pink flesh, can be found in some supermarkets as can the Finnish or Dutch yellow potatoes. What I would like to see more of are varieties of potatoes, clearly marked, rather than the anonymous piles of potatoes at the greengrocers.

THE BAKED POTATO

A plump baked potato with a crisp skin must be on everyone's list of comfort food. On a cold, rainy night the smell of a potato baking must be one of the most appetizing of all. Baked potatoes fit into this collection of fast-food recipes because of the absurdly small amount of work you need to do to them to make a meal. They take a good hour to cook, but it is an unattended hour, leaving you free to do other things. There is hardly a meal on earth that is less hassle than a baked potato and salad.

The best potatoes for baking are the big mealy ones. I have had some success with smaller ones but they lack the majesty of a real whopper. The russet Burbank, also called Idaho, is a very fine baking potato. You can also use long white potatoes.

I have exploded many baked potatoes in my time. Sometimes I have opened the oven door to find that just the skins remain, while the flesh has pebble-dashed the inside of my oven. The best way to avoid such potato bombs is to push a metal skewer straight through the middle. This will also cut down the cooking time as the heat travels along the skewer. Failing that, you can prick them all over with a fork to let out the steam.

The potato is done when the skewer pulls out easily and the skin is crisp. The best way to achieve perfection is by ensuring the potatoes are dry and the oven is set to at least 400 °F. A large potato will take about an hour. When it is cooked, cut a cross in the center and push hard with the fingertips of both hands. The quicker the steam leaves the potato, the better the chance of the flesh turning to a lovely fluffy pile.

► Some of the potatoes sold in plastic bags are very dull. Take a look at the organic offerings. Although they take longer to scrub, as they are usually caked in soil, your hard work may be rewarded by a better flavor

► I have a notion that cold, sweet, unsalted butter hard from the refrigerator is nicer than soft room-temperature stuff on a baked potato, but it may, of course, just be my imagination

► A delicious result can be obtained by slicing the potatoes through the horizon, scoring the flesh in lattice fashion, and then baking as normal. This method also cuts the cooking time by a third

► When the potato is cooked, try slicing off a "lid" and scooping out the flesh. Mash it with butter or plain yogurt and anything else you fancy, then stuff it all back into the potato shell. Sit the lid on top if you must

► Sweet potatoes are good, too. Bake them in the usual way, putting them on a tray to catch the drips of caramelizing sugar that leak from the sweet orange flesh. They need little in the way of adornment: butter and freshly ground black pepper are the most flattering, I think

Good things to top a Baked Potato

► Cold butter straight from the refrigerator

► *Fromage blanc*

► Garlic cream cheese, such as Boursin

► Grated Cheddar or Gruyère cheese with chopped fresh flat-leaf parsley and walnuts

► A spoonful of tapenade

► Garlic mayonnaise

► Crushed goat cheese and shredded baby spinach leaves

► Chicken or duck livers, sautéed in butter and sprinkled with balsamic vinegar

► Thinly sliced Mozzarella and chopped fresh oregano

► Bottled roasted sweet peppers, broiled till sweet and slightly charred, then chopped and drizzled with warm extra virgin olive oil and black pepper

► Eat the flesh from the potato, then pile a leafy, garlicky salad into the hollow skins

► Mash the flesh with pesto sauce from a bottle and sprinkle over a little grated Parmesan cheese; toast under the broiler till hot

► Sliced avocado and toasted sliced almonds

► Sliced onions sautéed in butter till sweet and golden

► Bacon cooked till crisp and then crumbled, with toasted pumpkin seeds and melted butter

MASH

I love mashed potatoes above anything else edible. I am not sure that you get any brownie points for admitting you are happier eating a plate of mashed potatoes than some boy- or girl-wonder's latest gastronomic creation. But mashed potatoes are my comfort food, one that I turn to when I feel the world is against me.

I mash them with butter or with cream and olive oil in the modern French manner, depending on my mood. Sometimes I melt grated cheese into them. Occasionally I let some of them go cold, then fry them for breakfast in butter till crisp and very hot. Comfort food indeed.

ENOUGH FOR 2, AS A SIDE DISH

1 pound long white potatoes, peeled
¼ cup heavy cream

2 tablespoons olive oil
salt
freshly ground black pepper

Cut the potatoes into even-sized pieces. Simmer them in salted water until they are tender, about 20 minutes, then drain well and mash or put through a ricer. Do not attempt to use the food processor: you will end up with glue. Warm the cream in a small pan, then stir into the mash. Beat in the olive oil, then taste and season with salt and pepper if you want.

ALIGOT

The most comforting, and to my mind the most delicious, supper of all. This cheesy potato purée will alter in texture as well as flavor depending on which cheese you use. In the Auvergne, where this recipe originates, mild Cantal cheese is used, though any good melting variety will do.

I mention Cheddar in the recipe, but I have had beautifully stringy results with other cheeses, particularly Gruyère and Taleggio. Use the heaviest-bottomed saucepan you have for this. The thick base will prevent the mixture from burning and keep it warm while you eat it from the pot.

SERVES 4

2 pounds long white potatoes
4 tablespoons butter
¼ cup creamy milk or half
*   cream and half milk*

1 clove of garlic, minced
¾ pound good melting cheese:
*   Cheddar, Gruyère, or similar*
salt
freshly ground black pepper

Put the potatoes in cold water and bring to a boil. Add salt and simmer till tender to the point of a knife, about 20 minutes, depending on the nature of the potatoes. Drain and pull away the skins, then discard them. Mash the potatoes with the butter using a masher, or use a ricer if you can be bothered with the dishwashing.

Return the pan to the heat and beat in the milk and garlic with a wooden spoon. Add the cheese, beating with a wooden spoon all the time, lifting the mixture up from the bottom of the pan. Taste and season with salt and pepper. The *aligot* will lighten and the cheese will melt into long strands. The mixture is ready when it is shiny and comes away from the sides of the pan. Put the pan on the table and eat the *aligot* from it with forks.

BROILED POTATOES

I cook these potatoes quite often, sometimes tossing them with chopped fresh thyme leaves before broiling. I have also eaten them for supper, lubricated with yogurt, say 1 cup, which I have stirred briefly with 2 minced cloves of garlic, 2 teaspoons grated fresh ginger, and ½ teaspoon cayenne pepper, fried till fragrant in a little olive oil. I stir in a tablespoon chopped cilantro just before the sauce meets the potatoes.

FOR 2 AS A GENEROUS SIDE DISH

2 medium potatoes, such as russet or long white
salt
2 tablespoons walnut or peanut oil

2 small cloves of garlic, minced and mixed with the oil

Slice the potatoes ¼ inch thick lengthwise. There will be about 4 slices per potato. Put the slices into cold water and bring them to a boil. Add salt, and turn the heat down to simmer until they are tender to the point of a knife. This will take about 4 minutes.

Drain thoroughly. Cut lattice slashes into the surface of each potato slice, and pour over the oil and garlic.

Cook under a preheated broiler till crisp and golden, about 10 minutes, then turn and cook for a further 5 minutes. Grind salt over the crisp potatoes and eat while still hot.

► For a light supper, lay soft blue cheese such as Gorgonzola over the potatoes while they are hot and return to the broiler till just melted. Eat with green salad

WALNUT OIL AND NEW POTATO SAUTÉ

Patricia Wells is the restaurant critic for *L'Express,* the French news-weekly. She once told me of a dish in her book *Bistro Cooking* where she cooked sliced potatoes in walnut oil. I tried and enjoyed her recipe and have since found it works well with new potatoes, which avoids the peeling and slicing involved with larger potatoes. Her book, a collection of recipes from the chic bistros in Paris, has since become something of a good friend.

FOR 4 AS AN ACCOMPANIMENT

6 tablespoons walnut oil
4 cloves of garlic, unpeeled, crushed flat
1 pound new potatoes, wiped clean

salt
freshly ground black pepper
2 tablespoons chopped fresh parsley

Warm the oil with the crushed garlic cloves in a shallow pan until it is hot, but not smoking. Add the potatoes and sauté them over a medium-low heat for about 15–20 minutes. Shake the pan from time to time. They are cooked when brown on all sides and tender to the point of a knife.

Season with salt and pepper. Sprinkle the parsley over as you toss them from the pan into a serving dish.

► I have often made supper by tipping the hot potatoes onto a plate of mixed salad leaves—the mixture you can buy from the super-market, often called *Salade Mesclun.* Bread, thin and crisp-crusted baguettes, is good here, too

POTATOES WITH ONIONS AND OLIVE OIL

I often make this dish with leftover cooked potatoes. Mealy baking potatoes will fall apart slightly as you toss them in the olive oil, and somehow the dish is better for it.

FOR 4 AS AN ACCOMPANIMENT

2¼ pounds mealy potatoes
4 medium onions, roughly chopped
2 large cloves of garlic, minced
½ cup olive oil

a small bunch of fresh parsley,
  roughly chopped
salt
freshly ground black pepper

Boil the potatoes in their skins. They are cooked when the point of a knife goes into them easily—about 20 minutes. Drain and cut them up roughly into bite-sized pieces. Keep warm.

In a shallow pan fry the onions with the garlic in the olive oil for about 5–7 minutes, until soft and shiny. Throw in the parsley and add some salt and pepper. Toss the potatoes in the onions and oil and, when bubbling, serve.

QUICK POTATO IDEAS

Fried Potatoes with Garlic and Salt

Peel 2 huge potatoes, or 4 large ones. Dice them into ½-inch cubes. Toss them in a shallow pan with a finger's depth of hot olive oil. Throw in 6 cloves of garlic, flattened with a knife but not peeled. Fry over a medium heat for about 12–15 minutes, till golden, shaking the pan from time to time. Drain on a paper towel, ditch the garlic, and salt the potato cubes liberally.

New Potatoes, Thyme, Garlic, and Cream

Put 1 pound new potatoes on to boil. Meanwhile, crush 3 or 4 sprigs of fresh thyme in your hand, just enough to bruise the leaves, and drop them into ¾ cup heavy cream in a small, shallow pan. Add 3 plump cloves of garlic, flattened but not peeled, and bring to a boil. Simmer for 7–12 minutes, until reduced by one-third. The potatoes should be cooked by now. Drain them, break each one in half and drop into the scented cream. Serve with something broiled, like fish or a chop.

SALAD ACCOMPANIMENTS AND DRESSINGS

In French and Italian street markets there is always at least one stall with a huge basket of assorted salad leaves: arugula, *frisée,* radicchio, escarole, and corn salad (*mâche*); sometimes a handful of chervil is thrown in for good measure. I think of it as just about the most perfect of all salads, a lightly dressed mixture of baby leaves, just right for accompanying a snack or for mopping up the juices of a main dish.

You can often find mixed salad leaves in specialty grocers and good supermarkets. I am particularly fond of a mixture of tiny oakleaf lettuce leaves, watercress, arugula, *frisée,* and escarole, all picked when very young. Salad leaves bought in this way work out to be surprisingly economical in comparison to buying five or six different salad ingredients. Cooking for one or two, I find I cannot use up several different kinds of lettuce in mixed leaf salads quick enough to prevent them turning the salad crisper into a swamp.

Dressings

The leaves require only a light dressing if their individual flavors are not to be lost. A delicately seasoned vinaigrette, with just the faintest waft of garlic, is just the job:

½ garlic clove, make it a small one
a little pinch of salt

1 tablespoon lemon juice
6 tablespoons light and fruity extra virgin olive oil

Crush the garlic with the salt using the flat blade of a large knife, grinding it to a fragrant, beige cream. Scrape it into a small bowl and whisk in the lemon juice, either using a fork or a small whisk. Whisk in the olive oil. The result need not be homogenous, though many people like it to be.

If the salad is to accompany something light and crisp, such as broiled fish fillets or vegetable fritters, then something rich and herby may fit the bill:

*1 tablespoon white wine vinegar, a
    tarragon-flavored one if you
    like*
1 shallot, minced
a large pinch of salt
2 tablespoons extra virgin olive oil

*2 tablespoons sharp, thick cream,
    such as* crème fraîche, *sour
    cream, or* fromage blanc
*1 tablespoon chopped fresh parsley,
    and another of chopped tarragon
    or chervil*

Mix the vinegar with the shallot and salt. Whisk in the oil and the cream, gently mixing till amalgamated. Stir in the fresh herbs.

Some of the bolder-flavored leaves, such as the bitter red and white chicories, piquant arugula, and lemony sorrel, respond better to an assertive but richly-flavored dressing. A drop or two from a bottle of balsamic vinegar, as precious as frankincense, will add a deep warmth to the other, more pedestrian ingredients.

1 tablespoon red wine vinegar
2 teaspoons balsamic vinegar
a small pinch of salt
freshly ground black pepper

*2 tablespoons hazelnut or walnut
    oil*
2 tablespoons peanut oil

Mix the vinegars with the salt and pepper. Whisk in both the oils and check the seasoning.

Many supermarkets now offer a selection of salads prepared at a central depot and delivered daily. Some of these ready-made salads, though expensive, can be convenient. Possibilities are *tabbouleh,* eggplant "caviar," grated carrot salad, and artichokes marinated in oil and lemon.

TOMATOES

Fresh Tomatoes

What are we to do about tomatoes? For the majority of the year they are flabby and tasteless, the result of supermarkets' desire for uniformity rather than flavor. Yet in high summer and autumn they can be superb: fragrant, firm, and flavorsome.

Tomatoes need sunshine: relentless scorching sun that burns their leaves to a crisp and concentrates the fruits' flavor. I have crept into fields in Italy and France and eaten the odd one straight from the vine, the tomato-eaters' version of "scrumping" apples. At the first twist of the fruit from the stem, the difference is clear: they are at once spicily fragrant, with a deep, rich taste. They have a tartness to them.

A tomato needs to fight for its flavor. When the fruit has a tough time, sharing fields with other crops and exposed to the vicious sun, the flavor sings out loud. The fruit's magic is lost when it is pampered under plastic and fed on fertilizer.

My answer is to look for knarled, odd-shaped fruit that occasionally appear in the supermarkets, or to go for the egg-shaped plum tomatoes. If you have a choice, buy the ones with their stems still intact, which to my mind taste better. Generally speaking the less perfect-looking the fruit the better the flavor. Beware, too, of those whoppers called beefsteak tomatoes, which can be as disappointing as the small ones, only more so. A tomato's flavor is richest when freshly picked. It can be kept for a few days on the windowsill; refrigeration seems to dull the flavor.

Canned Tomatoes

Some people are very sniffy about canned plum tomatoes. I think they are life-savers in the winter, when they will add much more flavor to a vegetable stew or sauce than fresh tomatoes. I always try to have a couple of cans in the kitchen, Italian brands by preference. I chop them up before adding them to a dish as they have an amazing resilience if tipped in straight from the can. Their copious canning juices are a bonus, but can be a nuisance if you try to chop the fruit on a board. I tend to attack them with a small sharp knife while still in the can, which is bad news for the knife blade (metal against metal) but saves losing all those valuable juices.

TOMATOES WITH GARLIC

I love to eat late-summer tomatoes when they are slightly warm, straight from the vine on my windowsill. This is an occasional treat, though, and for the most part I buy them from my local healthfood store, which has a good supply of small, organically grown ones all summer long.

I am not convinced that a tomato salad needs vinegar in the dressing. A good tomato has enough natural acidity, and really only needs a drizzle of olive oil to make a fine salad. This is the time to use some of that bottle of terribly expensive extra virgin olive oil.

FOR 2

2 large tomatoes, ripe but firm	*salt*
1 clove of new season's garlic—	*fresh basil*
mild, fresh, and sweet	*extra virgin olive oil*

Slice the tomatoes in half, without bothering to peel them. Score lines across the cut sides in a criss-cross pattern with a sharp knife. Peel the garlic and slice it very thinly—as thin as paper. Stick the slices of garlic into the cuts, and sprinkle with salt. Tear the basil into small pieces and scatter over the tomatoes. Drizzle over a little olive oil and eat immediately, preferably out of doors, in the sunshine.

BROILED TOMATOES

A piquant accompaniment to broiled meat or fish, I often eat these alone for lunch with just some very crusty white bread to mop up the buttery juices.

4 medium ripe tomatoes per person   *freshly ground black pepper*
salt   *butter*

Broil the tomatoes whole until the skins blacken slightly. Peel back the skins, which will be very hot, halfway down the fruits and squash the flesh slightly with a fork. Grind a little salt and black pepper over them and add a small piece of softened butter to each one. Serve hot.

POMODORI FRITTI

In her book *The Tuscan Year,* Elizabeth Romer describes her life during a year spent in a secret Tuscan valley. Her account is spiced with recipes from her cook, Silvana. This idea is hers.

4 large, slightly underripe   *fine cornmeal*
   tomatoes   *olive oil for frying*

Cut the tomatoes into thick slices. Scatter the cornmeal on a plate, then roll the tomato pieces in it.

Heat one finger's depth of olive oil in a shallow pan. Fry the tomatoes in it until golden and crisp. They will crackle and spit. Drain on a paper towel and serve hot. Eat with a mozzarella salad scattered with basil leaves.

DEEP-FRIED TOMATO AND PESTO SANDWICH

Prepare the tomatoes as for *Pomodori Fritti,* then sandwich between halves of a crusty baguette spread with mayonnaise into which you have stirred a little pesto sauce from the jar.

▶ These fried tomatoes make a fine accompaniment to any plainly broiled fish or meat or, especially, any of the eggplant dishes in this book

TOMATO AND ANCHOVY TOAST

One of my very favorite snacks. I sometimes add a few fresh basil leaves torn into shreds or a scattering of oregano if there is some around.

FOR 2

1 small onion, minced
1 tablespoon wine vinegar
4 tablespoons olive oil
salt
freshly ground black pepper

4 tomatoes
2 thick slices of crusty bread
1 clove of garlic, peeled
6 anchovy fillets

Put the chopped onion in a bowl with the vinegar. Stir in half of the olive oil. Season and set aside.

Slice the tomatoes into thick pieces. Sprinkle over a little salt and pepper and cook them under a preheated broiler. Toast the bread on both sides until golden. Cut the garlic in half and rub the cut side over the crisp toast. Pour over the remaining olive oil.

Place the broiled tomato slices on the slices of toast, crush them slightly with a fork, and put the anchovy fillets on top. Drizzle over the onion dressing and eat while hot.

TOMATO AND BASIL SANDWICH

This is the most basic of cheese and tomato sandwiches. Add to it what you will: watercress, scallions, cucumber, alfalfa sprouts, or garlic mayonnaise. I always use white bread—somehow brown bread with tomatoes is not the same.

MAKES 2 SANDWICHES

4 ounces sharp Cheddar cheese
2 ripe tomatoes
salt
freshly ground black pepper
*8 or so fresh basil leaves, torn into
   thin shreds*

*6 tablespoons mayonnaise—home-
   made or bought*
4 thick slices of crusty white bread
1 medium sweet onion, sliced thinly

Slice the cheese, though not too thinly. Wipe the tomatoes and slice them thickly. Grind over some salt and pepper and scatter over the basil leaves.

Spread the mayonnaise on the bread. Put the cheese and the tomato on two of the slices of bread. Place the onion rings over the tomatoes and cover with the remaining slices of bread.

CHERRY TOMATO AND WATERCRESS SALAD

I like the acidity of bright orange-red cherry tomatoes. If I can resist the temptation to eat them whole walking back from the store, they make a piquant addition to a leafy salad. Try them with young spinach leaves or watercress or those floppy, slightly furry, leaves of corn salad (*mâche*).

FOR 2

12 cherry tomatoes
*2 handfuls of watercress, washed
   and tough stems removed*

4 tablespoons virgin olive oil
salt
freshly ground black pepper

Cut the tomatoes in half; this is not strictly necessary, but they tend to have an annoying fork-dodging quality to them if you do not. Place them in a china bowl, strew the watercress on top, and drizzle over the olive oil. Add salt and pepper, toss gently, and eat with white crusty bread—one of those Italian loaves such as the holey *ciabatta* would be good.

TOMATOES FRIED WITH BUTTER AND SUGAR

I know the sugar sounds odd, but it really is worth trying.

FOR 2 AS AN ACCOMPANIMENT

2 tablespoons butter
1 pound (about 2½ cups) cherry
  tomatoes
scant ½ teaspoon sugar

salt
freshly ground black pepper

Melt the butter in a frying pan; when it foams add the tomatoes. Keep them moving while they cook, about 2 minutes. Sprinkle over the sugar, toss the tomatoes, and add salt and pepper, the coarser the better. Serve hot with French bread.

SUMMER TOMATOES WITH CREAM AND CHIVES

Allow 2 large or 3 medium tomatoes per person. Wipe them, slice them thinly, and lay on a cold plate. Snip 2 fresh chives per person into tiny pieces and stir into some heavy cream, allowing 2 tablespoons per person. Season the cream with a little salt and a grinding of black pepper and spoon over the tomatoes. A surprisingly good dish.

TOMATO SALAD

In summer, and only when we have had plenty of sun, I like to make a salad with nothing more than underripe local tomatoes and a slightly sweetened olive oil and parsley dressing.

FOR 2

1 pound tomatoes, ever so slightly
  underripe
salt
freshly ground black pepper
½ teaspoon sugar

1 tablespoon chopped fresh basil
  leaves
2 tablespoons chopped fresh
  parsley
3 tablespoons extra virgin olive oil

Slice the tomatoes, thinly or thickly, whichever you prefer. Sprinkle over some salt, pepper, and sugar and scatter on the herbs. Drizzle over the olive oil and leave for as long as you can before eating, but at any rate more than 15 minutes. This way the tomatoes can marinate in the slightly sweetened dressing.

EGGS BAKED IN TOMATOES

An idea adapted from a recipe of Margaret Costa's.

Cut some large tomatoes in half horizontally and scoop out the seeds. Sprinkle with salt and a little minced garlic. Break an egg, very carefully, into each tomato, but don't use more than a very little of the white. Season with salt and freshly ground pepper.

Spoon 1 tablespoon heavy cream over each egg, and season with salt and pepper and a few chopped fresh herbs (tarragon would be nice, if you have some).

Sprinkle over a little Parmesan cheese and bake in a preheated 350°F oven for 15–20 minutes, or until the egg has just set; they need careful timing. Serve, in Mrs. Costa's words, "on a croûton of bread fried crisp and golden in hot olive oil."

TOMATO STEW

I often make a double quantity of this juicy stew and eat it cold the next day.

FOR 4

4 tablespoons olive oil
1 medium onion, diced
2 cloves of garlic, sliced thinly
1 bay leaf
1¾ pounds ripe sweet bell peppers, red and yellow, cored, seeded, and cut into large pieces

1 pound tomatoes, chopped
salt
freshly ground black pepper

Heat the oil in a heavy-based pan, add the onion, and cook over a gentle heat until the onion is golden, about 5–7 minutes. Add the garlic and the bay leaf and continue cooking for 2 minutes, then throw in the peppers and cook for a further 10 minutes. Add the tomatoes and some salt and pepper and cook, stirring occasionally, for 10 minutes. Serve hot or cold.

BASIL, TOMATO, AND ANCHOVY DIP

The credit for this addictive dip goes to Lynda Brown, author of *The Cook's Garden*. She uses it as a sauce for broiled fish. I like it spread on pita bread or toast.

Combine 1 peeled large and very ripe tomato, a handful of fresh basil leaves, and 1 anchovy fillet with enough olive oil to make a thick sauce.

Five Fast Tomato Sauces

A FRESH TOMATO SAUCE

4 tablespoons butter
1 onion, sliced
2 pounds ripe tomatoes

salt
1 tablespoon chopped fresh basil
freshly ground black pepper

Melt the butter in a pan, add the onion, and cook gently until soft. Pour boiling water over the tomatoes, leave them to scald for no longer than 1 minute, then drain them and peel off the skins. Cut each tomato in half, scoop the seeds out with your fingers, and discard. Chop each tomato roughly and toss into the pan with the softened onions.

Add 1 teaspoon salt and the chopped basil, then simmer gently for 10 minutes. Season with a screw or two of black pepper.

AN UNCOOKED TOMATO SAUCE

2 pounds ripe tomatoes
½ small onion, chopped
1 clove of garlic, minced
1 wineglass of olive oil

10 or so fresh basil leaves, torn
   into little bits
salt
freshly ground black pepper

Pour boiling water over the tomatoes and leave them to scald for 1 minute. Drain them, peel off the skins, and cut the fruit in half. Scoop out the seeds and throw them away. Chop the tomatoes finely.

Put the tomatoes in a bowl and stir in all the other ingredients. Allow to sit at room temperature for a while before using; give it at least 20 minutes if you can.

CHERRY TOMATO SAUCE

Cherry tomatoes are bursting with flavor, especially the ones that are speckled with green. They make a quick, if slightly extravagant, sauce.

1 pound (about 2½ cups) ripe cherry
   tomatoes
1 wineglass of water
1 tablespoon olive oil

salt
freshly ground black pepper
a handful of chopped fresh parsley

Tip the tomatoes into a pan and cook until they start to burst. Pour in the water and leave them to bubble for 5 or 6 minutes.

Push the tomatoes through a strainer with a spoon, then stir in the olive oil, seasonings, and herbs.

CANNED TOMATO SAUCE

Come winter, I make this sauce at least once a week. All the ingredients are in the pantry, and it has been a life-saver on more than one occasion.

Peel and slice one large, or two small, onions. Put them in a pan with a generous piece of butter, cover with a lid, and simmer gently until the onion is soft.

Chop a large can of plum tomatoes and tip into the onions with the juice. Cook gently, uncovered and seasoned with a little sea salt, for 10 minutes. Grind over a bit of black pepper, add a further bit of butter, and use at once.

TOMATO-CHILI SAUCE

This is the ubiquitous tomato sauce of Mexico. I make it when I have bought tomatoes that do not taste as good as they look.

4 large ripe tomatoes
1 small onion, minced
2 fresh hot green chilies, seeded
   and chopped

a small handful of fresh cilantro
   leaves, chopped
salt

Chop the tomatoes finely—there is no need to remove the skins—and mix with all the other ingredients.

Broiled Tomato Sauce

Use this sauce with pasta or as an accompaniment to broiled vegetables, fish, or meat, or serve it, blisteringly hot, in individual bowls with very crusty bread as a snack.

Place washed whole tomatoes on the broiler pan. Place them under the broiler (or on the grill) and cook until they are soft and their skins are black and charred. They will probably have split, too. Drop the tomatoes, skins and all, into a food processor or blender. Whizz till puréed, a matter of seconds, then add a little sea salt.

GRAINS, LENTILS, *and* BEANS

T he most upwardly mobile of foods, these earthy,
comforting foods are all the rage. It has been
interesting to witness the way fashionable chefs have
embraced the humble lentil, even mushy yellow polenta,
for goodness sake, and elevated them to such heights.
Couscous is appearing on all the smart restaurant
menus, while rice pudding is moving in chic circles,
sometimes rolled into croquettes and fried in butter. No
doubt all these will suffer the same fall from grace as
other chefs' toys such as kiwi fruit. Fortunately, home
cooks are less fickle, and those who have recently
discovered these staples will hold onto them long after
the trendy chefs have focused on some other mundane
thing that many of us have been enjoying for years.

For grains, read comfort food. A bowl of steaming
oatmeal, a plate of risotto, or a bowl of sweet rice
pudding. Can there be a food that makes you feel more
secure, more at peace with the world?

I rank lentils and beans, along with potatoes and
pasta, as some of my very favorite foods. The fact that
they have to be soaked and take a good while to cook

should exclude them from a book on fast food. But I cannot think of life, or should I say meals, without them. Lentils cook quickly and canned beans, though not as good as homecooked ones, are perfectly satisfactory.

GRAINS

Bulgar, bulgur, or burghul wheat is a favorite of mine. It has a nutty taste and grainy texture that I find a pleasing change from rice.

I have also learned to love polenta, the Italian cornmeal mush. Whether I would have had the chance had it not become so fashionable in recent years I do not know. Like lentils, it has become difficult to avoid in trendy restaurants. Quinoa is an ancient Andean grain that has a most fascinating bobbly texture in the mouth and a very slight bitterness that I find refreshingly different. Buy it in health-food stores.

How relevant are grains to the cook in a hurry? Wild rice and whole wheat take almost an hour to cook, and are of little use unless they have been cooked earlier and can be incorporated into another dish. I have, though, cooked enough wild rice for two in just over half an hour, serving it with nothing but butter lest its very special texture and nutty flavor should be spoiled. Bulgur wheat, the grain cracked by boiling, needs only to be soaked before appearing with apricots, plums, lemon juice, and masses of brilliant green parsley for a *tabbouleh*.

Cooked rolled oats can be stirred into hot butter and seasoned with onions and black pepper for an earthy accompaniment. Some evenings after a taxing day I take solace in a warming bowl of rice, white, preferably the hugely fragrant basmati, into which I stir whatever I have at hand. A lump of garlicky soft cheese, a spoonful of *harissa* sauce, or cooked lentils and a handful of fresh mint. It is not a question of needless frugality; I thoroughly enjoy eating so simply. It is often worth cooking a little extra to reheat the following day. Rice can be fried and tossed with beaten egg, and almost all grains can be bound with beaten egg, spiced, and patted into cakes for frying.

I always like to keep some sprouted grain in my refrigerator. Sometimes I grow my own: mung beans are the easiest and taste like tiny fresh peas. Although I have a salad sprouter, a series of perforated trays over a tray filled with fresh water, you can easily sprout them in a jar. A bag of alfalfa or radish sprouts is useful to have around. They are good sandwich fillers, particularly for those involving cheese, and are notoriously nutritious. For a fast fix they can be piled onto whole wheat bread and topped with thick yogurt and a sliced avocado.

OATMEAL

I include oatmeal porridge in this collection at the suggestion of Derek Cooper, of BBC Radio 4's *The Food Programme.* The heat on which the oatmeal cooks is all important. It should not boil, but simmer peacefully, "gently erupting and heaving like gray lava," writes Mr. Cooper in *A La Carte* Magazine. "Giving the familiar 'plop' every few minutes just to show it is still cooking" is how Catherine Brown puts it in her book, *Scottish Cookery.*

ENOUGH FOR 2

2½ cups water   *salt*
⅔ cup Scotch oats or Irish oatmeal (too
fine a grain gives a pappy
consistency)

Put the water on to boil. A thick-based pan will help keep the mixture from burning. Dribble in the oatmeal with one hand while stirring with the other. A spurtle, a tapered wooden stick, is the traditional tool for this, but a wooden spoon will do. Tradition also decrees that oatmeal should be stirred clockwise.

Set the pan over a very low heat and leave to cook. The heat should be at a level where the surface hardly moves, giving only the occasional "glop." The consistency is determined by the length of time it cooks. Five minutes will give a sloppy texture, while 10 will ensure the oats retain some bite. Longer than 30 minutes and you will be able to cut it with a knife.

Taste and salt the oatmeal once it has reduced to your liking. Any earlier and the salt may cause the grains to harden. Eat hot, according to Ms. Brown, by dipping each spoon of hot oatmeal into cold milk, thus ensuring the oatmeal in your bowl keeps warm.

Good things to put in your Oatmeal

I make the following suggestions, some stolen and some unorthodox. Taste the oatmeal first, then add salt and any of the following. Do not omit the salt even though you may also be adding sugar. The salt is important to bring out the flavor of the oatmeal.

► Heather honey and butter

► Blackberries, honey, and cream

► Heather honey and Scotch whisky

► Thick plain yogurt and light molasses

► A warm compote of raspberries, blackberries, and blueberries with a spoonful of buttermilk

► Ground cinnamon and toasted hazelnuts

BULGUR WHEAT AND BLACK-EYED PEAS

I often use this earthy mixture, with its unusual texture of grain and bean, as a tool for soaking up the juices from a runny stew. Add shredded vegetables—dark green cabbage, crinkly spinach leaves, sliced zucchini, or florets of broccoli—and you have a feast.

FOR 2 AS A MAIN DISH, 4 AS AN ACCOMPANIMENT

2 tablespoons peanut oil
1 medium onion, roughly chopped
1⅓ cups black-eyed peas, precooked or canned and well rinsed

⅔ cup bulgur wheat
salt
freshly ground black pepper

Warm the oil in a deep pan, add the onion, and cook for 5–10 minutes, stirring occasionally, until soft and translucent.

Add the black-eyed peas and the bulgur wheat. Stir in 1¼ cups of water, or cooking water from the beans if you have cooked your own. Simmer for 15 minutes. Taste and check the seasoning.

BULGUR WHEAT AND EGGPLANT PILAF

A hearty main dish with half an eye to the Middle East. It is also an excellent accompaniment to broiled lamb or spiced chicken.

If you can remember to soak the bulgur wheat before you leave the house in the morning, you can cut down the cooking time. Remove the bulgur wheat from its water, wringing it out with your hands, and stir it into the eggplant and onion mixture. Heat through for 2 minutes and then add the seasonings. The consistency should be slightly runny, like a risotto. Add a minced clove of garlic with the onion if that takes your fancy.

FOR 4 AS AN ACCOMPANIMENT, 2 AS A MAIN DISH

4 tablespoons olive oil	1¼ cups vegetable stock or
1 bay leaf (optional)	water
1 small onion, sliced	2 tablespoons pine nuts
2 small eggplants, cut into	1 tablespoon minced fresh mint
1-inch cubes	about 12 leaves
1½ cups bulgur wheat	salt

Warm the olive oil, with a bay leaf if you have one, in a large pan. Add the onion and cook till it starts to soften, about 3 or 4 minutes. Add the eggplant cubes and cook over a medium heat, adding a drop more oil if necessary, until tender, about 4 minutes.

Tip in the bulgur wheat. Stir. Pour in the vegetable stock or water. If you are using fresh stock or water you should add salt, too. Simmer for 10 minutes, or until the water has evaporated. As soon as the liquid has disappeared, stir in the pine nuts and mint, taste for seasoning, and serve.

Bulgur Wheat with Mushrooms

I use Gruyère here because I particularly like its flavor and texture when slightly melted. It is far from essential, though, and sometimes I use Cheddar or whatever comes to hand. A warming, frugal dish this, and a great favorite of mine with a glass or two of red wine.

FOR 4 AS A MAIN DISH

½ pound mushrooms
2 tablespoons peanut oil
1⅓ cups bulgur wheat
4 ounces Gruyère cheese, cut into
   1-inch cubes

salt
freshly ground black pepper

Cut the mushrooms into quarters and cook them in a shallow pan with the oil for 3 or 4 minutes, until they are soft and golden brown. Remove them from the pan with a slotted spoon into a bowl. Keep warm.

Add the bulgur wheat to the pan, tossing the grains in what remains of the oil. Pour in 1¼ cups water and add a pinch of salt. Simmer the grains gently for 6 minutes. Taste the bulgur to see if it is tender; if not, cook for another couple of minutes.

Stir in the mushrooms and cheese, and season with black pepper and more salt if needed.

Fresh Plum *Tabbouleh*

The sumptuousness of ripe plums, the nutty bulgur grains, and the refreshing notes from the mint and lemon produces a salad of myriad flavors and textures.

FOR 4 AS AN ACCOMPANIMENT OR 2 AS A LIGHT LUNCH

½ cup bulgur wheat
a large handful fresh
   flat-leaf parsley
a small handful fresh mint
juice of 2 lemons
2 tablespoons olive oil

salt
freshly ground black pepper
4 small scallions, trimmed
½ pound (about 6) perfectly ripe,
   juicy plums

Cover the bulgur wheat with cold water and soak for 15 minutes. Mince the parsley and mint. Place in a salad bowl with the lemon juice, olive oil, salt, and a few grinds of pepper. Chop or snip the scallions into small pieces.

Halve each plum, pull or cut out the pit, and toss them into the herbs and dressing. Squeeze the water from the bulgur wheat with your hands. Drop the grains into the salad bowl and then mix gently with the plums and herbs.

BULGUR WHEAT WITH MANGO AND MINT

I tend to eat tropical fruits, such as mangoes, papayas, and passion fruit, for breakfast rather than chopping them up into after-dinner fruit salads. Finding hungry friends on my doorstep one summer lunchtime, there was little in the house other than the contents of the fruit bowl and the usual pantry stuff. Mint in the garden was sheer luck, but I could have done without it. As an accompaniment this goes rather well with broiled chicken.

FOR 2 AS A MAIN COURSE SALAD, OR 4 AS A SIDE DISH

⅔ cup bulgur wheat
1 large mango, ripe and fragrant
juice of 1 lemon
2 tablespoons olive oil

a handful fresh mint
4 scallions or 1 small sweet
* red onion*

Soak the bulgur wheat in cold water for 15 minutes. Peel the mango, over a serving bowl to save the rich, sweet juice, then remove the flesh from the pit with a small knife. Cut the flesh into small dice and add to the bowl.

Pour in the lemon juice and the oil, then chop the mint and add it to the mango. Chop the scallions or onion in small dice and add to the bowl. Wring the water from the bulgur wheat with your hands, then fold gently into the other ingredients. Leave for a few minutes for the flavors to marry.

Bulgur Wheat Pilaf with Butter and Almonds

The simplest imaginable winter supper. A perfect antidote to over-indulgence, and reassuringly frugal. Lift the spirits by serving it with a fruity, peppery salad of watercress and blood orange.

FOR 2 AS A MAIN DISH, 4 AS AN ACCOMPANIMENT

1⅓ cups bulgur wheat
1¼ cups water or vegetable
  stock
salt

freshly ground black pepper
4 tablespoons butter
⅓ cup sliced almonds,
  toasted

Put the bulgur wheat in a pan with the vegetable stock or water. Add salt—I think the grain needs it when served hot—and a few turns of the peppermill. Let it simmer over a low heat for 8 minutes, by which time most of the water will have been absorbed. Taste it; if it is not tender, then cook it for a minute or two longer.

Remove the pan from the heat. Stir in the butter and the toasted almonds and leave, with the lid on, for a further 10 minutes to absorb the butter. Taste the mixture and add more salt and pepper if you think it needs it, then serve.

Onion Skirlie

I was reminded of this simple accompaniment by Catherine Brown in her book, *Scottish Cookery.* It makes a fine side dish for roasted game or broiled oily fish such as mackerel.

FOR 2 AS A SIDE DISH

4 tablespoons drippings or butter
1 large onion, minced
⅔ cup Scotch oats or Irish oatmeal

salt
freshly ground black pepper

Melt the drippings or butter in a shallow pan over a medium heat. Add the onion and cook until soft, about 5 minutes. Sprinkle in the oatmeal, and season with the salt and pepper.

When all of the fat has been absorbed, which should take a couple of minutes, the skirlie is ready. Serve hot.

Date and Pistachio Couscous

I love cooking couscous the traditional Berber way: rinsing and soaking the grains of semolina, then drying and steaming them, separating the grains, then steaming them again.

I don't often have time to mess around with all that though. Here is a quick method.

FOR 4 AS AN ACCOMPANIMENT TO A SLOPPY, SPICY STEW

1⅓ cups couscous	*½ cup chopped fresh dates*
⅔ cup dried apricots	*butter*
½ cup pitted prunes	
½ cup shelled pistachio nuts	

Cover the couscous in a bowl with an equal volume of water. Stir occasionally until the grains have absorbed all the water, which will take about 15 minutes.

Cut the dried apricots and prunes into quarters. Rub the couscous through your fingers, smoothing out any lumps. Mix the grains and all the chopped fruit with the pistachios. Dump the whole lot into a shallow dish, cover tightly with foil, and bake in a preheated 425 °F oven for 20 minutes, till hot.

Remove the foil and fluff up the couscous with a fork while stirring in a large piece of butter.

QUINOA WITH BELL PEPPERS AND OREGANO

This comforting grain, available from healthfood stores, makes a fine supper when cooked with onion and garlic, and then tossed with broiled bell peppers. If you don't have the oregano, use marjoram, either fresh or dried. I have served it with Baked Feta and Thyme, see page 270, with some success.

FOR 4 AS AN ACCOMPANIMENT

2 red bell peppers, halved, seeds removed, and cut into long strips	*2 cloves of garlic, sliced*
	1 bay leaf
4 tablespoons olive oil	*2 teaspoons dried oregano*
¾ cup quinoa	*2 tablespoons chopped fresh*
1 medium onion, minced	*parsley*

Put the pepper strips on the bottom of the broiler pan, drizzle on half the olive oil, and cook under a preheated broiler for about 5 minutes on each side, turning once, till sweet, very tender, and black at the edges.

Pour the quinoa into a fine-mesh strainer and rinse under cold running water. Warm the remaining oil in a shallow saucepan or high-sided frying pan and fry the onion and the garlic till soft, 8–10 minutes, on a medium heat. Add the bay leaf, oregano, and quinoa. Pour over 2 cups water and simmer for 8 minutes. Almost all the liquid will have been absorbed.

Remove the peppers from the broiler, stir them into the quinoa and onion mixture with the parsley, and serve.

QUINOA WITH THYME AND TALEGGIO

The pleasure of this substantial supper is in the mixture of textures: the tiny bobbles of quinoa and the melting cubes of hot cheese. Almost any cheese will work well, but particularly Gruyère, Cheddar, and Mozzarella. Save a few thyme leaves for scattering over the top as you serve it.

FOR 2 AS A MAIN COURSE, WITH SALAD

2 tablespoons olive oil	*1 clove of garlic, sliced*
leaves from 4 sprigs of fresh thyme	*⅔ cup quinoa*
1 bay leaf (optional)	*1 wineglass of dry white wine*
1 medium leek, trimmed and shredded	*1¼ cups hot vegetable stock*
	4 ounces Taleggio cheese, sliced

Warm the oil with the thyme leaves, and a bay leaf if you have one, in a pan over a gentle heat. Add the leek and the garlic and cook for 5 minutes, covered, stirring from time to time.

Tip in the quinoa and the wine. Let the wine bubble away (you need its flavor, not its liquid), then pour in the hot stock. Simmer, stirring occasionally, for 10 minutes, watching that it does not stick on the bottom. When the stock has been absorbed by the quinoa grains, stir in the cheese. Serve right away.

RICE

My favorite rice is the fragrant basmati, which is pertinent to this book because it cooks quicker than some. I have had little joy from the boil-in-the-bag instant rices that I somehow manage to over-cook, even when I stick to the instructions like glue. I much prefer to wait slightly longer for basmati. Rice reheats reasonably well, at least better than pasta, and it may be worth cooking a little extra, cooling it quickly, and keeping it in the refrigerator for the next day. I have reheated many a bowl of rice in a colander over boiling water, then tipped it into a bowl and stirred in something savory from the cupboard.

PLAIN WHITE RICE

Exactly what it says. Serve as an accompaniment or as a main course if you are feeling decidedly delicate.

FOR 4 AS AN ACCOMPANIMENT

1 cup long-grain white rice   *1 teaspoon salt*

Put the rice into a heavy-based saucepan. Add the salt and 2 cups of cold water.

Bring to a boil, then turn the heat down to a simmer and cover with a lid. Cook for 12 minutes, no longer. Lift the lid: there should be no water left and little steam holes should have appeared in the rice. Lift a few grains of rice out with a fork and taste them to see if the rice is tender. It probably is. Replace the lid and remove the pan from the heat. Leave for 2 minutes.

Good things to stir into Rice

There are times when a bowl of steaming rice, perfumed basmati or pure and comforting white, is simply enough. When this is the case, try stirring in one of the following aromatic mixtures.

► Lots of butter and Parmesan cheese

► Sliced mushrooms sautéed in butter with a teaspoon ground coriander

► A handful of toasted pine nuts

► A can of lentils, drained and well-rinsed, warmed with a bit of butter

► Hot spinach, shredded and cooked in butter

► Shavings of Pecorino Romano cheese and shredded raw bulb fennel

► A spoonful of black olive paste and a couple of finely sliced sun-dried tomatoes

► Fresh tarragon leaves and a spoonful of tarragon vinegar

► Shredded carrot, toasted sliced almonds, and raisins

► Thin shreds of ham—Italian Parma or Spanish *serrano*—or cubes of cooked smoked pancetta

► Cubes of smoked bacon, cooked crisp, stirred in with their hot fat

► A tablespoon extra virgin olive oil and a dash of balsamic vinegar

► A lump of commercial soft garlic and herb-flavored cheese

► Herb butter and a squeeze of lemon juice

► A handful of fresh mint, chopped, and half an English hothouse cucumber, peeled and diced

► A rich, buttery cheese, such as Brie or Taleggio, cut into cubes

► A spoonful of basil pesto from a jar

► Minced hot chilies and chopped fresh cilantro

► A spoonful of spicy *harissa* sauce

FRAGRANT BROWN BASMATI RICE

Nutty brown rice scented with turmeric, cloves, and cinnamon is the perfect accompaniment for broiled meats, spicy stews, and soupy vegetable casseroles. The cooking method here is entirely unorthodox—but it works. The first boiling cuts out the long soaking, and the slightly reduced cooking time gives a chewy bite to the rice.

FOR 4 AS AN ACCOMPANIMENT

1½ cups brown basmati rice	*8 green cardamom pods*
1 tablespoon peanut oil	*2 bay leaves*
½ teaspoon ground turmeric	*salt*
3 whole cloves	*juice of ½ lemon*
½ stick of cinnamon	*2 tablespoons butter*

Put the rice in a deep pan and pour in enough water to cover the rice by about 1 inch. Boil hard over a high heat for 5 minutes. Meanwhile, warm the oil in a saucepan and fry the spices and bay leaves for 2 minutes, till fragrant.

Pour the rice into a strainer over the sink. Tip the drained rice into the pan containing the spices, cover with fresh water, add salt, and bring to a boil.

Turn down the heat, put on a lid, and cook slowly for 15 minutes. By this time the rice will have absorbed all the water. Remove from the heat and allow the rice to stand, still covered, for a full 10 minutes.

Remove the lid, add the lemon juice and the butter, and fluff up the grains of rice with a fork. Discard the bay leaves. Tip into a warm bowl and serve.

RISOTTO WITH PARMESAN CHEESE

The risotto only just makes it into this collection. It requires half an hour of your undivided attention. Even so, I find it perfectly possible to throw a salad together while keeping a very close eye on the rice. Radicchio and bulb fennel or mushrooms would be my choice. You will need Italian *arborio* rice if your risotto is to have an authentic consistency.

FOR 4 AS A MAIN DISH

1 small onion, minced	*1 quart hot vegetable or*
4 tablespoons butter	* chicken stock*
1¼ cups arborio *rice*	*4 tablespoons butter*
1 wineglass of dry white wine	*½ cup grated Parmesan cheese*

Cook the onion in the butter over a medium heat until soft, about 5 minutes. Add the rice, stir, and then pour in the wine. Continue cooking until the wine has reduced by half, then pour in a ladleful of stock.

Let the risotto simmer gently, adding another ladle or two of stock each time the liquid is absorbed into the rice. Stir, almost constantly, ignoring the telephone or anything else demanding attention, until the rice has taken up all the stock. If you intend to follow with a salad, make it near to the stove, so that you can keep a watchful eye on the rice.

After 25 minutes cooking time, stir in the butter and grated cheese. The risotto is ready when the rice is *al dente,* that is, when tender but retaining some bite, and the consistency is creamy.

Good things to put in a Risotto

Add to the above recipe:

Asparagus

1 pound freshly boiled asparagus can be added after the onion has been sautéed. Half the stock should be replaced with the asparagus cooking water. Serve Parmesan cheese at the table

Zucchini

Add 4 medium zucchini, sliced into thin rounds, cooked till golden with the onions

Celery
Add 4 stalks of celery, sliced as thick as coins, when the onions are soft. Include some of the celery leaves, a small handful, which add a delightful aroma

Artichoke Hearts
Probably the best use for bottled, canned, or frozen artichoke hearts is to cut them into quarters and toss them in a risotto. You will need at least 12 for 4 people. Add them when the onions are soft. Throw in lots of fresh parsley, too

Fennel
The loveliest of all. Add finely shredded raw bulb fennel and the merest hint of Pernod or Ricard if you have some, after the onions. Throw in a handful of minced fresh parsley. Oh, and be generous with the Parmesan

BASIC FRIED RICE

I have watched Shanghai-born chef Kam-Po But make this in his restaurant kitchen. Traditionally, it is more likely to be eaten at home than in a restaurant, where the savory dishes are better for being eaten with plain boiled rice.

FOR 2 AS AN ACCOMPANIMENT

2 cups cooked white rice
2 tablespoons peanut oil
*2 scallions, trimmed and cut
  in fine rounds*

1 egg, beaten with ½ teaspoon salt
salt

If the rice is very cold, fork it through to separate the grains. Heat the wok or frying pan, pour in the oil, and swirl it around the pan. Lower the heat and drop in the scallions. Fry for 30 seconds, stirring constantly.

Tip in the egg all at once, leave for a few seconds, and then stir to break up the setting egg. (Chopsticks are easiest for this.) Add the cooked rice. Toss the pan, pushing the egg and rice around the pan for 3 minutes. Taste, and add salt if necessary. Serve hot.

LENTILS *and* BEANS

Lentils take mercifully little time to cook, and few need soaking. The fashionable *lentils de Puy* are the ultimate. Their slate blue-green flesh has a deep spiciness and an earthy, nutty aroma. In summer I add red currants to sharpen a bowl of brown lentils. In winter I toss them into a tomato sauce spiced with hot chili if I am feeling too lazy to do more, or serve them as a side dish with a Middle-Eastern mint dressing.

Beans, though lacking the bite of homecooked ones, emerge from a can relatively unharmed as long as you rinse them thoroughly of their emetic brine and cook them only briefly to keep them *al dente*. I have made a dish of rich, creamy beans by warming cannellini beans from a can with cream, thyme, and tarragon, which is now a great favorite.

Pale green flageolet, white cannellini, and motley pink pinto beans all come in cans, and are an invaluable pantry staple. Drained, rinsed, and stirred into a spicy tomato sauce, then topped with grated cheese; they make a comforting winter supper that needs no recipe. Warm them with your best olive oil and a handful of fresh green beans, and you have a multi-textured side dish.

Canned chick peas (garbanzos) are virtually indistinguishable from the home-soaked and cooked ones. Open a can and you will save hours in soaking time and a fortune in fuel. I turn to them for whizzing up a garlicky dip for warm pita bread when I need a snack in seconds.

Much is made of the bean family's ability to induce flatulence. There are all sorts of methods for reducing this property, and I have even heard of research into producing beans that have had their remarkable phenomenon bred out of them. Personally, I am amazed at all the fuss. So, beans give you wind. And what is wrong with that?

LENTILS WITH TOMATOES

This pantry supper is a life-saver when the refrigerator contains nothing but the cat's milk and an old package of Japanese soy paste.

FOR 2

½ cup brown lentils
1 bay leaf
3 tablespoons olive oil
1 onion, chopped
1 fresh hot red chili, chopped

a 16-ounce can plum
  tomatoes, chopped
salt
freshly ground black pepper

Rinse the lentils in a strainer under running water. Cook them with the bay leaf and a tablespoon of the oil in boiling salted water for 15 minutes. Drain them in a colander.

Meanwhile, fry the onion in the remaining oil for about 5–7 minutes, until soft and golden. Add the chili and cook for a further minute or two. Add the drained lentils and the tomatoes with all their juice, plus some salt and pepper. Simmer gently for 10 minutes, and serve hot.

► Once associated with slow-cooking, the lentil, which cooks to perfection in 15–20 minutes and sometimes less, is good snack material. Sometimes I boil them with a bay leaf and a little oil, then just drain them and smother in soft butter and black pepper. How to feel indulgent at almost no cost

HOT BROWN LENTILS WITH MINT VINAIGRETTE

Small brown lentils will cook in about 20 minutes. Canned ones are quicker, but are somehow less toothsome and seem to lack the natural spiciness of freshly cooked ones.

FOR 2

1 heaped cup brown lentils	*salt*
1 bay leaf	*freshly ground black pepper*
a sprig of fresh mint	*1 shallot, minced*
leaves from 2 sprigs of fresh mint,	*2 tablespoons white wine vinegar*
chopped	*6 tablespoons extra virgin olive oil*

Rinse the lentils in a strainer under running water. Cook them (there is no need to soak them) in boiling salted water with the bay leaf and mint sprig until tender, about 20 minutes.

Meanwhile, make the dressing. Crush the mint leaves with a little salt in a small bowl. Add the minced shallot and pour in the vinegar. Mix in the oil with a fork. Season with pepper.

Drain the lentils and pour the dressing over them while they are still warm.

LENTIL AND RED CURRANT SALAD

Red currants have a short season during June and July. I like the different textures in this salad, with its spicy, nutty lentils and tart, fresh currants. Snap up white currants if ever you see them—they are even better.

FOR 2

1 cup small lentils, de Puy *or small*	*2 tablespoons extra virgin olive oil*
brown	*juice of 1 lemon or lime*
1 cup red currants	*salt*
4 fresh chives, chopped	*freshly ground black pepper*

Rinse the lentils in a strainer under running water. Cook them in boiling salted water for 12 minutes; they are cooked when tender but still firm to the touch. Drain and place in a bowl.

Trim the currants and add to the lentils. Snip the chives into ½-inch lengths and add them with the olive oil, lemon or lime juice, and some salt and pepper to the lentils. Mix all the ingredients gently so as not to crush the currants.

WARM TWO-BEAN SALAD

Inspired by David Scott, who runs the Everyman Bistro in Liverpool, the warm flageolet beans are given bite by the addition of a few crisp green beans. A good way to use up leftover beans. The better the olive oil, the more fragrant the dish.

FOR 2

⅔ cup canned or cooked flageolet beans
4 ounces green beans
2 tablespoons extra virgin olive oil

juice of 1 lemon
salt
freshly ground black pepper

Place the cooked flageolet beans in a saucepan and add just enough water to cover them. Put them on a low fire and bring gently to a simmer. Trim the green beans, and cook for 3 minutes in boiling salted water. Drain both types of beans and mix, while still warm, with the olive oil, lemon juice, and some salt and pepper.

WHITE BEANS WITH TARRAGON AND CREAM

A comforting dish of herby, creamy beans. You will need some bread to wipe up the juices from the plate, or serve it on toast.

FOR 2

a bit of butter
1 small onion, finely diced
1 bay leaf
1 small carrot, finely diced
2 sprigs of fresh thyme
leaves from 4 branches of fresh
  tarragon

a 16-ounce can cannellini
  or flageolet beans
⅔ cup light cream
salt
freshly ground black pepper

Melt the butter in a saucepan and fry the onion gently until it is soft and golden. It must not burn, or it will become bitter.

Add the bay leaf, carrot, thyme, and tarragon. Tip in the beans, well rinsed and drained. Pour in the cream and slowly bring to a boil. As soon as the mixture starts to boil remove it from the heat, correct the seasoning—it may need a good grinding of pepper—and serve hot.

HUMUS

An earthy-tasting purée of chick peas that can become addictive.

SERVES 5–6 AS A FIRST COURSE

1½ cups canned chick peas (garbanzos)
6 tablespoons tahini paste
2 cloves of garlic, peeled
6 tablespoons lemon juice
3 tablespoons olive oil

cayenne pepper
freshly ground black pepper
salt
olive oil, for drizzling

Whizz the chick peas in a food processor or blender with a little of the liquid from the can until they are smooth. Add the tahini, garlic, lemon juice, and olive oil and work in the processor or blender until very smooth. Season with the peppers and salt. Turn into a dish, scraping out all of the humus from the mixer bowl with a rubber spatula. Flatten the top slightly, then drizzle over some olive oil and serve with warm pita bread.

MICHAEL'S BEANS

I am always suspicious of recipes that "tart-up" commercial products, remembering the maxim about the uselessness of throwing good after bad. That said, I have found several canned or frozen products can be useful as a springboard for your own invention and whim. Canned baked beans are one of them. I prefer not the bland sweet beans that sell in their millions, but the ones available from healthfood stores. These contain no added sugar, have a lightly spicy sauce, and harbor no weird preservatives. This recipe is named after the friend whose idea it was.

FOR 2

1 tablespoon peanut or olive oil
6 thick slices of smoked bacon,
  diced
2 medium onions, thinly sliced
2 16-ounce cans best-quality
  baked beans, preferably unsweetened

2 fresh medium-hot red chilies,
  split, seeds removed, and
  chopped
4 tablespoons light or dark molasses
salt

Heat the oil and fry the bacon for about 3–4 minutes, till the fat turns golden in color. Add the onions and cook over a medium heat till they soften and sweeten, about 5–7 minutes. Tip in the beans. Add the chilies and simmer until the beans are thoroughly hot. Stir in 2 tablespoons of the molasses and taste, then add more molasses and some salt if you wish. Serve hot.

LAMB CHOPS WITH FLAGEOLET BEANS AND CILANTRO-PARSLEY SAUCE

I admire those who know what they will be eating the following day. They are the sort who remember to soak the beans overnight. I rarely have a clue what will be for supper tomorrow, which is why canned flageolet beans intrude into my recipe for lamb with beans.

FOR 2

4 plump cloves of garlic, peeled	*a 16-ounce can green flageolet*
2 large lamb sirloin chops, 1 inch	*or cannellini beans*
thick	*1 onion, thinly sliced*
salt	*1 bay leaf*
freshly ground black pepper	*1 small handful each of fresh*
7 tablespoons extra virgin	*parsley and cilantro leaves*
olive oil	

Put the garlic cloves in a small pan, cover with water, and simmer for 15 minutes. Season the chops and brush them with a little olive oil.

Drain the beans of their liquid, rinse them well and tip them into a medium saucepan. Add a little salt, and simmer with the onion, bay leaf, a sprig of the parsley, 1 tablespoon of olive oil, and enough water to cover. They are already cooked and need only gentle simmering for 5 minutes to heat through.

Broil the chops until brown on both sides, about 3 minutes per side; they will be pink in the middle. Drain the garlic and whizz in the food processor or blender with the cilantro, remaining parsley, and a little salt. Pour in the rest of the olive oil. Transfer to a small saucepan and warm through, but do not bring to a boil. Drain the beans, stir in half the garlic and parsley purée, and divide between 2 warm plates. Put a chop on each plate and spoon over the remaining purée.

CHICKEN

C hicken is the most versatile meat for the quick cook. Any cut—thigh, drumstick, whole leg, or breast half—is both accessible and easy to deal with. There is no need to embark on any butchery yourself; the butcher will cut exactly the pieces you need from a fresh bird. Prepacked pieces are available from any supermarket. Chicken also has the added advantage of being extremely low in fat compared to red meats.

There are broadly two types of chicken available. The best of these is range or free-range, where the birds are given more space indoors, are fed a vegetarian diet free of antibiotics, and are allowed to roam outdoors and forage for at least part of their food. Free-range chickens, which are available from butchers, wholefood markets, and some supermarkets, are more expensive than the alternative, mass-produced birds. These "battery" chickens live their short lives in large windowless sheds, a more uncomfortable existence than that of free-range birds, as they grow from chicks to full-sized chickens. Their feed is laced with antibiotics to guard against disease, though many birds die before slaughter. The flavor of these chickens is thought to be much blander (some would describe it as tasteless) than that of free-range birds.

CHAPTER SEVEN

Free-rangers mature more slowly without the growth promoters added to mass-produced birds' feed, and are therefore sold at a premium. These birds are hardier breeds than those used in intensive farming, which combined with their opportunity to feed naturally and take some exercise, results in a better-flavored bird. Unfortunately the free-range system is open to abuse, so it is best to buy from a reputable supplier.

The chicken recipes that follow were all developed using free-range chickens. The meat is matched with its natural partners, such as garlic, olives, butter, spices, cream, and fresh herbs like tarragon and parsley.

One final point, when buying chicken: beware of the pieces in the stores that have had their skin removed. The skin is a valuable asset, crisping deliciously and keeping the flesh moist during cooking.

CHICKEN IN HOISIN SAUCE

An approximation of a dish I ate in a Chinese restaurant in Paris. I asked for the recipe, but was none the wiser after they had told me. Ask the butcher to chop the chicken through the bone, or do it yourself if you are good with a cleaver, but take care not to leave any sharp splinters of bone in the chicken.

FOR 2

2 tablespoons peanut oil
2 cloves of garlic, peeled and
   minced
4 ounces chicken pieces, chopped
   through the bone into
   1-inch pieces
4 ounces mushrooms, cut
   into quarters
4 ounces broccoli, split into large
   florets (about 1 cup)

2 tablespoons dry sherry
1¼ cups chicken or vegetable
   stock
1 tablespoon light soy sauce
2 tablespoons hoisin sauce
2 teaspoons cornstarch mixed with
   2 teaspoons water

Heat a frying pan or wok until hot, pour in the oil, and add the garlic. Stir quickly, with chopsticks or a large spoon, so that the garlic cooks for 20 seconds without standing still. It must cook without burning. Add the chicken and brown lightly, then add the mushrooms and broccoli. Fry for 3 minutes, stirring all the time.

Add the rest of the ingredients except the cornstarch. Cook until the chicken is tender and the broccoli cooked but still crisp, about 4 minutes. Add the cornstarch mixture, and serve when the mixture thickens. Serve with rice or noodles.

CHILI-CHICKEN PITA

A wonderful snack, spicy and substantial, of chicken pieces with chili, dribbled with mint-flecked yogurt, then stuffed into Middle-Eastern pita bread. Don't be put off by the long list of ingredients because you will probably have most of them.

FOR 2 PITAS

1 small onion or 4 scallions,
   chopped
4 cloves of garlic, minced
3 tablespoons peanut oil
juice of 1 lemon
½ teaspoon salt

1 tablespoon clear honey
1 teaspoon paprika
½ teaspoon mild chili powder
1 small, fresh hot red chili,
   seeded and minced
½ pound boneless chicken

FOR THE SAUCE:

6 tablespoons plain yogurt
1 tablespoon chopped fresh mint
1 teaspoon paprika

2 scallions, trimmed and
   chopped
crisp lettuce and hot pita bread or
   hamburger buns, to serve

Mix together the onion, garlic, oil, and lemon juice. Add the salt, honey, paprika, and chili, dried and fresh. Cut the chicken into lumps about 1 inch or so square, and stir into the above ingredients. Leave as long as you can, but at least 20 minutes. Mix the ingredients for the yogurt sauce.

Heat a cast iron ridged grill pan, which should be red-hot. Scatter the chicken over the pan and cook till the pieces are crisp and shining golden brown on the outside, yet still juicy within—about 8 minutes, turning once. Cram the lumps of chicken into hot pita bread with the spiced yogurt and some shredded crisp lettuce.

SPICED CHICKEN WITH BROWN BUTTER

Ground coriander, cumin, and both mild and hot chili are used here to lend warmth to a simple broiled chicken. Use an ovenproof dish that will hold the spicy brown butter, which is an integral part of the dish and can be spooned over any accompanying rice or perhaps some bulgur wheat with mint.

FOR 2

2 teaspoons paprika
½ teaspoon cayenne pepper
1 teaspoon ground cumin
½ teaspoon coriander seeds,
   crushed

3 cloves of garlic, minced
salt
4 tablespoons butter, at room
   temperature
4 chicken thighs

Mix together all the spices, the garlic, and salt and beat them into the butter. Spread the butter all over the chicken skin and put each piece in a heatproof dish that will fit under the broiler. Drizzle over the oil. Cook under the broiler, about 5 inches away from the heat, till the skin is crisp and slightly blackened, about 10 minutes on the first side and 6 on the other.

Spoon the nutty brown butter over the chicken regularly as it cooks. The chicken is cooked when its skin is crisp and golden brown, and the meat is moist and just short of being undercooked. Serve hot, with boiled rice and the butter and juices from the dish.

CHICKEN WITH SPICES AND CREAM

Nothing raises purist eyebrows quite like the mention of curry powder. I will say in its defense that I have eaten some delicious meals where the main dish was spiced with a commercially blended powder. I prefer to toast and grind my own spices, but when short of time I use a "proprietary" powder, then add a few spices of my own.

FOR 4

4 chicken pieces: breast halves or thighs
salt
freshly ground black pepper
2 tablespoons butter
1 tablespoon peanut oil
2 medium onions, roughly chopped
3 plump cloves of garlic, minced
2 tablespoons curry powder, from
   a recently opened jar

½ teaspoon ground cinnamon
4 medium tomatoes, seeded and
   chopped
1 cup chicken stock
½ cup heavy cream
juice of ½ lemon

Rub salt and pepper into the chicken. Heat the butter and oil in a shallow pan, add the chicken, and cook till the skin is golden. Add the onions and garlic and cook over a medium heat until soft, about 7 or 8 minutes.

Stir in the curry powder and cinnamon. Cook for 4 minutes, until the spices are cooked. Add the tomatoes and the stock, then simmer until the chicken pieces are tender and cooked right through, about 15 minutes.

Stir in the cream. Taste the sauce. Add salt, pepper and the lemon juice, a little at a time, tasting as you go. Simmer for 1 minute, then serve hot, with basmati rice.

TARRAGON CHICKEN

Make sure that the tarragon you are buying, or picking, is the French variety, which has a refined aniseed smell and flavor. There is also a Russian tarragon that has a coarser flavor and a light aroma only. You can spot it by its narrower leaves, and its slight bitterness. Avoid at all cost skinned chicken breast halves; you need the skin to keep the moisture in the flesh as it cooks.

FOR 4 WITH A GREEN SALAD OR GREEN BEANS

4 large boneless chicken breast halves	*salt*
4 tablespoons butter	*2–3 teaspoons wine or tarragon*
8 healthy sprigs of fresh tarragon	*vinegar or lemon juice*
1 cup heavy cream	

Slice the chicken breasts into strips about ½ inch wide. Melt the butter in a shallow pan over a medium heat. Strip the tarragon leaves from their stems.

When the butter starts to sizzle, add the chicken pieces and tarragon. Cook until the chicken has colored slightly, about 3 minutes. Move the chicken around the pan, but remember that the skin must turn golden in order to give a good flavor. Check that it is almost cooked through by cutting a strip in half. Pour in the cream and let it simmer until it thickens slightly, about another 3 minutes. Add salt and a teaspoonful vinegar or lemon juice, then taste and add a second. Taste again and add a third if you wish.

Half a dozen sublime Chicken Sandwiches

Chicken with Watercress and Mushroom Sandwich

Slice a boneless chicken breast half into thin strips about ½ inch wide. Season with salt and pepper and sauté in butter in a frying pan. Remove the chicken when it starts to brown, after about 1 minute, and set aside to keep warm. (On a plate with a glass bowl on top will do.) Add a little more butter or a drop of oil to the pan, then cook a handful of sliced mushrooms until softened, about 2 minutes. Lift them out with a slotted spoon and add to the chicken. Soften a few shredded lettuce or watercress leaves and stems in the butter left in the pan, lift them out, and stir in a couple of tablespoons of mayonnaise. Spread two hamburger buns or crusty rolls, split and toasted, with the mayonnaise and then pile on the chicken, mushrooms, and leaves.

Hot Chicken with Cream and Garlic Sandwich

Slice a chicken breast half into ½-inch strips. Sauté with a sliced clove of garlic in a little butter till the strips start to brown, about 1 minute. Stir in some chopped fresh herbs, whatever you have, and enough heavy cream to make a thick "glop." Check for seasoning, then spoon over split, toasted rolls or slather into hunks of French bread.

Yesterday's Roast Chicken Sandwich

Stir-fry small strips and hunks of roast chicken in a little oil, butter, or drippings in a frying pan. Shred any cooked greens, such as broccoli, collard greens, or spinach, and throw in with the chicken. Season generously (these are leftovers, remember) and cook for 2 or 3 minutes. Scoop in any leftover gravy and pan juices, then when very hot, pile onto halves of a split French stick or English muffins. Eat while still steaming.

Chicken with Basil Mayonnaise Sandwich

Make a basil mayonnaise, either by stirring shredded basil leaves into mayonnaise or mixing bottled pesto with an equal amount of a good-quality, ready-made mayonnaise. Spread it over thick slices of good white bread, then top with thick slices of well-salted cooked cold chicken and spicy salad leaves such as arugula. Crisp iceberg lettuce will do if there is nothing else.

Hot Garlic Butter and Chicken Sandwich

Lay thin slices of cooked chicken on toasted English muffins or bread. Spread with garlic butter, then flash under the broiler until the butter melts.

Toasted Blue Cheese and Chicken Sandwich

Cream a little blue cheese (anything will do) with some butter at room temperature. Add a few chopped walnuts if you have some (a spoonful of cognac wouldn't go amiss either). Spread this mixture on thick slices of cold chicken. Lay the chicken on crisp toast and broil till bubbling, then top with another slice of hot toast. Occasionally you come across people who mutter darkly about eating meat and cheese at the same time. Ignore them—they don't know what they are missing.

CHICKEN PO' BOY

The po' boy, or poor boy, is the classic New Orleans snack of French bread stuffed with fried fish or meat. Oysters, fried in cornmeal, were the original main ingredient, though the really poor boys had only fried potatoes. Good mayonnaise, and plenty of it, is essential. This is the basic chicken version.

FOR 2

2 small baguettes
1 skinless chicken breast half
fine cornmeal or flour
a little peanut oil for frying

mayonnaise
shredded lettuce, such as iceberg or romaine
½ lemon

Split the baguettes lengthwise, put the halves together, and warm them in a hot oven. While they are heating, slice the chicken breast into six pieces and roll in the cornmeal or flour. Alternatively, put the cornmeal or flour in a bag and shake the pieces in it.

Fry the chicken in hot shallow oil till crisp, about 4 or 5 minutes, turning once. Remove the bread from the oven and spread all the cut sides generously with mayonnaise. Add some shredded lettuce to the bottom half of each baguette, then pile on the fried chicken pieces. Squeeze over the lemon juice and fit on the top halves. Press down firmly and eat while still warm.

BROILED CHICKEN WITH MUSCAT WINE AND THYME

These chicken pieces will be especially delicious if you let the sweet wine caramelize slightly on the skin as they cook. Use an orange muscat wine, such as Essensia or Australian Brown Brothers for a change, drinking the rest of the bottle with nuts and fruit afterwards. I serve this dish with sautéed potatoes and a blood orange and watercress salad.

FOR 2

1 small carrot
1 small onion
a stalk of celery
4 cloves of garlic, lightly crushed

the leaves from a few fresh sprigs
* of thyme*
2 wineglasses of muscat wine
4 chicken pieces: breast halves or thighs

Dice the carrot, onion, and celery. Toss them together in a bowl with the garlic cloves, thyme leaves, and muscat wine. Put in the chicken pieces and turn them over in the wine. Set them aside while you prepare the rest of the meal.

Heat the broiler, place the chicken pieces on the broiler pan, and set it about 4 or 5 inches from the heat (or a little further if the pieces have a bone in them). Spoon over plenty of the herb and wine juices and broil for about 12 or 15 minutes, turning once and basting with the wine. They are ready when the juices from the chicken run clear and the skin is golden and crisp. Spoon the wine and herb juices over the chicken as you serve it.

BROILED CHICKEN WITH GARLIC AND LEMON

A quick way to liven up supermarket chicken pieces. A green salad, the sort you find already mixed in the produce section, is a fair accompaniment. Even better is a bowl of lentils—well-rinsed canned ones will do—dressed with a workaday vinaigrette and brought to life by a generous seasoning of chopped fresh mint leaves.

FOR 4

8 chicken pieces: a mixture of
* thighs and drumsticks*
2 juicy lemons, halved
1 plump clove of garlic, sliced
* finely*

4 tablespoons olive oil
salt
freshly ground black pepper

Put the chicken pieces in a shallow dish. Squeeze over the lemons, add the garlic and the olive oil, and set aside while you prepare the rest of the meal.

Heat the broiler. Season the chicken with salt and pepper. Put the pieces in the broiler pan, spoon over some of the juices, and place under the broiler. The chicken should sit between 4 and 6 inches from the heat source. Turn once, basting with more of the juices.

The chicken is cooked when the skin is crisp all over, and cara-melized in places, and the juices from the meat run clear when pierced with a metal skewer. Serve hot or cold, with the cooking juices poured over.

Broiled Chicken with Red Chili, Garlic, and Yogurt

A flattering side dish for this spicy chicken is zucchini with yogurt. Stir-fry coarsely grated zucchini, squeezed dry, with a little peanut oil and a few mustard seeds until tender, about 4 or 5 minutes. Stir in a few spoonfuls of thick yogurt and a sprinkling of paprika. Or try the Bulgur Wheat with Butter and Almonds recipe on page 198, with a dollop of thick yogurt on the side.

FOR 2

2 cloves of garlic, peeled
a piece of fresh ginger, about
   1 inch long, peeled and
   chopped
1 tablespoon ground cumin
½ teaspoon ground cardamom
½ teaspoon hot chili powder

2 teaspoons paprika
⅔ cup plain yogurt
salt
4 large chicken pieces: breast halves,
   drumsticks, or thighs

Throw all the ingredients, except the chicken, into the food processor or blender and whizz till smooth. Put the chicken pieces in a shallow dish and smooth over the spicy "glop." Set aside for at least 15 minutes, or longer if you can, while you prepare the rest of the meal.

Place the chicken under a preheated broiler, about 4 inches away from the heat, then cook until the juices run clear—about 15 minutes for boneless pieces, 20–25 for those with the bone in—turning once. Let the ocher-colored skin char a little.

CHICKEN WITH CHILI, LIME, AND PARSLEY AND QUINOA SALAD

I love this salad with chicken, and the lime's bright citrus notes lift the grain's earthy blandness. Use chili oil, instead of the oil and chilies, if you have some, to marinate the chicken.

FOR 2

*2 chicken breast halves, preferably with
 the wing attached*
juice of 2 limes
2 tablespoons olive oil

*2 small fresh hot red chilies,
 seeded and very thinly sliced*
salt
freshly ground black pepper

FOR THE QUINOA SALAD:

⅔ cup quinoa, see page 192
leaves from 2 handfuls of parsley
grated zest and juice of 1 lime

2 tablespoons extra virgin olive oil
salt
freshly ground black pepper

To make the salad, rinse the quinoa, then cook it in boiling salted water until it is tender but still has some bite to it. This will probably take about 15 minutes, but start tasting after 12. Drain and cool under running water. While the quinoa is cooking, chop the parsley, but not too finely. Mix together the lime zest, juice, and oil and add salt and pepper to taste.

Salt and pepper the chicken, and cook with the chilies under a preheated broiler, 4–5 inches from the heat, for about 7–10 minutes on each side, spooning over the juices. When you test the chicken for doneness, stick in the skewer nearest to the bone, to make sure it is cooked right through. Let the skin char a little.

Dress the grain with the lime and oil and mix with the parsley. Serve with the hot chicken.

DEVILED CHICKEN

Buy a cooked chicken in France and you will get a juicy, savory bird that will most likely still be warm when you get it home. Supermarkets elsewhere usually have those rather hard, cold, shrink-wrapped numbers. But they can be useful, and here is a way to perk one up quickly. The idea is far from new, but somehow particularly relevant today. Deviled cooked meat recipes can be found in old cookbooks.

FOR 2 WITH GREEN SALAD

2 cold cooked chicken legs

FOR THE PASTE:

1 tablespoon Dijon mustard
2 cloves of garlic, minced
2 tablespoons fruity chutney:
  apple, mango, or whatever

1 tablespoon Worcestershire sauce
  or mushroom ketchup
a good shake of hot pepper sauce

Mix the ingredients to a paste. Slash the skin and flesh of the chicken with a sharp knife and spread the spicy goo over the meat and inside the slashes.

Broil, 4 inches or so from the heat, till sizzling and hot right through—about 10 minutes, turning once.

► Chicken cooked in this way makes a wonderful sandwich. Slice the meat from the bone while still warm and pile into a crusty roll or hamburger bun, then spread with lots of mayonnaise and add a few crisp green leaves

CHICKEN MARSALA

Quick and creamy. The flour used here has two important tasks: it protects the chicken and seals in its moisture, and helps form savory deposits on the bottom of the pan, which dissolve into the Marsala or sherry to deepen the flavor of the sauce.

FOR 2, WITH A SALAD

2 boneless chicken breast halves
4 tablespoons butter
flour
1 wineglass of Marsala or dry
  sherry

⅓ cup heavy cream
salt
freshly ground black pepper

Put the chicken between two sheets of plastic wrap and pound them out to a ¼ inch thickness with a rolling pin.

Melt the butter in a shallow pan. Dust the chicken with flour on both sides and lay in the sizzling butter. The butter should be quite hot. Cook for 2 or 3 minutes—no longer—on each side, until golden brown. Remove the chicken to a warm plate.

Tip away most of the butter, turn up the heat, and pour the Marsala or sherry into the pan. Let it bubble while you scrape away at the morsels of chicken that have stuck to the pan. When only half the Marsala or sherry is left, tip in the cream. Season with salt and pepper. Return the chicken to the pan. Taste, adding more pepper or salt if you wish, then cook for 1 minute more. Done. A bulb fennel and raw mushroom salad dressed with lemon juice and a bland oil would be fine with this.

BROILED CHICKEN LIVERS WITH MUSTARD AND THYME BUTTER

A fine sandwich that will double as a light supper if you have eaten substantially earlier in the day. English muffins or hamburger buns are a doughier substitute for the crisp toast.

FOR 2 AS A SUBSTANTIAL SNACK

4 tablespoons butter, softened
1 shallot, chopped
1 tablespoon grain mustard
2 teaspoons chopped fresh thyme
  leaves

1 tablespoon chopped fresh parsley
½ pound chicken livers, cleaned
salt
freshly ground black pepper
English muffins or toasted bread

Soften the butter so that it is sloppy but not liquid. Mix in the shallot, mustard, and herbs. Lay the livers on the broiler pan, skewered if you wish, and brush them with a little of the herb butter. Season them well with salt and pepper and cook them under the broiler, 2–3 inches from the heat, for 2 or 3 minutes, turning once, till crisp outside, pink within. Test a liver by cutting it in half. Pile them on split muffins or slices of toast with a dollop of the remaining herb butter.

WARM CHICKEN LIVER SALAD

FOR 4 AS A FIRST COURSE OR LIGHT MAIN DISH

4 large handfuls of assorted leaves:
  spinach, escarole, dandelion,
  arugula, or whatever
1 cup thinly sliced mushrooms
6 tablespoons vinaigrette, made
  with salt and freshly ground
  black pepper, mustard, red wine
  vinegar, and olive oil

1 tablespoon olive oil
½ pound chicken livers, cleaned
2 tablespoons red wine vinegar
salt
freshly ground black pepper

Wash the leaves, toss them with sliced mushrooms and vinaigrette, and divide among 4 plates.

Heat the olive oil in a frying pan. Add the chicken livers and cook until brown on the outside, about 3 or 4 minutes. They must remain pink in the center. Tip the livers onto the salad leaves. Pour the vinegar into the pan, scrape up any crusty bits, and add a little salt and pepper. Pour the contents of the pan over the livers.

Roast Turkey, Hot Bacon, and Chutney Sandwich

Now we're talking. Butter two slices of hot toast. Cover one with thinly sliced cold roast turkey. Spread the turkey with mango chutney. Cover the mango chutney with bacon that is both hot and crisply fried. Slap on the second piece of hot buttered toast.

Quick things to do with leftover Roast Turkey

You have eaten the best bits already, with nutty stuffing and proper gravy. Here are some ideas for the rest of the bird:

► Cut the largest, flattest slices of breast you can. Lay them on a broiler pan. Spread them with pesto sauce from a jar. Cover with thin slices of Gruyère cheese and broil till it starts to melt. Catch the cheese before it goes rubbery; it should be just melting

► Cut chunks of brown and white turkey meat into bite-sized lumps. Melt a tablespoon of the drippings from the turkey pan in a frying pan. Fry a handful of diced bacon and button mushrooms till golden. Throw in 2 minced cloves of garlic and a handful of cooked broccoli florets. Throw in twice as much turkey meat as mushrooms and greens. Fry until everything is hot. Pour in a wine-glass of red wine and let it bubble till syrupy. Taste it; you may need salt and pepper. Eat as it is or pile it over a plateful of salad leaves

► Strip the carcass. No, I don't know why you bought such a big bird. You will be left with lumps of brown and white meat of all sizes and some wonderful jelly. Melt a large piece of butter in a frying pan and gently cook a tablespoon dried tarragon, which you have reconstituted with an equal amount of boiling water. Stir in ½ cup of heavy cream. Boil until it starts to thicken. Throw in the turkey scraps and the jelly. Warm through, then taste and add salt and pepper. A drop or two of lemon juice would not go amiss. Serve with chunks of bread and glasses of dry white wine

CHAPTER EIGHT

MEAT

T raditionally, it is the meat recipes that form the bulk of a cookbook. In this one I have included approximately 40, which is somewhat less than those for chicken or fish. I feel that this is very much in line with modern eating patterns. I know of no one who eats as much red meat now as they did ten, five, or even two years ago. Almost without exception, people are eating more fish and poultry, and I feel bound to respect that trend. I suspect that meat's repositioning in our diet is due to a number of reasons.

It is now recognized that we should cut down on fat consumption to reduce the risk of heart disease. The healthy eating campaign has highlighted the World Health Organization's recommendation that we should all eat less fat, particularly saturated fat—the type in meat. Their suggestion that no more than 30 percent of our energy should come from the fat we eat in meat and dairy products is way below the actual figure. It is regrettable that in order to be really succulent, meat needs a significant percentage of fat.

Secondly, many more people are now aware of the unpalatable side of intensive farming methods. More of us now understand that if we are to enjoy the benefits of cheap meat, it is the animals who must pay. My objection to intensive rearing is that the animals are often kept in totally unnatural conditions, and their feed may contain growth hormones and antibiotics.

The food scares of recent years have also left their mark. Disease has become rife in the intensive farming of poultry and some fish. Concerns are also expressed about the use of hormones to increase milk production in dairy cows, and pesticides and chemical fertilizers on grazing lands for cattle.

The more adventurous we become in our eating and cooking the less likely we are to rely on meat as the most important feature of a meal. Many cuisines make more of fish, vegetables, and grains than we historically do, and meat is often no longer such a prominent part of our shopping lists.

There is much talk about "natural" meat. This is a term used to signify meat from old-fashioned breeds, which have been reared in the traditional manner. That is to say the animals spend their lives on something nearer to what we imagine a Western ranch to be like, without being subjected to the degrading procedures of intensive farming. Most animals feed on rangeland, with all the grasses and wild herbs that go with it, and homegrown, often organic, feedstuffs. The animals graze where clean water is available, and are not given growth promoters or routine antibiotics.

"Natural" meat is usually produced by small-scale operations, often on family ranches and farms, and it is important to note that those who produce meat in this way are a growing band, not a dying breed. As you would expect, meat produced in this way is more expensive, but it should come as no surprise when people say that it tastes like "meat used to." It is my hope that the trend away from quantity in favor of quality will mean that one day all meat may be produced this way.

At its best, meat can be a succulent and substantial addition to a fast meal: pork chops sizzling from the pan, lamb steaks charred crisp outside and juicy and pink within, or a thin slice of liver glistening with savory onion gravy.

LAMB

I am not convinced that slow-cooking or a cream-based sauce does much for lamb. Lamb should be cooked quickly by fierce heat so that the outside is crisp, with the edges very lightly charred. The inside must be sweet, juicy, and pink. I have no doubt that this is best attained by cooking over a charcoal fire. Lamb offers itself to this type of cooking better than almost anything else. But a charcoal fire takes time to prepare.

For quick cooks, myself included during winter months, a broiler that cooks from above is all there is. A ridged, cast iron grill pan that fits over the heat works to good effect, but is not suitable for all meats. The recipes in this section contain instructions for those with oven broilers. The result will, of course, be better if you have a charcoal grill, but timings must then be taken with a pinch of salt as I have no idea how much heat you have harnessed in your wonderful charcoal brazier.

Lamb seems to me to be at its best when robust herbs, like thyme or rosemary, are involved. When lamb is not grilled with olive oil and these hardy aromatics, then it requires a bold spicing from a sweet or hot pepper, or the warmth of ground cumin and coriander. I have enjoyed lamb best in Morocco and Greece, less in Italy, and even less so in France. Roast lamb, which does not come within the realm of this book, cooked with garlic and herbs and served with pan juices and roasted potatoes, is another matter.

For the quick cook there are several cuts to bear in mind. Chops from the rack, of course, and thicker sirloin chops from the rear of the saddle, are good for broiling and frying. Cubed lamb is best known for casseroles, but is even better spiced and broiled. If you thread the meat onto a skewer, choose a flat one so that the meat does not slip around when you turn it.

Ground lamb often ends up in shepherd's pie and spaghetti bolognaise, which is a shame, as it makes the best meatballs, especially when spiced with mint and cumin. Choose meat that has been finely ground; it sticks together better during cooking. Generally, I avoid ready-prepared lamb kebabs, as butchers are often too timid with their spicing for my taste.

Rack of lamb is the quickest of roast meats, cooked in 20 minutes or less. Steaks, cut from the leg, are fine pieces of meat and good value. Cut into strips for a stir-fry or broil them whole.

▶ Lamb discolors quickly once sliced. This means that you can often find it marked down in supermarkets at the end of the day. A good buy for a late shopper

▶ I have to say that I never buy frozen lamb. It looks so depressing in the supermarket freezers

▶ Good-quality lamb should have crisp, white fat with a waxy feel to it. The meat should be a soft pink in young lamb, deepening to an orangey-red at one year

▶ Lamb is the one meat that has escaped the attention of the "factory farmers." The animals thrive on rough, often inaccessible grazing, often made up of short grass and wild herbs

BROILED LAMB SIRLOIN CHOPS

FOR 2

2 large lamb sirloin chops, 1 inch
    thick
1 clove of garlic, peeled

olive oil
salt
freshly ground black pepper

Lay the chops on a plate. Crush the garlic to a paste with a pestle and mortar or on a board with the flat of a large knife blade. Smooth a little olive oil over both sides of the chops with your fingers and spread over half of the crushed garlic, then set aside while you prepare the rest of the meal.

Heat the broiler. Spread more olive oil and the rest of the garlic over the chops. Cook the chops under the broiler, about 3 inches from the heat for a minute on each side, then move them a little farther away from the heat and continue broiling for 4 minutes, without turning. Remove from the broiler and season lightly on both sides with a little salt and a few grinds of pepper. Eat at once.

Serve with zucchini sautéed with mint, followed by a leafy salad.

Lamb Noisettes with Thyme and Black Olives

FOR 2 AS A MAIN DISH

4 noisettes of lamb (boneless loin chops), about 1 inch thick
olive oil
1 tablespoon chopped fresh thyme leaves

½ cup small black olives, pitted
freshly ground black pepper
½ lemon, cut into quarters

Brush the noisettes of lamb with olive oil. Sprinkle both sides of the chops with chopped thyme.

Heat a small amount of olive oil in a heavy shallow pan, just a thin film on the bottom of the pan. When the oil is hot sear the noisettes on both sides, cooking them for about 3 minutes on each side.

Just before the lamb is cooked, toss the olives into the pan. Grind black pepper quite coarsely over the lamb, squeeze over a little lemon, and eat immediately. Eat with:

► Wide noodles tossed in parsley and butter

► Tomato Stew, page 186

► Pasta with Whole Garlic, Goat Cheese, and Thyme, page 117

► Mashed Potatoes, page 171

Moroccan-Spiced Broiled Lamb

The effect that the Moroccan-inspired spice paste has on the lamb here depends on the length of time the lamb spends in the marinade. Some may like the light spicy notes you have when the lamb is marinated with the spices for 20 minutes or so. Others will prefer the deeper flavors of a 2-hour soaking. This is particularly good when the meat is seared on a hot cast iron ridged grill pan over a gas flame.

FOR 2

2 lamb sirloin chops or ¾ pound cubed boneless lamb
1 small onion, grated or minced
1 clove of garlic, minced
½ teaspoon ground cumin
½ teaspoon paprika

a pinch of cayenne pepper
2 tablespoons each of chopped fresh flat-leaf parsley and cilantro
4 tablespoons olive oil
juice of ½ lemon

Put the lamb in a shallow dish. Mix the other ingredients and toss with the meat. Leave for as long as you wish before cooking. The flavor will become stronger the longer the meat is left in the marinade.

Shake any liquid from the meat and cook under a preheated broiler till firm and lightly crisped on the outside and pink and juicy within, about 3–4 minutes on each side. Eat with:

► Fresh Plum or Apricot *Tabbouleh,* page 196

► Bulgur Wheat and Eggplant Pilaf, page 195

► Tomato Salad, page 185

Spiced Lamb Kofta with Pine Nuts and Red Cabbage

Crisp red cabbage, shredded really fine and lubricated with a good dollop of thick plain yogurt, makes a change from lettuce as the ubiquitous pita-stuffer. Throw in a few raisins, too, if you like. These are rather moist and may break up a little during cooking, but they are none the worse for that.

MAKES ABOUT 12 SMALL PATTIES, ENOUGH FOR 2 WHEN STUFFED INTO 4 PITAS

½ pound ground fresh lamb
1 medium onion
1 clove of garlic, fresh and plump
1 teaspoon ground cumin
1 teaspoon cayenne pepper
1 medium egg, lightly beaten
1 heaped tablespoon pine nuts

¼ teaspoon each salt and freshly
  ground black pepper
peanut oil, for shallow-frying
juice of ½ lemon
pita bread, thick plain yogurt, and red
  cabbage, for serving

Put the ground lamb in a large mixing bowl. Peel the onion and garlic and work in the food processor till minced, or grate them coarsely. Mix with the lamb, spices, egg, pine nuts, salt, and pepper.

Knead with your hands until the mixture comes together. It will be quite wet. Roll into small rounds, no bigger than ping-pong balls. Flatten them slightly. Warm a finger's depth of oil in a shallow pan. When it is very hot add the balls, in small batches, and fry till crisp and brown on the base—4–5 minutes. Turn carefully and fry the other side for about 2 minutes. Drain on a paper towel, then squeeze over the lemon juice.

Serve hot, in split warm pita breads, with red cabbage, as above.

LAMB BROILED WITH MUSTARD AND LEMON

A mild enough seasoning that does not overpower the flavor of the lamb. Steaks cut from the leg usually come nearly 1 inch thick; for anything thinner or thicker alter the cooking time accordingly.

FOR 2

2 plump cloves of garlic, peeled
a large pinch of sea salt
1 tablespoon fresh thyme leaves
* or 2 teaspoons dried thyme*
2 tablespoons grain mustard

2 tablespoons lemon juice
4 tablespoons olive oil
4 lamb steaks or chops, weighing
* about 4 ounces each*

Crush the garlic with the salt in a pestle and mortar or in a small bowl with the end of the rolling pin. Add the herbs, mustard, and lemon juice. Whisk in the oil with a fork, or small whisk, until the mixture is sparkling and has slightly thickened.

Pour one-third over the lamb, turn the meat over, and anoint that side, too. Heat the broiler. Broil the lamb, 3–4 inches from the heat, for 3–4 minutes on each side, depending on how thick the meat is. Brush with the remaining mixture as you turn the meat. The lamb should be a little singed outside, and rare within.

Serve with:

► Tomatoes with Garlic, page 181
► Broiled Mushrooms, page 157
► any of the green salads, pages 178–9

LIVER WITH ONION CHUTNEY

You will need a chutney that is thick with onions and raisins, rather than a sweet fruity one. The coarser the chutney the better. Coriander seeds, which often appear in these products, are a bonus. Don't expect anything even vaguely edible from a dark-brown, vinegary, sugar-laden commercial product.

FOR 2

2 tablespoons olive oil
2 tablespoons butter
10 ounces lamb's liver, thinly sliced
1 wineglass of red wine

⅓ cup coarse-cut oniony
* chutney (if you have a hot chutney*
* use 3 tablespoons, plus 2 of a*
* mild fruity one)*

Heat the oil and butter in a frying pan. When it sizzles, fry the liver very quickly until brown on both sides, probably a minute on each side. Remove the liver to warm plates. Pour the wine into the pan. Scrape up any residue from the pan with a spatula as the wine reduces over the heat. Stir in the chutney. As soon as it bubbles, spoon over the liver.

If you have the time, mashed potato is good with liver cooked this way, or in any other for that matter. If not, I would serve a salad of floppy pale green lettuce, dressed with plenty of lemon, and bread to mop up the sauce.

KIDNEYS COOKED WITH SHERRY

Most *tapas* bars serve a version of this recipe; some use flour in the sauce while others prefer bread crumbs. In Spain, this recipe is made with veal kidneys, hardly the things you have just lying around or can pick up on a last-minute dash to the supermarket. Lamb kidneys make an accessible substitute.

FOR 2, WITH MASHED POTATOES

8 lamb kidneys, halved and cores	*1 tablespoon flour*
removed	*1 wineglass of dry sherry*
juice of 1 lemon	*1 tablespoon chopped fresh flat-leaf*
2 tablespoons olive oil	*parsley*
1 medium onion, chopped	*salt*
2 cloves of garlic, minced	*freshly ground black pepper*

Drop the kidneys into the lemon juice and mix well. Leave for at least 10 minutes.

Heat the olive oil in a shallow pan and cook the onion until soft and translucent, about 5–7 minutes. Add the garlic and cook briefly over a medium heat. Turn the heat up to boil away any liquid. Drain the kidneys, dry them on a paper towel, and add them to the pan. Brown the kidneys on all sides, then stir in the flour and add the sherry with an equal amount of water. Bring to a boil. Reduce the heat and simmer for 10 minutes. Add the parsley, taste, and season with salt and pepper.

SOUVLAKIA

For several years I spent much of each summer in Greece. It now seems as if I lived on these little lamb parcels bought from street vendors. I have better results when using a ridged cast iron grill pan; left over a gas flame until really hot, then brushed with a little oil, than when I attempt to cook under a broiler. Marinate the lamb for as long as possible.

FOR 2

1 medium onion, peeled
4 cloves of garlic, peeled
4 tablespoons peanut oil
½ teaspoon ground cinnamon
1 teaspoon ground cumin
1 teaspoon ground coriander
1 teaspoon ground paprika, and a
   little more
salt
¾ pound boneless lamb: leg or shoulder,
   cut into 1-inch cubes

2 tablespoons loosely packed
   minced fresh mint
⅓ cup plain yogurt
4 pita breads, toasted while the
   lamb cooks
a handful of crisp shredded lettuce
a little cayenne pepper, for sprinkling

Whizz the onion and garlic with the oil in a food processor till they are reduced to a slush (failing that, you will have to grate the onion and mince the garlic). Mix in the spices, adding about ½ teaspoon salt. Stir into the cubed lamb, and set aside for as long as you can, tossing it around in the dry marinade from time to time.

Heat a grill pan until it is very hot (or heat the broiler). If the pan or broiler is not hot enough the lamb will cook through before the outside is crisp. Shake the cubes dry and grill or broil until slightly charred without and pink and juicy within. It will take about 2 minutes on each side in a hot pan or 4 minutes on each side over charcoal or under the broiler. Sprinkle with salt.

Stir half the mint into the yogurt in a small bowl. Split each warm pita bread to reveal a pocket and pile in the hot lamb with the shredded lettuce. Spoon over the yogurt and the rest of the mint and sprinkle lightly with cayenne. Eat with your hands.

PORK

Pork is not the meat it was. Cross-breeding and intensive farming have taken their toll, and the great drive to produce leaner pork has resulted in a loss of the meat's inherent richness and succulence. Pigs often spend their lives on concrete floors, never allowed out to forage for their own food, and sometimes permanently tethered. The stress of modern slaughter, too, can result in a bland and dry meat.

The good news is that some small-scale farmers are producing pork by traditional methods. This free-range pork is a different product altogether. Many of the old breeds renowned for their flavor are being used and are allowed to roam in the open air. The combination of humane rearing and traditional pure breeds gives a product that has a deeper flavor and more succulent texture. Free-range pork is available from specialist butchers and whole food markets.

Cuts of pork suited to the short-of-time are steaks cut from the leg or tenderloin and chops from the loin. Steaks are sometimes pounded thin to form a cutlet, which can be used in place of veal cutlets. Pork cuts such as these can be pan-fried or broiled, being served with their pan juices or a quickly made cream sauce, or stir-fried.

► Friends of pork include garlic, lemon, fresh sage leaves, pears and apples, plums and apricots. Peppercorns, either soft green ones from a jar or crushed black ones, and aniseed notes from star anise, fennel, or tarragon are flattering seasonings for pork, too

PORC AU POIVRE

A richly aromatic dish for an autumn or winter's night. The pork chops are best if cut thin, no more than 1 inch, and the fat is allowed to crisp in the butter. Crushing the peppercorns coarsely is best done with a pestle and mortar; the process is marginally slower, but it is easier to control than an electric mill. Ground too fine and the spice will burn.

FOR 2

4 tablespoons butter
2 pork chops, about 1 inch thick
2 tablespoons roughly crushed black peppercorns
3 shallots, minced

1 tablespoon cognac
4 tablespoons red wine
½ cup canned consommé or chicken stock
walnut-sized piece of cold butter, to finish the sauce

Melt half the butter in a shallow pan over a medium heat. Press the chops into the crushed peppercorns; make sure that as many as possible stick to the chops. When the butter sizzles add the chops. Cook until the juices run clear, about 8–10 minutes, turning once during cooking.

Remove the chops from the pan and keep warm. Melt the rest of the butter in the pan and cook the shallots till soft, about 2 minutes. Pour in the cognac. Stir. Cook for 1 minute at a good boil. Add the wine and bubble for a further minute. Pour in the consommé or stock and leave at an enthusiastic simmer until the liquid has reduced to 6 tablespoonfuls, about 4 minutes.

Stir in the cold butter. This will give a shine and richness to the sauce. Pour the sauce over the chops. Serve with mashed potatoes and a plate of salad afterwards.

Pork Steaks with Fennel

The lemon in this recipe is quite pronounced. To enhance the aniseed notes you could add a teaspoon, but no more, of Pernod with the lemon juice. Serve with a dish of white mushrooms, buttons or large cups, sliced thin and dressed with a little olive oil and lots of chopped fresh parsley.

FOR 2

2 tablespoons olive oil
2 pork steaks, about
  ½ inch thick
salt
freshly ground white pepper

1 medium fennel bulb, weighing
  about 11 ounces, thinly sliced,
  green fronds saved
juice of 1 large lemon

Warm the olive oil in a sauté or frying pan. Season the meat with salt and pepper. When the oil is hot, add the pork and fry quickly on one side to a proper golden brown, about 1–2 minutes. Then turn over, without piercing the flesh, and seal the other side. Turn down the heat, throw in the fennel, apart from the fronds, and cook until it has softened and browned slightly. Check that the meat is cooked through but still juicy. It will take about 7–9 minutes.

Remove the meat to warm plates with a slotted spoon. Throw in the fennel fronds and the lemon juice, scrape any crusty bits from the bottom of the pan with a spatula, boil for a couple of minutes, and then pour over the pork.

PORK AND PEARS

The garlic is used here purely to scent the cooking oil. A faint whiff more than anything. A fluffy pile of puréed potatoes, mashed without butter or oil, and a few sharp leaves would be my choice for a side dish. It is important that the pears are ripe.

FOR 2

2 pork loin chops, about
 1 inch thick
salt
freshly ground white pepper
2 tablespoons peanut oil
2 cloves of garlic, crushed flat but
 unpeeled

2 ripe pears, peeled if you wish,
 cut into eighths, and cored
6 tablespoons dry white wine
6 tablespoons vegetable or chicken
 stock or water

Season the chops with salt and pepper. Heat the peanut oil with the crushed garlic cloves in a shallow pan over a high heat. Slide in the pork chops—take care, they will spit at you—and seal on both sides.

Turn down the heat, add the pears, and cook until both are tender and browned, about 10 minutes. Remove the chops and pears to a warm plate. Pour most of the fat from the pan and return to the heat. Pour in the wine, scraping away at the bits of pork and pear that are clinging to the pan. Add the stock, or water, and simmer until reduced by half, about 2–3 minutes. Pour the pan juices over the chops and pears.

Eat with:

► a salad of bitter leaves, such as arugula

► Belgian endive leaves dressed with lemon and chopped walnuts

► spinach leaves, cooked for a few seconds with some drops of water till they wilt, seasoned with black pepper, no butter

Five-Spiced Pork Buns

Not pork buns as in *dim sum*, but pork buns as in spiced broiled pork sandwiches.

ENOUGH FOR 2 AS A SNACK

10 ounces boneless pork leg or shoulder, cut into 1-inch dice
3 cloves of garlic, minced
2 tablespoons dark soy sauce
2 tablespoons lemon juice
2 teaspoons five-spice powder
2 tablespoons clear honey
freshly ground black pepper
2 handfuls of torn bok choy *or* watercress
4 hamburger buns with sesame seed or English muffins, for serving

Put the pork in a bowl and mix with the other ingredients.

Heat the broiler. Line the broiler pan with foil, put in the lumps of pork, and broil till crisp on the outside, but still juicy within, about 5–6 minutes, shaking the pan regularly to turn the meat.

Split the buns or muffins horizontally, dip their cut sides in the cooking juices in the broiler pan, and then pile on the chunks of pork. Eat while hot.

VEAL

Veal is the meat of a one-to four-month-old calf. It is inclined to be lacking in flavor and dry. Baby beef, calves six-to twelve-months-old, give meat with a stronger flavor and deeper color.

There are no recipes for veal in this book *per se.* Many of the pork recipes, particularly those for chops and steaks, and a few for lamb, such as the pan-fried or broiled steaks, are quite suitable for veal. The *Porc au Poivre* and Pork Steaks with Fennel would be especially suitable.

BEEF

Lean does not necessarily mean flavorsome. Beef needs a fair marbling of fat in among the meat if it is not to be dry. Little veins of creamy fat are a sure sign that the meat is likely to be succulent. Meat from grain-fed, or grain-finished, cattle will have more marbling than that from grass-fed animals. Dark, almost purple meat means that the carcass has been hung for about two weeks and should have some flavor.

There is a great deal of talk about breeds, and whether the black Angus has a better flavor than the Hereford or the Charolais. The answer is, of course, the one you like best. The only way to discover which you prefer is to taste them all.

The recipes for beef here are all very simple. There is no need to cook beef beyond recognition or cover up its flavor with an overpowering sauce. Steaks are useful for those who have little time to cook. In the absence of a charcoal grill you may find a ridged cast iron grill pan that sits on the heat a sound investment. The trick is to get the pan very hot before you add the (oiled) meat.

CARPACCIO

In my youth I was a waiter at The Savoy Hotel in London. I watched with amazement and disgust as pallid businessmen lunched on steak tartare. To this day I still cannot stomach the mixture of ground raw beef and raw, barely beaten, egg.

Carpaccio is also raw beef, served with a sauce made from raw eggs. But somehow it is a very different beast. The paper-thin slice of beef, with its soft texture and gentle flavor, is drizzled with a mustardy mayonnaise. I like *ciabatta,* that floury flat Italian bread, with it. And arugula leaves dressed with lemon juice, or a spinach salad.

FOR 4

½ pound beef tenderloin or filet mignon, scrupulously trimmed of fat
1 teaspoon lemon juice
1 teaspoon Worcestershire sauce
1 heaped teaspoon smooth mild mustard

1 cup mayonnaise—homemade or bought
a drop of milk

The beef is easier to slice when it is very cold. You can put it in the freezer for 15 minutes or so. Slice it very thinly with a long sharp knife. By thinly I mean as thin as you can go without the beef looking like a lace tablecloth. By sharp I mean like a razor. Lay the paper-thin slices on large cold plates.

Mix the lemon juice and seasonings into the mayonnaise. Thin to drizzling consistency with a little milk. Pour ribbons of sauce over the meat.

► An unsophisticated but equally good (better actually) way to eat this dish: split a piece of *ciabatta,* spread the bottom half with the sauce, then pile on the thin slices of meat with a few arugula or spinach leaves and more sauce. Cover with the top half of the bread

THE HAMBURGER

This is the basic hamburger, made with ground beef and seasoned only with salt and pepper. Tomato paste, garlic, mustard, and soy and hot pepper sauces are all worthwhile additions, but not really necessary.

The leaner the meat, the drier the hamburger. Choose beef that has a fair amount of fat, perhaps more than you would usually prefer. I suggest at least 10 percent, which is not a lot. Chuck or round usually provides the ideal amount of meat and fat. If you buy the meat cubed to grind yourself, beware of overprocessing it, which will reduce it to a sticky paste.

These basic burgers are fried so that you can make a gravy, but grill or broil them if you prefer, and sacrifice the best bit.

FOR 2

½ pound ground beef
salt
freshly ground black pepper

2 tablespoons butter
1 tablespoon peanut oil

Mix the beef with the salt and pepper. Be frugal with the salt. Use your hands to form two loose but not untidy patties, and set aside.

Heat the butter and oil in a shallow pan. They must be hot and sizzling when you add the burgers. Fry them till crisp on each side and springy to the touch, about 3 or 4 minutes if you like them rare. If you want to know exactly to what degree they are cooked inside, you will just have to cut one of them open.

Lift out the burgers and keep them warm. Sprinkle ¼ cup of water into the pan and stir it around over the heat for a few seconds, scraping up all the bits of burger that have stuck to the pan. Let the gravy bubble for a minute, then pour over the meat and serve.

More Hamburger ideas

Consider these hamburger ideas, too, all of which are fine but hardly orthodox. Some may consider them pure heresy.

Add to the raw hamburger mixture:

► 2 teaspoons chili sauce: Moroccan *harissa* or Indonesian *Sambal Olek*

► a walnut-sized lump of blue cheese stuffed into the middle of each burger

► 1 tablespoon heavy cream, a minced clove of garlic, and 1 small minced onion

► 2 teaspoons Dijon mustard and a teaspoon Worcestershire sauce

► 2 tablespoons chopped fresh parsley and 2 tablespoons grated sharp cheese

And for serving over the meat or for dipping the bun in, toasted or not:

► Cream Gravy: remove the hamburgers from the pan, sprinkle in a tablespoon flour, and scrape up any crusty bits of meat clinging to the pan. Pour in ½ cup heavy cream, bring to a boil, and then season with freshly ground black pepper

► Add 2 tablespoons seedy mustard and ½ cup heavy cream to the pan juices

► Rinse the pan out with 2 tablespoons lemon juice, then throw in a handful of chopped fresh flat-leaf parsley

► Remove the hamburgers from the pan. Add a handful of quartered mushrooms and fry till tender, adding more butter if necessary. Scoop them out and add them to the burgers. Rinse out the pan with cognac, not forgetting to scrape at the best bits. Spread the split and toasted buns thickly with some of that mushroom pâté that comes in a tube, pile on the burgers and mushrooms, and pour over the boozy juices from the pan. Slam the other half of the bun on top and eat

Burger in a Bun

Buy the right bun for the job: no crisp baguettes here, thank you. A soft bun is crucial. I like floury, doughy ones, and have on occasion used an English muffin. Avoid the *very* airy sesame-sprinkled numbers; they are like eating cotton wool.

To my mind, it is essential the bun should be split horizontally and toasted, then dipped in the pan gravy before it meets the burger. The unsophisticated gravy above is ideal. Extras layered between burger and bun are a matter of choice, but consider the following classics:

► Sliced unpeeled tomatoes, seasoned with black pepper

► Tartare sauce instead of gravy, made by mixing capers, pickled gherkins, mustard, and lemon juice into mayonnaise, slathered copiously onto the toasted bun

► Gruyère, Cheddar, or Roquefort cheese melted on top of the burger

► Iceberg lettuce, cold and crisp, shredded and piled on the bun

► Tomato sauce, one of the quick ones on pages 187–9, spooned over the bread

► Sliced pickled gherkins, like the ones you find all over the sidewalk outside McDonald's, thrown away by horrified youngsters

► Tom Ketch (lots of it)

SLOPPY JOES

I love messy food—the sort that runs down your chin or up your arms. This particular mess looks like a hamburger that hasn't worked. American friends assure me that my omission of chopped green bell peppers from the classic recipe is sacrilegious.

FOR 4

1 pound ground beef	*2 tablespoons tomato ketchup*
1 onion, chopped	*¾ cup tomato juice or chopped*
½ pound dark mushrooms,	*plum tomatoes from a can*
chopped	*salt*
1 tablespoon Worcestershire sauce	*4 hamburger buns*
hot pepper sauce	

Heat a frying pan, nothing flimsy, over a high heat until it is really hot. Add the beef and cook until it starts to brown. Add the onion. Stir. Cook till the meat has browned properly; there should be no raw streaks. Add the mushrooms, Worcestershire sauce, a few shakes of hot pepper sauce, the tomato ketchup, and juice. Turn down the heat and simmer for 15 minutes. Taste and add salt. Add water if the mixture is at all dry.

Toast the hamburger buns. Sandwich the filling between the toasted buns as best you can. It will spill out all over the place, but that is the point of the whole thing.

STEAK COOKED IN THE TUSCAN MANNER

The Tuscans know how to cook steak. They rub the raw meat with olive oil and then squeeze on lemon when it is cooked. On the very rare occasions I cook a steak, this is how I do it.

The steak should be no more than 1¼ inches thick. It should be cut from the round or sirloin, which have more flavor. I suggest you allow ½ pound per person. Rub the steak with olive oil. Not too much, but enough to make it shiny and slightly slippery all over. Grind a little black pepper over the meat, coarsely.

Heat a grill, ridged grill pan, or broiler. The meat is best cooked over charcoal. When hot, cook the meat on the grill or under the broiler for 3 or 4 minutes on each side. A bit less if you like it very rare. Put the steaks on warm plates. Squeeze a quarter of a lemon over each steak and grind over a little salt.

STEAK SANDWICH

Mayonnaise, ketchup, or mustard often lurk in steak sandwiches. None of them is necessary. The juices from the pan are good enough.

MAKES 2 LARGE SANDWICHES

4 small boneless sirloin steaks, weighing about 3 ounces each, cut ½ inch thick
a little olive oil
salt
freshly ground black pepper
2 small baguettes, about 8 inches long

Fry the steaks in just enough oil to stop them sticking to the pan. They will need barely 2 minutes on each side. Salt and pepper the cooked steaks and add a tablespoon or two of water to the pan. Slice the baguettes in half horizontally. Scrape any crisp sediment from the meat into the liquid as it bubbles. Dip the soft sides of the bread into the meat juices and pile the steak on the two bottom halves. Press on the lids.

► A variation that seems to be exceptionally popular is to spread the halved baguettes with garlic butter, then warm them in the oven as you would garlic bread (that is, wrapped in foil). Lay the sliced steak on the garlic bread and pour over the pan juices

► A dab of mustard, rather than a dollop, can be a good addition, as is a thin spreading of anchovy sauce or *Patum Peperium*

BEEF STROGANOV

This late-nineteenth-century recipe was created for, and named after, the famous Russian family by their chef. The recipe found its 15 minutes of fame in the 1960s, when it became, along with coq au vin and profiteroles with chocolate sauce, standard bistro fare. Perhaps it was then that tomato paste, chopped tomatoes, and tarragon found their way into the recipe. They are not in this one. Quartered mushrooms, rather than sliced, are unorthodox, but juicier. You will need two pans.

FOR 4

½ pound beef tenderloin, trimmed
of all fat
1 teaspoon paprika
salt
freshly ground black pepper
6 tablespoons butter
1 tablespoon olive oil

1 yellow onion, sliced
6 ounces brown mushrooms,
quartered
1 tablespoon smooth French
mustard
½ cup sour cream

Cut the beef into fingers 2 inches long and ¼ inch wide. Roll the strips in the paprika, salt, and pepper. Heat half the butter with the oil in a shallow pan, add the onion, and cook till soft but not colored, about 5–7 minutes. Add the mushrooms and cook till tender, around 2–3 minutes.

In another similar pan melt the remaining butter. When it sizzles add the beef strips and cook over a high heat until the outsides are browning and the inside is pink; a minute or two is all it takes. Stir the mustard into the onion and mushroom mixture. Transfer the beef and its spicy buttery juices to the first pan and stir in the sour cream. Taste, add salt or pepper, bring to a boil, and serve, with wide, plain noodles.

STIR-FRIED BEEF WITH BROCCOLI AND MUSHROOMS

I claim no great knowledge of Chinese cooking. I scribbled the recipe down during a demonstration by a visiting Chinese chef. I have probably forgotten a few things, but I think it tastes good enough to set down here. Assemble all the ingredients in little bowls and cups before you start.

FOR 2

¾ pound boneless beef: chuck or sirloin
2 tablespoons thick soy sauce
2 tablespoons medium dry sherry
2 scant teaspoons cornstarch
4 tablespoons peanut oil, plus 2
   teaspoons
salt
freshly ground black pepper
2 tablespoons oyster sauce

a 2-inch lump of fresh ginger,
   peeled and cut into
   matchstick-sized shreds
a 1-pound head broccoli, halved through
   the stem and cut into large
   florets
4 ounces button mushrooms
3 cloves of garlic, thinly sliced
3 scallions, trimmed and cut
   into 1-inch pieces

Cut the beef into pieces ½ inch thick and 2 inches square. Put them in a bowl with 1 tablespoon soy, half the sherry, 1 teaspoon cornstarch, 2 teaspoons oil, and 1 tablespoon water. Add a pinch of salt and a few turns of the peppermill. Leave for 15 minutes.

Mix the remaining cornstarch and soy in a cup with the oyster sauce and 4 tablespoons water. Heat a wok or light frying pan. Add 2 tablespoons oil. Over a high heat, add the ginger, broccoli, and mushrooms. Fry and stir till the broccoli turns bright green. Add a pinch of salt and 4 tablespoons water. Cook for 3 minutes.

Remove, and wipe the pan clean. Reheat the pan and add the remaining oil. When hot add the garlic and the scallions. Stir. Throw in the beef and cook till brown. Throw in the remaining sherry. Keep stirring. Stir the sauce in the cup and add to the pan. Stir till it thickens. Return the broccoli to the pan and serve.

ROAST BEEF HASH

The simplest form of hash is where yesterday's roast beef and potatoes reappear as a crisp fry-up. American friends who make it in my kitchen include other leftovers from the refrigerator. Sometimes this is not a good idea. My advice is to keep it simple, but most of all, crisp.

FOR 2

4 tablespoons drippings from the beef pan or butter
1 medium onion, minced
3 cups leftover cooked potatoes, cut into ¼-inch dice
1 tablespoon flour

1 cup hot beef stock or leftover thin gravy
1 pound cold roast beef and its fat, cut into ¼-inch dice (about 3 cups)
salt
freshly ground black pepper

Melt the drippings or butter in a large nonstick frying pan and sauté the onion until soft, 5–7 minutes. Turn up the heat and brown it lightly. Add the potatoes to the onion and fry for 10 minutes, till golden and crisp at the edges. Stir in the flour and cook for a further minute. Pour in the hot stock or gravy and simmer for 2 minutes, then add the diced beef.

Cover and simmer until a crust forms on the bottom. Stir it in, then simmer again, tasting and adding salt, pepper, and extra liquid if it appears dry. The hash is done when the bottom is crisp but there is a little liquid left, too.

▶ A few greens, such as broccoli, collard greens, or cabbage, may be chopped and added with the beef

▶ Dried hot pepper flakes, or a chopped fresh hot chili, can be stirred in when you add the beef

▶ A fried egg is a popular addition. Cook it in a separate pan and perch it on top of the hash when you serve

Cold Roast Beef Salads

When a roast is awkward to slice thinly for eating cold, I find it easier to hack lumps off the bone, then cut them into 1-inch squares. Again, it is important that the meat is not cold from the refrigerator. When too chilled the flavor is often dull. A lively dressing is most important if the salad is not to give you the feeling that you are eating leftovers.

Beef Salad with Orange-Mustard Dressing

Toss 2 cups diced cold beef in a dressing made from ½ cup plain yogurt, 2 teaspoons mustard (a seedy honey one would be ideal), a teaspoon cider vinegar, and the juice and a little of the grated zest of a small orange. Mix the beef and dressing with 1 large tart apple, cored and sliced into thin segments but not peeled, 1 small sweet onion, cut into thin rings, and 2 handfuls of trimmed watercress

Warm New Potato and Bean Salad

Boil 1 pound new potatoes till tender. Drain and cut them in half. While still warm, mix them with 4 ounces cooked green beans, a 16-ounce can flageolet or cannellini beans, drained and well rinsed, and 1 tablespoon rinsed capers. Toss with 2 cups diced cold beef and 1 cup vinaigrette, see pages 179–80

Double-Walnut and Beef Mayonnaise

Whizz 1 cup mayonnaise in the blender with 6 medium leaves of baby spinach or sorrel, 8 fresh mint leaves, a handful of chopped fresh parsley, and 1 tablespoon hot water. Scrape the mayonnaise into a bowl, stir in 3 pickled walnuts, halved and sliced, and a small handful of coarsely chopped walnuts. Stir in 2 cups diced cold beef

COLD ROAST BEEF SANDWICHES WITH CARAMELIZED GARLIC AND BASIL SAUCE

A wonderful sandwich where the toasted bread is dipped in warm sweet garlic and basil dressing. *Poilâne,* that expensive, dense, sour bread sold in posh food emporiums, is just the thing for this (despite some wag once writing that it tastes like stale cake). You may like to sharpen the dressing with lemon juice or wine vinegar to taste.

ENOUGH FOR 2 AS A SNACK

4 plump cloves of garlic, sliced in half
½ cup olive oil
a good handful of fresh basil leaves
1 tablespoon balsamic vinegar
salt

8 slices of interesting bread: sour dough, ciabatta, or olive
lemon juice or wine vinegar
8 thin slices of rare, cold roast beef, at room temperature

Sauté the garlic cloves in half the olive oil in a small shallow pan till golden and soft, about 15 minutes. Shred the basil leaves and put them in the blender with the vinegar and a little salt.

Toast the bread lightly. Pour the soft garlic and its cooking oil with the remaining olive oil into the blender and whizz with the basil and salt. Taste and adjust the seasoning with salt, pepper, and either lemon juice or wine vinegar. Spoon the dressing over the toasted bread. Lay the cold roast beef on the toast and eat.

CHEESE

I would hate to live in a world without cheese. I particularly enjoy the artisan cheeses made by small producers, some of which are made with unpasteurized, or raw, milk. These cheeses are becoming more accessible through specialist grocers, health food stores, and wholefood markets. They are made on farms to traditional methods and have a far more complicated and interesting character than the modern "block" cheeses. Each artisan-made cheese will vary according to the milk and the production methods, lacking the boring standardization of the big dairies.

Cheeses made in this way have a far deeper flavor and more interesting texture than their factory-produced pasteurized counterparts. The French, whose taste in such matters is more adventurous than our obsession with blocks of Cheddar, have many hundreds of cheeses made in this way. Elsewhere, we must rely on the enthusiasm of a small group of cheesemakers who are working to come up with a finer product than that of the "cheese giants." A cheese of this quality is especially appropriate for those with little time. The better the cheese, the less you need to do to it. Try eating a thick piece of Maytag Blue from Iowa with a slice of pear or tart apple and you need not much else apart from some decent bread.

I love British and Irish blue cheeses, such as Beenleigh and soft and tangy Cashel, either with bread or oatcakes or in a salad that includes radicchio and *frisée*. A trip to a cheese specialist is well worth the effort for the delights of cheeses that range from soft and creamy to rich and spicy.

Goat cheeses have become popular of late. It is a smart cook who has learned to broil rounds of soft white goat cheese and toss them in a bowl of green leaves with a mustardy dressing for a five-minute supper dish. They marry surprisingly with sweet beets and dark rye bread, too.

Where unpasteurized and artisan-made cheeses are not available, then go for a farmhouse pasteurized one. The last resort is the shrink-wrapped blocks of bland hard cheeses that sometimes seem to differ in color only. Although uninteresting they are regrettably often the only alternative. Even unpromising blocks, such as white Greek Feta, can come to life when sprinkled with thyme and baked in a hot oven, and the solid Swiss cheeses are perfect for melting and scooping up with soft, doughy English muffins.

Although cheese prefers a cool place to live, I think the refrigerator is too severe. The flavor of cheese is dulled by cold storage; a cool room with good air circulation is best. Plastic wrap and a cold refrigerator sound the death knell for a cheese that has been made with love.

CHEESE SUPPERS

Of all fast suppers, "Cheese and Something" is the one that I turn to more than any other. A piece of cheese, a little salad, and some fruit and I often need nothing more. It would not sustain everyone. But it is enough for me. Granted, it satisfies only if all the parts are fine. Good cheese is not difficult to locate, though you had best forget most of the supermarkets, which store their cheese in too cold a cabinet and refuse (with few exceptions) to have any truck with cheeses made from unpasteurized milk.

Go to someone who will let you taste their cheese before you buy. With rare exceptions is a vast display of cheese a good sign. My local grocer carries hardly more than six cheeses, all sold in pretty near-perfect condition. His wife may increase the choice at weekends to include a couple of soft fresh goat cheeses. A lovely summer combination is white goat cheeses, with their gray coating of ash, sharing a plate with a pile of fresh cherries on their stems.

I have had problems finding a perfect Camembert lately, but similar British cheeses such as Bonchester fill the gap admirably. I have eaten those funny little triangles of Camembert rolled in corn-meal or bread crumbs and fried in hot oil. The crunchy coating hides a warm oozing mess of cheese. I have so far avoided the addition of a jammy purée such as cranberry or gooseberry, which seem to have found favor lately.

Match the salad to the cheese. Sweet tomatoes with salty Feta, nutty sweet apples with Cheshire, and sweet winey grapes with sharp rich blues. A bowl of soft green corn salad (*mâche*) works nicely alongside cheeses such as milky Taleggio and Cantal. A soft fresh ricotta is a gentle stuffing for canned jalapeño peppers; you don't even have to stuff them, just serve the ricotta alongside the fat hot pepper.

Occasionally I throw cheese into a salad. Cheese coleslaw can be good, especially if you use bitingly crisp white cabbage and a blue cheese, perhaps a Stilton. I make red cabbage coleslaw, tossing in toasted pumpkin seeds, bite-sized lumps of Irish Cashel Blue, Italian Gorgonzola, or French Roquefort, and huge dark raisins. I then pour over a warm dressing of hazelnut oil and cider vinegar. Or even simpler, spinach and arugula leaves with huge flat shavings of Parmesan, drizzled with some very good olive oil.

Plowman's Lunch

I am sure most plowmen would be horrified to see what is served nowadays in their name in some British pubs. But the cheese need not be a slice from a sweaty block, sitting next to a pool of sweet caramel-brown relish. Neither does the bread have to be a hunk of hard French bread or cottage loaf. Sticky coleslaw, lurid rice salad, and potato chips have helped this traditional British snack to sink to new depths.

A plowman's lunch needs nothing more than good white or brown bread, cut from a fresh loaf, or individual rolls, a lump of farmhouse cheese, not necessarily Cheddar, and a spoon or two of sharp relish. An apple is a welcome addition in the field, less so as part of a pub lunch.

Choose a Caerphilly, Cheshire, or Cheddar cheese and break off one large lump. Thin slices just curl up and laugh at you. A pickle or relish, pickled onions (if they are crisp), pickled walnuts, or a spicy chutney is fine. A sweet relish is most unsuitable. It goes without saying that the apple should be an old-fashioned variety, and not one of those polished, waxy numbers that shine lime green or red from greengrocers' shelves. An English russet apple with a lump of unpasteurized Cheshire is a favorite of mine. I prefer hard cider to drink here, but beer of some sort is probably the most appropriate.

Deep-Fried Mozzarella

Use the less expensive Mozzarella for this, rather than the more fragile and flavorsome *Mozzarella di Bufala*. Serve with a salad of bitter leaves such as radicchio or Belgian endive.

FOR 2 AS A LIGHT LUNCH OR SUPPER

2 balls of Mozzarella cheese   *peanut oil, for deep-frying*
1 egg, beaten
½ cup fresh bread crumbs

Cut the cheese into slices ½ inch thick. Dip each slice in the beaten egg, then into the bread crumbs. Heat the oil in a large deep pan or in a deep fryer, slide in the breaded cheese slices, and fry till lightly browned, about 2–3 minutes.

DEEP-FRIED CAMEMBERT

Camembert, the sort that comes not just in a wooden box but also cut into triangles and wrapped, can be deep-fried, too. Bread in much the same way as above, then fry in hot oil till crisp and golden, with the molten cheese bulging at the seams. Remove from the oil and eat immediately, with salad leaves and a handful of green olives. Reckon on about 3 triangles per person, that is, 2 portions to the box.

BAKED FETA WITH THYME

Even the most mundane of grocers seem to stock plastic-wrapped planks of Feta cheese; more sophisticated stores may also sell Halumi, a similarly salty white cheese most often found in Cyprus. Although firmer and saltier than the norm found in Greece, they can be turned into a good supper with a little olive oil, some crusty white bread, and a glass or three of red wine, as rough as you like.

FOR 2

a 7-ounce block of Feta or Halumi cheese
1 tablespoon olive oil

2 healthy sprigs of fresh thyme leaves

Cut the cheese into 2 thick slices using a large knife. Place each slice on a piece of foil, dribble over the olive oil, and scatter over the thyme leaves.

Put the cheese under a preheated broiler or in a 425 °F oven, with the foil very loosely wrapped around the cheese, and cook until the cheese is warm and soft and slightly colored here and there, 7–10 minutes. Eat with crusty bread and, perhaps, a tomato and cucumber salad.

Oven-Melted Gruyère, or Cheat's Raclette

Butter an ovenproof dish, preferably ceramic or glass, and quite shallow. One of those brown earthenware dishes would be perfect. Put a 1-pound block of Gruyère cheese in the dish and place in a very hot oven till it melts, about 15 minutes. Scoop up the molten cheese, spreading it over crusty bread or boiled new potatoes. Return any unmelted cheese to the oven for second helpings. To drink: beer.

Cheese on Toast

The best thing about cheese on toast is that it is cooked almost as quickly as you can think about it. A good example is one where the bread is cut thickly from a proper white loaf and the cheese is sliced from a sharply flavored Cheddar. The trick of turning a good cheese on toast into a sublime one is to char the edges of the bread while melting the cheese to a patchy golden brown without it overcooking and turning to leather. This is how to do it.

Cut slices from a white loaf (you can use brown but I think white is better here), about ¾ inch thick. Toast the bread on one side under the broiler till pale brown. Turn the bread over and toast again. Spread with butter if you wish, though I am not convinced it makes that much difference. Pile at least ¾ inch high with thin slices of cheese—a good sharp Cheddar or a Caerphilly is probably best— then return to the broiler. Cook until the cheese has melted and starts to brown in patches and the crusts of the bread have charred. Eat immediately.

WELSH RABBIT

I have had a number of minor disasters with traditional recipes for this savory little delicacy, mostly involving mixtures that will not thicken or that turn irretrievably lumpy. This is not a particularly authentic version, but it is the one that never fails for me, and is far quicker than the norm. The best flavor will come from cheeses that have some bite to them, though virtually anything will work. Stilton or a very sharp Cheddar have enough of a tang to be interesting, Caerphilly or Wensleydale slightly less so. Eat as a snack with the rest of the beer.

FOR 2 AS A SNACK

½ pound cheese
2 tablespoons butter
1 tablespoon Worcestershire sauce

1 tablespoon English mustard
2 tablespoons beer
4 slices of toast

Grate or crumble the cheese and mix to a rough paste with the butter, Worcestershire sauce, mustard, and beer. Spread over the toast and broil for a minute or so, till it singes in patches. If the toast is slightly charred at the edges, then even better.

Different Rabbits

Chutney Rabbit

Instead of butter, spread the toast under the cheese mixture with a thick layer of chutney. Tomato or apple chutney is particularly good sandwiched between the toast and cheese.

Bacon or Salami Rabbit

Strips of bacon, cooked crisp, or slices from a salami can be laid on the toast before pouring on the cheese mixture.

Poached Egg Rabbit

A poached egg lurking under the cheese, while being somewhat heavy on the cholesterol count, turns the snack into something altogether more substantial. Serve with crisp salad leaves such as *frisée* or Belgian endive.

Pesto Rabbit

A spoonful or two of pesto from a jar can be stirred into the cheese mixture instead of the mustard. Be generous with the basil sauce, and use dry white wine instead of ale.

Asparagus Rabbit

The late British food writer Jeremy Round made a version of this for a secret snack. It is certainly almost the only use I can think of for canned asparagus. Lay the spears, which will probably overhang a little, over the buttered toast and top either with Welsh rabbit mixture or just grated cheese *à la* Round, then broil till bubbling.

► Use crumbled ends of cheese—any sort will do nicely—instead of Cheddar. Blue cheeses such as Stilton work splendidly, but my experience with some Swiss cheeses is that they tend to go leathery and hard.

If you prefer not to use booze, then use thinly sliced or grated cheese as a blanket for toast loaded with:

► Thick slices of big, browny-black pickled walnuts

► Bottled artichoke hearts, sliced, drizzled with walnut or olive oil

► A mash of chopped black olives and anchovies

► Cold leftover ratatouille

► A mixture of chopped ham, pickled gherkins, and a few capers

► Sliced very ripe pears scattered with chopped fresh walnuts and a drop of Kirsch

CROQUE MONSIEUR

According to the *Larousse Gastronomique,* the first Croque Monsieur was served in Paris, in 1910, in a café on the Boulevard des Capucines. This most popular of French fast foods comes in sandwich form, either toasted or fried, or as a rich cheese sauce on a slice of toast. Either way, it consists of bread, cheese, and ham. Frying produces a crisper result, but toasting offers the benefit of less fat. *Croquer,* incidentally, means to munch, which suggests to me that the snack could delight in the name "Mr. Munch."

Butter two thin slices of white bread. Cover one with a thin piece of Gruyère or Cheddar cheese, add a slice of ham and another of cheese, and then the second slice of bread, buttered-side down. Press the sandwich together with the palm of your hand, then toast under a preheated broiler. The sandwich is ready when the bread is golden and crisp and the cheese is oozing out from the join.

BROILED GOAT CHEESE

Most goat cheese does not melt; it just softens and oozes tantalizingly. Broiled goat cheese on toasted French bread is now a rather passé *amuse-gueule.* A shame really, because sharp *chèvre* and crisp bread make such a good snack, and even better when served atop a salad of trendy little leaves such as oakleaf lettuce, chervil, arugula, and *frisée.* Until the whirligig of food fashion comes around again you will just have to eat your broiled goat cheese by yourself, on those black octagonal plates you seem to have been hiding recently.

FOR EACH PERSON

1 slice of brown or white bread or four slices cut from a French stick

1 small goat cheese, about 4 ounces in weight

a little olive oil

Toast the bread under the broiler. When golden on both sides, slice the cheese into 4 thick slices. Drizzle a little olive oil over the toast, cover with the cheese, and place under the broiler. When the cheese has browned a little, about 2–3 minutes, serve with a leafy salad.

BEET AND GOAT CHEESE SAVORY

I was invited on a very smart Press trip to Paris, where I stayed in an enormous and impossibly luxurious hotel. As my vacation accommodation usually consists of a sleeping bag, I was most grateful to my absurdly generous hosts. The highlight of the visit was dinner at The Bristol, an understated hotel with an innovative chef, Emile Tabourdiau. The unlikely combination of beets and cheese, which he presented as an elegant-striped terrine, is his.

Cover a slice of wholegrain toast with slices of cooked beet (not the vinegary ones though), about the thickness of silver dollars. Add a layer of goat cheese slices cut from a log, and drizzle over a little walnut or olive oil. Toast under a preheated broiler, and serve with some floppy green leaves such as spicy arugula or tender *mâche*, sometimes known as corn salad, dressed with nothing more than lemon juice and nut or olive oil.

A SALAD OF BITTER LEAVES, BLUE CHEESE, AND WALNUTS

A crunchy salad of bitter leaves and salty cheese in a thick mustard dressing. Bold flavors indeed. Piquant leaves are a bonus, but make this salad with whatever ones you have. Use one or a mixture of blue cheeses, and make sure, if the walnuts are from a package, that they are fresh; they become rancid very quickly after opening.

FOR 2 AS A LIGHT LUNCH, SUPPER, OR SNACK

1 tablespoon Dijon mustard	4 ounces blue cheese: Dolcelatte,
1 teaspoon red wine vinegar	Roquefort, Stilton, or Beenleigh
salt	Blue
4 tablespoons peanut oil	1 cup walnut pieces
2 large handfuls per person of:	
Belgian endive leaves, radicchio, and	
frisée, torn into bite-sized pieces	

Mix the mustard, vinegar, and salt in a salad bowl. Pour in the oil and stir until thick. Add the bitter leaves, crumble in the cheese, and drop in the walnut pieces. Toss the leaves, cheese, and nuts in the mustard dressing.

RICOTTA WITH FAVA BEANS

Ricotta has a texture rather like a smooth and crumbly cottage cheese and a mild and creamy flavor. This white Italian cheese is made from either cow's or sheep's milk. It must be very fresh if it is to be good, and there should be no yellowing around the edges, which indicates ageing.

For me it is at its best when eaten as an accompaniment to baby fava beans. Just put the beans on the table with a lump of the ricotta, and let everybody scoop up the cheese, and shell the beans themselves.

This snack becomes a celebration when eaten outside, with friends, sitting in the first summer sunshine.

Cheese Plates

Deli counters in supermarkets can be the home of really good cheese. A slice or two cut from a whole cheese and picked up on the way home can make a substantial snack, especially if following a bowl of soup. Well-made farmhouse cheeses, as opposed to shrink-wrapped factory blocks, respond to careful matching of accompaniments and the right glass of wine.

Taleggio with Grapes and Walnut Oil

Taleggio is a delicate Italian cow's milk cheese, usually found in its red-and-white-paper-covered gray rind. It is slightly firmer than Brie. Choose a little more than you think you will need because its rind is not good to eat, and anyway the paper sticks to it. Lay a slice, about ½ inch thick, on a plate, scatter over a handful of halved and seeded black grapes, and then drizzle with a little walnut or gentle olive oil.

Gorgonzola with Warm Potato Salad

Lay a ½-inch slice of ripe Gorgonzola on a plate. Accompany it with a potato salad made by slicing warm boiled new potatoes in half, mixing them with a few torn arugula or spinach leaves, then tossing in a little olive oil and lemon.

Feta with Raw Peas

Cut a slab of Feta in half horizontally. Drop a handful of shelled raw green peas over the salty white Greek cheese and drizzle with extra virgin olive oil.

Farmhouse Cheshire with Walnuts and Pears

A good English farmhouse Cheshire takes some beating. Put a wedge, large enough for one, on a plate. By its side lay a ripe pear, sliced into eight and the core removed. Chop a handful of freshly shelled walnuts roughly, and sprinkle them over the pears. Season with a few crushed black peppercorns and a few drops of cider vinegar.

Mascarpone with Fruit

Scoop a large dollop of sweet, creamy Mascarpone onto a plate. Surround it with sliced pears, sweet apples, and a small bunch of muscat grapes. Dip the fruit into the cheese.

Ricotta with Apricots and *Amaretti*

Go for the freshest ricotta in the deli; it should be soft, crumbly, and white. Put a slice in the center of a plate and eat it with pitted fresh apricots and the little Italian almond cookies called *amaretti*.

FRUIT

I often turn to the fruit bowl in search of dessert. Bananas can be baked with spices and butter or whipped into a yogurt-based fool; oranges can be sliced and drizzled with melted chocolate; while apples might be best pan-fried with brown sugar and thick cream.

Old-fashioned apples have become a retailing success story in Britain recently. For years the supermarkets here have insulted us with the shiny green and red imported numbers, with their cotton-wool texture and utter lack of scent. Growers are now being encouraged to produce the less profitable but hugely flavorsome old varieties, many of which had died out commercially. We can now enjoy the apple's true seasons, tasting the nutty yellow-fleshed Blenheim Orange, the heavily scented, white-fleshed Egremont Russet, and the aromatic Ashmead's Kernel.

CHAPTER 10

Matching fruits to cheese can be a joy. Try a real Parmesan *(Parmigiano Reggiano)* with a William's or Bartlett pear, an eighteen-month-old Cheddar with a Newtown pippin apple, or Flame Tokay grapes alongside some Brillat-Savarin.

Treats like pineapple should be handled gently: just peeled and sliced, then spiked with alcohol. Grapefruit, especially the dawn-toned pink variety, are a perfect partner for the crisp white fennel bulb, and orange works wonders with spinach. Orange has the added advantage of helping the iron in the spinach to be more easily absorbed. Remember, too, that bananas make a substantial sandwich filling with alfalfa sprouts, peanut butter, or bacon.

APPLES AND PEARS

STEAMED APPLES WITH BUTTER SAUCE

An unfiltered, cloudy apple cider is best for this. The taste is simply better than those thin clear brown juices. Use whatever apples are in the fruit bowl, although Winesap has a very good flavor when cooked.

FOR 2

1 cup unsweetened apple
  cider

2 apples
3 tablespoons unsalted butter

Pour the apple cider into a non-corrosive pan and bring to a boil. Cut the apples in half, peeling them if you wish. Take out the cores and lay them flat in a steamer basket to fit the pan.

Steam them over the apple cider for 4 or 5 minutes, a minute or two longer for large ones. Remove the apples from the steamer basket with a slotted spatula. Place in a warm dish. Remove the steamer basket and turn up the heat under the cider.

When the cider has reduced a little, cut the butter into small cubes and whisk into the apple cider, a couple of cubes at a time. As you whisk, the sauce will start to thicken. Pour the apple sauce over the steamed apples.

APPLES WITH BUTTER AND SUGAR

PER PERSON:

2 medium apples
2 tablespoons unsalted butter
1 tablespoon white or brown sugar

Peel, core, and slice the apples into 8 pieces. Melt the butter and add the apples and sugar as soon as it starts to foam. Cook the apples till they are soft and golden, about 5–7 minutes.

APPLES WITH ORANGE SAUCE

Omit the cream if you wish, or serve it separately.

FOR 2

1 large orange	*2 tablespoons brown sugar*
2 apples	*⅔ cup heavy cream*
4 tablespoons unsalted butter	

Finely grate the zest and squeeze the juice from the orange. Peel and core the apples and cut them into segments, about 8 per apple if the fruit is a good size.

Melt the butter in a shallow pan; when it starts to sizzle, add the apple pieces. Cook for about 5–7 minutes, until they are soft to the point of a knife and golden brown. Transfer to a warm shallow dish with a metal spatula.

Add the sugar to the butter left in the pan and place it over the heat until the sugar starts to melt, about 2–3 minutes. Stir while it is caramelizing to stop it burning. Pour the orange juice and zest into the pan, and stir in the cream. When the mixture bubbles and thickens, pour it over the apples.

APPLE, WALNUT, AND CARROT SALAD

Use the salad as a base, adding crunchy, nutty things as you will. Pumpkin seeds are good, and so too are raisins, golden sultanas, and poppy seeds.

FOR 4 AS A SIDE DISH, 2 AS A SNACK

2 carrots, crisp and hard	*2 tablespoons nut oil, preferably*
2 apples	*walnut*
½ cup roughly chopped walnuts	*1 teaspoon cider or white wine vinegar*
juice of 1 small orange	*salt*

Scrub the carrots and grate them coarsely. Grate the apples, without peeling them, core and all. Stir the walnuts into the apple and carrot. In a cup, mix the orange juice, oil, and vinegar. Season with salt and toss gently with the carrots, apples, and walnuts.

Pan-Fried Apple and Cheese Salad

A rather smart way to eat an apple and a lump of cheese. Crumbly farmhouse Cheshire cheese is the one I recommend for this salad, but a Caerphilly would be fine, too. Or use whichever hard well-flavored cheese you have.

FOR 2 AS A SNACK OR LIGHT LUNCH OR SUPPER

1 large or 2 small apples
1 tablespoon walnut or peanut
* oil*
2 tablespoons broken walnuts
2 handfuls of salad leaves, perhaps
* oakleaf lettuce*

2 ounces crumbly farmhouse cheese,
* such as Cheshire or Cheddar*
½ lemon

Wipe the apple(s), but do not peel. Cut in half and then into quarters. Remove the core and cut the fruit into thick slices, about 6–8 slices per apple.

Warm the oil in a large shallow pan; when it is hot add the apples and walnuts. Cook the apples for about 3–4 minutes, until they are golden, turning them once. Place a few salad leaves on each of 2 plates. Remove the apples from the pan with a metal spatula and scatter them among the leaves. Crumble the cheese over the hot apples—it will soften rather than melt. Squeeze the lemon juice into the pan and drizzle the resulting dressing over the salad. Eat immediately.

What to do with leftover Baked Apples

Finding a cold baked apple in the refrigerator in a hungry moment can be a good thing. Leftover baked apples look so sad, punctured and deflated, especially when you remember how good they were when hot and fluffy and straight from the oven. I often have a baked apple leftover; in fact, sometimes I deliberately put in an extra one.

Scrape the fluffy chilled apple flesh away from the skin. Then either:

▶ Mash the flesh with a fork, then fold it into an equal amount of thick, cold, plain yogurt, and eat it then and there

► Cream the flesh to a purée with a fork and place in a small dish. Sprinkle a tiny pinch of cinnamon and a grating of nutmeg (go easy on the nutmeg) on top, stir it in, and then pour over a spoonful or two of cream

► Mash the apple flesh really well with a fork, toss in a few plump raisins, and add a spoonful Calvados or cognac. Spread it on a hot English muffin, thick buttered toast; or, best of all, on sweet, dark British malt loaf

► For each 1 cup of apple purée you have, beat 2 egg whites till stiff and shiny. Fold in the apple and continue beating till the mixture holds its shape softly in a spoon. Serve with cream or, even better, a purée of blackberries or raspberries whizzed in the blender with a little lemon juice

HONEYED PEARS

FOR 4

3 ripe pears
6 tablespoons unsalted butter
2 tablespoons clear honey

Cut the pears in half and remove their cores. Chop the fruit into chunks, roughly 1-inch cubes, but don't be too precise about this—the uneven size of the pear pieces is part of the dessert's charm.

Melt the butter in a pan, add the pears, and cook for 7–8 minutes over a medium heat, tossing gently without breaking the fruit to a mush. When the chunks are golden, dribble over the honey and serve hot.

BANANAS

DATE AND BANANA CREAM

The sweetness of the dried dates is important here as fresh dates do not give the same result. If you have the time, give the assembled fruits and cream an hour or two in the refrigerator before you eat. The preparation time is barely 5 minutes.

FOR 4

4 large bananas, ripe but still
* firm, peeled*
½ pound dried dates
1¼ cups light cream

2 teaspoons orange-flower water
2 tablespoons sliced almonds,
* toasted*

Slice the bananas about as thick as silver dollars. Pit the dates and chop them. Toss the fruits together in a serving dish. Stir the orange-flower water into the cream and pour over the fruits. Scatter over the almonds. The dessert is best eaten after at least an hour in the refrigerator, but it will still be good after 25 minutes or so.

BAKED BANANA WITH CARDAMOM AND ORANGE

FOR 4

4 ripe bananas, peeled
⅓ cup brown sugar
4 tablespoons butter

2 cardamom pods
the juice from 1 large orange

Cut the bananas into slices about ½ inch thick. Put them into a baking dish, sprinkle with sugar, and dot the butter, in little pieces, on top.

Bake the bananas for 7–8 minutes, depending on their ripeness, in a preheated 400 °F oven. While the bananas are baking, remove the little black cardamom seeds from their husks and crush them roughly. If you do not have a pestle and mortar, then put them in a paper bag and bash them gently with the end of a rolling pin. When the bananas are hot and have softened somewhat, take them out of the oven, scatter over the crushed cardamom, and sprinkle with the orange juice. Return to the oven for a minute. Serve immediately.

BROILED BANANA WITH LIME AND HONEY

FOR 4

4 ripe bananas
2 limes
2 tablespoons clear honey

Peel the bananas and place them in the bottom of a foil-lined broiler pan. Squeeze the juice of one of the limes over the bananas and brush with the honey. Place the bananas under a preheated hot broiler, rolling them over from time to time as they cook. They are ready to eat when they have turned golden but still hold their shape. Cut the other lime in quarters.

With a slotted spatula, transfer the bananas to plates, then pour over any juices from the pan. Eat while warm, with a squeeze from the limes.

HOT BANANA BRIOCHE

Panettone, the open-textured Italian Christmas bread, is even better than the brioche, should you have some around after the festivities.

FOR 4

4 slices of brioche or panettone,   *4 ripe bananas, peeled*
 ½ inch thick   *juice of ½ orange*
rum, which is quite optional   *thick yogurt, for serving*

Preheat the broiler. Put the slices of brioche or *panettone* on the broiler pan. Sprinkle with rum if you wish. Slice the bananas into pieces as thick as silver dollars, and lay them, slightly overlapping, on top of the bread.

Squeeze over the orange juice and place the bread under the broiler until the banana starts to turn golden brown, about 5–7 minutes. Serve hot with thick yogurt.

BANANA-YOGURT FOOL

FOR 2

4 soft, ripe bananas, peeled
1¼ cups thick, creamy
  plain yogurt

Drop the bananas in the blender and whizz till smooth, but stop before they turn gummy. Add a spoon of yogurt if they refuse to move, or use a food processor. Scrape into a bowl with a rubber spatula and fold in the remaining yogurt, which should be chilled and thick. Spoon into wine glasses and chill till you are ready to eat.

BANANA SANDWICH

The banana sandwich, of which there are many versions (I recently found one with cheese and jam), seemed to start life with the fruit mashed to a sticky pulp. I think this is a shame as the banana's texture is quite unlike anything else, being meaty and delicate at once. To my mind a banana sliced for a snack should be a firm one, on the underripe side even, and should be cut into pieces at least as thick as a silver dollar.

Bacon and Banana Sandwich

The bacon must be crisp and the bananas ripe. This is one of those sandwiches that should be filled to capacity, even if the filling does sound a littlè eccentric. The sort of sandwich to devour alone.

thin bacon slices
crisp lettuce leaves: iceberg or romaine
bread, sliced from a white or
  whole wheat loaf

mayonnaise
mango chutney
bananas, peeled and sliced as thick
  as silver dollars

Fry the bacon slices until they are crisp. Shred the lettuce finely. Spread the bread with mayonnaise, then with mango chutney. Pile on the shredded lettuce followed by the bacon and the sliced banana. Cover with another slice of bread.

Banana, Cream Cheese, and Walnut Sandwich

*bread, sliced thickly from a
   whole wheat loaf*
*cream cheese such as Mascarpone or
   Philadelphia*
*slightly underripe bananas,
   peeled*

*walnut halves, freshly chopped
   (prepacked chopped nuts are
   often stale)*

Spread the bread with the cream cheese, as thickly as you dare. Add the banana, sliced, and cover with the chopped walnuts. Top with another slice of bread.

Banana, Alfalfa, Cottage Cheese, and Date Sandwich

brown bread, thickly sliced
cottage cheese
alfalfa sprouts

*fresh dates, sliced or roughly
   chopped*
ripe bananas, peeled and sliced

Spread the cottage cheese on the bread with extreme generosity. Cover with a layer of alfalfa sprouts, scatter over the dates and sliced bananas, and cover with another slice of bread.

BANANA SPLIT

Some people come over all superior about ice cream sundaes. Their loss. A sundae made with the best ice cream, fresh fruit, and thick cream is fast food of the first order, and not to be sniffed at. Reckon on 1 banana, 1 large scoop of ice cream, and ¾ cup berries per person.

bananas, ripe but firm
vanilla ice cream, the real thing

*raspberries, or better still
   blackberries, whizzed in the
   blender with a little lemon juice*

Peel the bananas and slice into thick chunks. Place a large ball of vanilla ice cream in a small dish, place the sliced banana around the side, and then pour over the raspberry or blackberry purée, strained if you must.

CITRUS FRUITS

BROILED GRAPEFRUIT

I was a child of the 1960s, and I can assure you that broiled grape-fruit was the height of sophistication in Wolverhampton, England. (It probably still is.) Almost as a joke, I prepared it the other night, and, dare I say, rather enjoyed it. To remind:

Cut a yellow grapefruit (the whirligig of fashion being what it is, I feel obliged to insist upon the color) in half across the horizon. Sprinkle it with sugar—white will give a thin, crisp crust—and dash it under a very hot broiler, close to the heat. Don't give it long enough to heat the fruit through, just to caramelize the sugar—barely a minute.

PERFUMED PINK GRAPEFRUIT JUICE

FOR 1

1 teaspoon orange-flower water
1 tall glass of pink grapefruit
  juice, either freshly squeezed or
  from a carton

ground cinnamon
crushed ice

Stir the orange-flower water into the grapefruit juice, dust with a very little cinnamon, and serve over plenty of crushed ice.

GRAPEFRUIT, BEET, AND WATERCRESS SALAD

Slice small cooked beets into disks as thick as silver dollars. Put them in a bowl with the grated zest and the juice of an orange. Peel a grapefruit with a small sharp knife and cut into sections. Pour a spoonful olive oil into the bowl with the orange juice and beets. Toss gently—this is not a dressing that needs to be emulsi-fied—then add the grapefruit sections and a few good handfuls of trimmed watercress or *mâche* (corn salad). Salt or pepper are unnec-essary. Serve with cold meat (duck is good), or with a sliced goat cheese.

PINK GRAPEFRUIT AND FENNEL SALAD

The sweetness of the grapefruit, the aniseed notes of the fennel, and the creamy dressing work together to surprising effect. The colors are pretty, too.

FOR 4 AS A SIDE DISH

1 pink grapefruit	*salt*
1 large fennel bulb, fat and round	*freshly ground black pepper*
⅓ cup heavy cream	*a small handful of green olives*

Peel the grapefruit with a sharp knife, taking care to remove all the pith. Slice the peeled fruit crosswise, putting the slices into a china bowl. Catch all the juice in a second smaller bowl; you will need it for the dressing. Slice the fennel into quarters and then into thin strips. Add them to the grapefruit. Scatter over the olives.

With a fork, mix together the grapefruit juice, cream, and seasoning. Drizzle this over the fennel, grapefruit, and olives, and serve.

CITRUS FRUITS WITH HONEY

A salad made from the Christmas fruit bowl, with a dressing of the fruits' own juices sweetened with honey. A neat first course, or the perfect accompaniment to roast pork, hot or cold. When the salad is chilled, a few sprigs of fresh mint would not go amiss.

FOR 4 AS A SIDE SALAD

3 satsumas, clementines, and	*3 small oranges*
* tangerines*	*1 grapefruit*

FOR THE DRESSING:

the juices from the fruit	*juice of 1 lemon*
2 tablespoons light, fruity olive oil	*2 tablespoons clear honey*

Peel the fruits, taking care to remove all the pith, and slice them into rounds. Collect any juice that runs from the fruit in a bowl. Whisk the oil into the collected juices, add the lemon juice, and stir in the honey. Dress the sliced fruits with honey, oil, and fruit juice, and chill for as long as you can.

CHILLED ORANGES

Leave firm Navel, Shamouti, or Valencia oranges in the refrigerator. When they are thoroughly chilled (we are talking hours rather than minutes), slice them through into quarters from stem to flower end. Eat them with your hands.

SPINACH AND ORANGE SALAD

FOR 4 AS A LIGHT LUNCH DISH WITH CHEESE TO FOLLOW

4 handfuls of small spinach leaves, washed
4 oranges, small and firm
3 tablespoons virgin olive oil
freshly ground black pepper
a small handful of tiny black olives

Remove the stems from the spinach, but leave any tiny ones. Peel the oranges with a knife, taking care to remove the pith and to collect the juice for the dressing. Cut the oranges in half, then each half into thin semi-circular slices.

Stir the olive oil into the orange juice and season with freshly ground black pepper and the tiny whole olives. Toss with the spinach and oranges.

AN ORANGE PLATE

Peel and slice 1 blood orange per person, taking care to remove all the pith. Serve the slices in little mounds on plates, arranged with an assortment of sweet and sticky dates, squares of darkest chocolate or little chocolate truffles, strips of crystallized orange and lemon peel, and crisp cookies such as brandy snaps. Set before your guests on your most beautiful plates, as an instant dessert, with hot dark-roast coffee.

AN ORANGE SNACK

Slice a large juicy orange, or whatever orange you have in your fruit bowl and sprinkle it with a spoon or two of granola and a spoon of roughly chopped dark chocolate. A bizzare-sounding snack perhaps, but it works.

FOIL-BAKED ORANGES

Peel 1 large orange per person with a small sharp knife, removing all the pith. Slice the orange into sections, then place on a square of foil. Sprinkle with a little orange-flower water, or cognac if that is more to your taste, and pull the sections together to reform the orange. Wrap up in the foil, scrunching and twisting it at the top. Bake in a preheated 400 °F oven until heated through, about 10–15 minutes.

DAMSONS

Although damson plums are hard to come by in Britain nowadays, I include them here as I think a bowl of hot poached damsons, with a pitcher of cream, is one of the finest and fastest of fruit desserts. Damsons share with red bell peppers the almost magical ability to be transformed from the hard and tasteless to the sensuously rich and sweet by the application of heat. I must also declare a probably slightly romantic memory of the huge damson tree at home, when we would harvest the slightly overripe fruits on wet and misty autumn mornings, with all around the smell of rotting leaves and mushrooms.

HOT DAMSON COMPOTE

If you are lucky enough to find fresh damsons in the market, and plan to use them for a fast dessert, then I suggest you make sure they are ripe. Some of them can be like purple-black bullets, and need a long, slow cooking to be good.

Remove the little stems from the fruit, discarding any squashed ones. Put them in a saucepan, stainless steel for preference, and add a small amount of water, to come no more than a third up the side of the pan, and a generous quantity of sugar. Bring quickly to a boil, then turn down the heat and simmer gently till the fruits have burst their skins and their juices have worked with the sugar to produce a rich purple sauce, about 15 minutes. Serve hot with cream.

FIGS

The best figs I have ever eaten were in a national park in Yugoslavia, straight from the tree in a meadow filled with hummingbirds and butterflies. Figs appear in the shops in this country during the autumn, mostly imported from Italy and France. Although there are many varieties, it is the fat, round, purple ones and the pointed, soft, green variety that we see most often. Eaten as a snack they are good enough, but they make a fine end to a meal when served on a plate with freshly shelled almonds and hunks of jewel-like pomegranate.

For me, along with the peach, they are the most sensual of fruits, and I can make an entire meal of a few figs and some flat floury bread such as Italian *ciabatta*. Try them split and dressed with a dollop of thick plain yogurt or scattered with thin slivers of air-dried ham.

Check the fruit for ripeness by pressing very, very gently with your fingers—if they are soft they are ready. If they are oozing very slightly at the base, then eat them soon. To ripen them quickly, store in a paper bag at room temperature.

Dried figs, with the possible exception of dates, are the sweetest of all the dried fruits. I prefer the loose-packed ones that you find in ethnic grocers to the bags of smaller ones from healthfood stores, good though they are. Snack on them instead of sugary candies, or add them to winter fruit salads with bananas, purple grapes, and sweet Navel oranges.

PURPLE FIGS WITH WARM HONEY

A snack to share with someone special, in bed, on a cold winter's night.

Split two bulging purple figs per person. They must be seriously ripe. Gently warm a small pot of clear honey—thyme or orange-blossom if you have it—in a pan of simmering water. Carefully remove the pan from heat, twist the lid off the pot, using oven mitts or a dish towel, and spoon the warm honey over the ripe figs. Eat with your fingers, sucking the purple-red flesh from the skins.

FIGS WITH PARMA HAM AND WALNUTS

FOR 2 AS A LIGHT LUNCH OR FIRST COURSE

6 ripe figs, green or purple
¼ cup chopped walnuts
⅔ cup thick plain yogurt

2 paper-thin slices of air-dried ham
such as Parma, shredded

Wipe the figs, then cut a cross in the top of each one, to go at least halfway down the fruit. Squeeze gently to open the fruit like a flower. Fold the chopped walnuts into the yogurt, and stir lightly.

Spoon the yogurt dressing over the opened figs. Scatter the shredded Parma ham over the yogurt.

HOT POACHED FIGS

SERVES 2

6 figs, green tinged with purple
2 cups red wine
⅓ cup clear honey

Put the figs into a stainless steel or enameled pan. Pour the wine over them and spoon in the honey. Bring gently to a boil. Simmer until the figs are hot and tender, about 15 minutes. Serve tepid.

Figs with Navel Oranges

Cut 2 figs per person into quarters. There is no need to peel them, provided you have taken the trouble to wipe them. Place them in a bowl.

Peel a small orange per person, catching the juice as you cut away the peel and pith in the fig bowl. Cut the orange thinly into round slices, then add to the figs. Chill for as long as you can before eating.

A Plate of Dried Figs

Choose the plumpest, softest dried figs you can. You will probably find them in ethnic grocers. Slice them in half across to produce two seedy rounds. Sprinkle them with a few fennel seeds. Arrange on plain white plates with the new season's fresh walnuts and a sprig of muscat grapes. Serve with strong black coffee.

Canned Figs with Pernod

Figs come from a can relatively unscathed, and are actually rather good if served very cold. Try not to think of fresh figs when you eat them.

SERVES 2

1 16-ounce can whole green
  figs in syrup
½ teaspoon Pernod

Place the figs in a plain china dish using a slotted spoon. Tip the Pernod into the syrup in the can. Stir the syrup or shake it gently, then pour it over the figs. Serve with cream.

PEACHES

From May to October, markets offer many different varieties of peach, with skins that may be red-blushed creamy-white or golden. You may also find the rare white-fleshed peaches, altogether too good to miss.

A ripe peach is a fragrant one. There is no need to squeeze, just sniff. Their aroma is rich and sweet, and some varieties, particularly white peaches, have a deep fragrance of roses and raspberries. Unforgettable. Carry them carefully, and bring them gently to ripeness in a brown paper bag. Only the very ripest need refrigerating, but bring them back to room temperature before you eat them, for it is then that they are at their most fragrant.

I have never had the same fondness for the nectarine, whose smell I find flat and the flavor not up to that of the peach. Many prefer them, disliking the fuzzy skin of the peach. For me that is one of the delights of the fruit, first the fluffy skin, then the sweet flesh with its juices that dribble down my chin. The choice is yours, and they are interchangeable in all recipes.

In savory form the peach broils well. Try stuffing a pitted peach with soft cheese such as Dolcelatte and Mascarpone, then flashing it under the broiler till the cheese melts. Or toss a few crisp romaine leaves with sliced peaches and dress them with a lemony vinaigrette.

And what faster food is there than a ripe peach sliced into the last glass of the red wine that accompanied dinner?

DOLCELATTE, MASCARPONE, AND PEACHES

The blue- and white-striped cheese "cake" found in specialty cheese stores is a layered concoction of mild blue Dolcelatte and sweet Mascarpone, called Torta Dolcelatte. Although this first appears bizarre, it makes good eating. Try breaking off chunks of the creamy cheese and placing them in the hollows of pitted peach halves. Scatter over a few roughly chopped walnuts and serve as a snack or first course.

PEACHES WITH BASIL

Slice fresh peaches, peeled if you wish, into a china dish. Squeeze over a little lemon juice, then toss very gently with a few shredded fresh basil leaves. Allow 4 leaves of basil per peach, and 2 teaspoons lemon juice.

BROILED PEACHES WITH HONEY

Both the fragrance and flavor of a truly ripe peach seem to be retained by cooking them quickly under the broiler.

FOR 4

⅓ cup clear honey	*4 ripe peaches*
juice of 1 lemon	*4 teaspoons butter*

In a small bowl mix the honey with the lemon juice. Cut the peaches in half and remove the pits. Lay them, flat-side up, in a shallow baking dish.

Dot half a teaspoon butter on top of each peach half. Brush the lemon and honey mixture over the peaches and place under a preheated broiler, 5–6 inches from the heat. They are done when the honey starts to bubble and the peaches turn golden brown in patches, about 5–7 minutes. Serve hot with thick plain yogurt.

BROILED STUFFED PEACHES

Follow the previous recipe but forget the butter. Before you spoon over the honey and lemon, stuff the peach halves with the following filling.

FOR 4

¼ cup ricotta cheese
6 amaretti cookies, crushed in
  their papers with a rolling pin

Spoon the honey and lemon over the stuffed peach halves and place under the preheated broiler until the almond-cheese filling begins to brown, about 5–7 minutes. Serve hot, spooning the syrup from the baking dish over the peaches.

WHITE PEACHES WITH BEAUMES DE VENISE

A white peach, fragrant and warm from the windowsill rather than cold from the refrigerator, is a perfect partner for a glass of chilled Beaumes de Venise or other sweet wine. You could, of course, slice the fruit into the chilled wine, then eat the wine-soaked peach with a teaspoon, and drink the rest.

A WHITE PEACH PLATE

Make a dessert plate to end a high-summer meal. Arrange deeply perfumed white peaches on a pretty plate with a handful of fresh almonds, shelled but not skinned, and a little pile of deep red loganberries or raspberries.

PINEAPPLES

I cannot think of pineapples without transporting myself, just for a few minutes, to the beach in India. There, every morning of my vacation, I watched an awesomely dextrous man peel and slice a ripe pineapple for me. He would offer me one slice, then bag the rest in blue plastic and send me off along the beach.

► Canned pineapple is usually very sweet, but I have eaten a perfectly passable dessert made by chopping up canned pineapple, first drained of its juice, and putting it into a shallow dish. Thickly whipped cream was spooned over and spread level to the top of the dish. Sugar was dusted over the top and it was broiled under a very hot flame till the sugar caramelized—3–4 minutes. There was probably a drop of Kirsch in among the fruit, now I come to think of it. I have heard of the same being done with canned peaches

► I don't know why this is so good. Spread large plain crackers, quite ordinary ones are fine, with a thick swirl of cream cheese. Add a slice of fresh pineapple. That's it

► Pineapple with Kirsch is still one of the most popular desserts in the less pretentious Parisian restaurants, though it has long disappeared in Britain—no doubt in favor of "a symphony of fruit sorbets with a purée of their fruits." It is very important that the pineapple is ripe and chilled. Peel and slice the fruit and place it on a plate. Upend a measure of Kirsch, or rum if you prefer, over the fruit

PLUMS

HOT BUTTERED PLUMS

I enjoyed this dish as a child, although I remember it as plums on toast. Elizabeth David recorded it forty years ago, and I think it so good as to give my version here.

Make sure the plums are ripe; they should dribble juice (which you will catch in the dish) if they are ready. If your plums are not yet ripe, but for some reason you must use them, then you had better make a fruit crisp instead.

FOR 2 AS A DESSERT OR SNACK

2 slices of white bread	*4 ripe plums, dark and juicy*
butter	*⅓ cup sugar*

Butter the bread thickly. Remove the crusts. Halve and pit the plums. Lay the bread in a shallow dish, and sprinkle it with most of the sugar.

Place the plums, flat-side up, on the bread and dot over a few bits of butter. Sprinkle over the remaining sugar. Bake in a preheated 400 °F oven for 15–20 minutes, until the butter has melted and the juices from the plums are bubbling. Serve hot, with cream.

SCARLET FRUITS AND BERRIES

Raspberries, mulberries, loganberries, red currants, black currants, and strawberries form the backbone of fast summer fruit desserts. Nothing good will come of fancy recipes for these glorious fruits. Raspberries with blackberries and soft white Petit Suisse cheese, blackberries crushed and folded into thick cream with toasted hazelnuts, or a hot fruit crisp made with black currants and mint is sophisticated enough.

I try not to add anything to these fruits that will interfere with their fragrance. I see little point in adding *framboise,* the raspberry liqueur, to the fresh fruit, though black currants are assertive enough to benefit from a touch of cassis. A sharp cream such as *crème fraîche* or *fromage blanc* is a favorite accompaniment, though even better, I think, is a half-and-half mixture of thick plain yogurt and softly whipped cream. The cream should barely hold its shape, and the yogurt should ideally be a thick Greek one, perhaps a strained sheep's milk variety. Sweet wines, especially the muscats and Sauternes, and a few peppery herbs such as basil and mint are other natural partners for red fruits.

With figs, muscat grapes, and peaches, I think of the raspberry as among the finest fruits we have. I often eat a handful balanced on fresh white bread that has been spread with a soft, fresh cream cheese such as ricotta or Mascarpone. At their most heady and luscious, raspberries need no sugar or cream, just a white bowl and a spoon.

Strawberries need more help than the softer berries. Deeply flavored berries are a rare find nowadays. A squeeze of lemon juice or a splash of rosewater will lift a slightly dull berry, though there is little that will improve an out-of-season berry if it is really not ripe. The fact that strawberries can be eaten with cucumber in a salad is hardly news, but have you ever thought of giving them a richer flavor with a sprinkling of precious balsamic vinegar or sharpening their edge with the juice and seeds of a passion fruit?

On a sunny day there can be few better ways of eating these deeply perfumed, rich scarlet and purple fruits than setting them out on the table, in the shade, with a bowl of *crème fraîche* and a glass of muscat wine for those who wish for it.

CHERRIES

I am sure that cherries, yellow- and red-tinged, are at their best eaten straight from your hand. I remain unconvinced that their flavor is better for the application of heat. Fruit crisps are better made with plums, and pies with apples and blackberries, and tarts are surely the vehicles for soft scarlet fruits. The pits, which take up most of the cherry, drive me quite mad.

I find the next best way to eat this fruit is: pit a handful of slightly sour cherries per person. Put half of the fruit in the bottom of a large wineglass. Fill the glass two-thirds with a soft fresh cheese such as a French *fromage blanc,* then pile on the remaining fruit. Toast a few sliced or shredded almonds until they smell nutty and turn light brown in color, and sprinkle them over the top.

STRAWBERRIES WITH ORANGE AND *FROMAGE BLANC*

Choose plump red strawberries. Wipe or quickly wash them, then remove their green leaves and stems. (To do so before would allow water to enter the berries.) Pile into a bowl and squeeze the juice from an orange over the fruit. Serve with a separate bowl of *fromage blanc* or ricotta.

STRAWBERRIES WITH RED WINE

Slice washed strawberries into a china bowl. Sprinkle with red wine—a light and fruity Beaujolais would be ideal—and set aside in a cool place for as long as you can. Half an hour is about long enough.

STRAWBERRY FOOL

A fool, lumpy with chunks of fruit and sharpened by *fromage blanc,* is I think preferable to the usual concoction of a smooth, sweet, pink paste.

FOR 2

½ pound strawberries
1 cup fromage blanc

½ cup crème fraîche *or*
      heavy cream

Crush the berries in a bowl with a fork. Fold in the *fromage blanc* and the *crème fraîche,* slowly but thoroughly. Spoon into glasses or small pots and chill before serving—leave it for as long as possible. An almond cookie or shortbread would make a flattering accompaniment.

STRAWBERRIES WITH ORANGE JUICE AND GRAND MARNIER

Cut the berries in half. Place them in a china bowl. Pour enough freshly squeezed orange juice over the berries just to cover them. Stir in enough Grand Marnier to be interesting, then set aside to macerate for as long as you can, but half an hour should do it. If you get the chance to leave them overnight, they will taste even better, though the berries will soften.

Little things to wake up a bowl of out-of-season Strawberries

► A very light grinding of black pepper

► A squeeze of lemon

► A shake from the balsamic vinegar bottle

► A spoonful of orange-flower or rosewater

► A little shredded fresh mint

► The juice and seeds from a passion fruit

RASPBERRIES

It is difficult to imagine that there could be anything more fragrant than a bowl of warm and perfectly ripe raspberries, eaten without the gilding of cream or sugar. Perhaps, though, at the height of the season, you may want to try something more adventurous.

RASPBERRIES WITH RICOTTA

FOR 4, WITH SECOND HELPINGS

1 pound (2 cups) ricotta, very white and fresh
¼ cup clear honey or confectioners' sugar

2 tablespoons Grand Marnier
6 tablespoons cream, softly whipped
1 pound (about 4 cups) raspberries

Push the ricotta through a strainer, or whizz it in a food processor. Stir in the honey or confectioners' sugar and Grand Marnier. Blend well. Fold in the whipped cream.

Pile the ricotta cream into a glass or china dish and scatter raspberries around. Serve with a bowl of extra raspberries.

SCARLET FRUIT "MESS"

Eton Mess, sometimes called Clare College Mess, is in its simplest form a concoction of strawberries and cream made by mashing the two together with a fork. Purists would say that it does not need the grated orange zest, crumbled meringues, or other foreign bodies that appear in recipes from time to time. Although I like the idea of simply whipping cream and folding smashed strawberries into it, I do think that purchased meringue shells are a sound addition.

The best Mess to my mind is one where raspberries, rather than strawberries, are crushed gently with a fork until they bleed, next folded into lightly whipped cream, then the whole mixture lightened and sweetened with a couple of meringue shells, broken up into little pieces.

The crucial point lies in the whipping of the cream. It should be as rich as possible, and should be gently half-whipped, that is, until it is just about capable of holding a little shape, but by no means stiff enough to form peaks. Oh, and it really must be eaten quickly if it is to be good.

Hot Raspberry and Mascarpone *Brûlée*

Pile raspberries into a shallow ovenproof dish (a gratin dish is fine). Dot scoops of Mascarpone over the fruit and sprinkle with sugar. Place under a very hot broiler, 3–4 inches from the heat, until the Mascarpone has started to melt and the sugar begins to caramelize, about 2 minutes. Serve hot.

Raspberry Fool

Whizz raspberries in the food processor till smooth. Squeeze in a little lemon juice, then fold in some softly whipped cream. Reckon on an almost equal volume of whipped cream to berries.

Vanilla Ice Cream with Raspberry Sauce

Whizz a pint of raspberries in a food processor, or push them through a nylon strainer. Stir in a squeeze of lemon juice. Serve over the best vanilla ice cream you can find.

Raspberries in Wine

Drop a handful of ripe luscious raspberries into a glass of chilled sweetish wine, preferably a Gewürztraminer.

Raspberry Compote

*1 pound (about 4 cups)
   raspberries
2–3 tablespoons sugar*

1 teaspoon Kirsch

Tip the berries into a china or glass bowl. Sprinkle with sugar and Kirsch. Leave in a warm place such as the back of the stove for a few minutes, then serve with a pitcher of cream.

Ten-Minute Trifle

Real trifle, made with homemade sponge cake, syllabub (or sabayon), and a gallon of sherry must be one of the most delicious desserts known to man, but it takes an age to make from scratch. The commercial alternative contains lurid orange gelatin topped with a substance akin to shaving foam, only sweeter. It is topped with rainbow-colored sugar-strands or, if you are really unlucky, those teeth-breaking silver balls.

The following recipe is almost as quick as its name and has some of the alcoholic creaminess of the former without any of the horrors of the latter. I serve it unadorned, just a soft creamy mass in a plain bowl, scattering crystallized violets or rose petals over the surface only if I am feeling like being tacky.

FOR 4, AND IT IS EVEN BETTER THE NEXT DAY

10 ladyfingers, broken into
   1-inch pieces
1 cup chilled sweet white
   wine, such as Moscato, or cream
   sherry
1 heaped cup raspberries, loganberries,
   or juicy blackberries

2 ripe bananas, peeled and sliced
2 eggs, separated
¼ cup sugar
½ pound (1 cup) Mascarpone cheese
a little vanilla extract or brandy

Put the ladyfingers in a 1-quart dish. You can use that cut-glass thing Auntie Connie gave you if you must, but the trifle looks far more elegant in a plain white china bowl. Pour over the wine, gently pressing the fingers down into the liquid, then throw in the raspberries or other berries and the bananas.

Cream the egg yolks with the sugar, add the Mascarpone, and beat with an electric mixer till light and creamy. Tip in the vanilla or brandy. Beat the egg whites till they form stiff peaks and fold gently but thoroughly into the cream. Tip the Mascarpone cream over the fruit and ladyfingers. Shake the bowl gently for a few seconds. Set aside for as long as you can. A minute should suffice.

Blackberries and Raspberries with Petit Suisse

The most charming of all the cream cheeses must be the little pots of Petit Suisse. Unwrap one of the cheeses and place it in the center of a small plate. Scatter a handful of raspberries and blackberries around the cheese, then pour over a dash of light cream. The effect of the sharp white cheese, the sweet cream, and the scent of the purple fruits is positively ambrosial.

Blackberry Fool

Crush, or rather bruise, the blackberries with a fork. Stir in a little sugar (reckon on ¼ cup sugar to 1 pound fruit), then fold gently into ¾ cup heavy cream, softly whipped. Scatter over halved and toasted hazelnuts, if you like. It is most important that the cream is not overwhipped; it should barely stand in peaks, or perhaps drifts, and should fall lazily from the spoon.

Blackberries in Cassis

If you find any blackberry liqueur *(crème de mûres)* at the back of the cupboard, then it would be just perfect here. Cassis, or black-currant liqueur, turns a bowl of berries into a wonderfully heady treat.

Tip the blackberries, which will probably be the large and juicy cultivated ones, into a glass bowl. Pour over a few glugs of liqueur and sprinkle with sugar. Leave for as long as you can. Serve with a pitcher of cream.

Blackberries with Melon and Muscat

If you have come home with some wild blackberries, ones that have missed being eaten en route or squashed on the carpet in the back of the car, try them the following way. Serve them, freed from their prickly gray stems, in a simple bowl of china or glass, with cubes of ripe golden and fragrant Charentais (or other) melon, macerated for a little while in Beaumes de Venise or other chilled deep-golden muscat wine.

Blackberry and Yogurt Burnt Cream

You will need either those sweet little white ramekin dishes or a shallow dish similar to a quiche mold. Two-thirds fill the dish with blackberries, or other berries if that is what you have. Cover with a layer of thick Greek-style yogurt and smooth flat with a knife. Sprinkle a thin layer of sugar over the yogurt and put under a preheated broiler, close to the heat, till the sugar caramelizes to a golden crust, around 2–3 minutes.

Fruits *Brûlée*

This summer dessert really excels when it is made with soft fruits, berries (black, blue, and rasps), peaches if they are really ripe, and bananas. Red currants look like glistening jewels if a sprig or two is laid on top of the peaks of cream. Sheer indulgence, this fruit and cream mess has been known to seduce even confirmed dessert-haters.

FOR 6

1¼ cups sugar
1½ pounds mixed soft fruits, to
   include bananas, peaches, and
   raspberries

1½ cups chilled heavy cream

Put the sugar in a heavy pan and pour in enough water to cover. Set over a high flame to boil, while you prepare the fruit. Peel the bananas, pit and slice the peaches, and remove the stems from the raspberries. Put all the fruit in a serving bowl. Whip the cream until it forms soft peaks. If it starts to look grainy, then you have over-whipped it. Spoon the cream in waves over the fruit.

The sugar in the saucepan will start to turn to a pale golden caramel after about 10 minutes—watch it carefully as it is prone to burning, but do not stir it, which would make it crystallize. The caramel is ready when it turns a rich golden brown. Take off the heat before it starts to smoke, or it will turn bitter.

Immediately, taking care not to splash or burn yourself, pour the caramel over the cream and fruit. It will at once set to a crisp shiny coat. Serve within 30 minutes.

Black Currants

Black currants, removed from their stems and sold in neat plastic boxes, are to my mind the most successful of frozen fruits. They are probably the only ones I ever really use.

Hot Black-Currant Bread and Butter Pudding

FOR 2

Butter 4 thin slices of white bread very generously. (I think you had better remove the crusts.) Lay half of them on the bottom of a shallow ovenproof dish. Cover with ½ pound (about 1¼ cups) fresh or thawed frozen black currants and sprinkle rather lavishly with sugar, about 3 tablespoons. You can use raw cane brown sugar if it makes you feel better, but it will change the flavor of the finished dish.

Place the remaining buttered bread, butter-side up, over the currants, sprinkle with a little more sugar and 2 tablespoons cassis, *eau de vie,* or cognac, and dot with a bit more butter. Bake in a preheated 425 °F oven for 20–25 minutes, until the black currants have started to burst and their glorious juices have stained the bread. The result is juicy bread reminiscent of summer pudding underneath the crisp top. Serve with cream.

Vanilla Ice Cream with Hot Black Currant Sauce

Cook some black currants with a very little water until they start to burst. Stir in enough sugar to make them palatable but far from sweet, simmer for a couple of minutes to melt the sugar, then pour into a pitcher. Serve hot with balls of vanilla ice cream, which will melt slightly at the edges and swirl beautifully into the steaming purple compote.

Black Currant Crisp

Plums probably make the finest fruit crisp. Or perhaps gooseberries. This black currant version is pretty serious stuff, and is just as good cold. A glug from the cassis bottle will not go amiss, nor will a few fresh mint leaves tucked in among the fruit, for that matter.

FOR 4, WITH SECONDS

1¼ cups flour
½ cup plus 2 tablespoons butter
¼ cup plus 3 tablespoons sugar

1 pound (about 2½ cups) black currants, fresh or frozen, removed from stems

Whizz the flour and ½ cup butter in the food processor. When they look like bread crumbs stir in the ¼ cup sugar. Pile the currants into a baking dish, sprinkle over the 3 tablespoons sugar, and dot with the 2 tablespoons butter. Cover the currants with the crisp mixture and bake in a preheated 400 °F oven until the topping is golden and the fruit is bubbling, about 25 minutes. Serve hot with cream or thick, creamy yogurt.

Red Currants

Red currants mean only one thing to me—Summer Pudding. Squashed with raspberries and a handful of black currants between layers of bread, it really must be the most sublime of English puddings, though it takes too long to prepare to be included in this book.

Hot Red Fruits

Perhaps unexpectedly, these fruits retain their individual flavors if not cooked for too long. The ensuing syrup is tart and rich, and any leftover makes a good kick-start for breakfast, with yogurt.

FOR 4

½ pound (about 1¼ cups) red currants, removed from stems
¼ pound (about ⅔ cup) black currants, removed from stems
⅓ cup sugar

1 pound (about 4 cups) raspberries or loganberries

Put the currants and the sugar into a stainless steel saucepan with 2 tablespoons water. Bring slowly to a boil. When the currants start to burst and flood the pan with color, tip in the raspberries or loganberries. Simmer for 2 minutes, no longer, and serve hot in a white china dish, with a pitcher of cream.

White Currants

You are extremely lucky if you can find some white currants; I have not seen any for at least two summers. When I next see a punnet, I shall serve the sprigs with tiny crisp water biscuits (the almost flavorless crackers often served with cheese), on pretty plates, surrounding small mounds of Petit Suisse cheese. I shall put a little scoop of the sweet white cheese onto a water biscuit, pile on a few golden currants, and eat them in the garden, in the shade, with a glass of chilled sparkling Moscato.

Incidentally, a well-made currant jelly can make a delightful snack eaten with cream cheese and water biscuits.

SECRET SNACKS
AND THE QUICK FIX

Visitors from other countries must be amazed at Britain's selection of cheap sugar-laden confectionery surrounding the checkouts in shops. In France or Italy, one might leave the office for a few moments to stand at a bar and swig an espresso or munch a toasted sandwich, while here in Britain it seems people are more likely to return with a chocolate bar or even a packet of cookies. All that fat and sugar is bad news for everyone except the huge cookie and candy companies.

Here are some salty or sweet alternatives that will hit the same spot, but which are, for the most part, better for you, and whose flavor means there is some point in snacking on them.

► **Sun-Dried Tomatoes**, for a deeply savory nibble

► **Pumpkin and Sunflower Seeds**, for toasting or eating straight from the jar

► **Black and Green Olive Pastes**, for dipping bread into

► **Tahini**, a paste made from toasted sesame seeds: drizzle on dry toast

► **Scottish Oatcakes**, eat them as they are from the box, or dip them, in totally unorthodox fashion, into olive pastes, or spread them with honey

► **Caviar**, forget the silly accompaniments such as chopped onion, and eat in generous heaps on hot toast

► *Patum Peperium*, a secret blend of anchovy and spices, for spreading in minute amounts on hot toast

► **Bottled Tomato Juice and Cans of Consommé**, for mixing with Worcestershire and Tabasco sauces and making extra-thick Bloody Marys, see page 42, which are almost as good as a meal

► **Umeboshi Plums**, Japanese salted plums, which will keep in the refrigerator for months; good for when only something simultaneously salty and sour will do. Buy them from health-food stores or Asian grocers

► **Yogurt**, keep a tub of thick plain yogurt in the refrigerator for sprinkling with nuts and honey; try it with thickly sliced bananas, too

► **Condensed Milk**, boiled in its can for 1 hour till thick. It will keep for weeks in the refrigerator. An index finger is preferable to thin cookies, which break in the thick sweet gunge

► **Marshmallows**, toast till soft and warm. For serious sugar attacks

► **Chocolate**, the dark and fruity Manjari or Carré de Guanaja from Valrhona is pure chocolate with very little sugar and none of the fat and milk-powder padding of the cheaper varieties

► **Hunza Apricots**, tiny fawn-colored wrinkly fruits from Pakistan, the wild Hunza apricot is chewy and addictive; available in health-food stores

► **Turkish Delight**, make sure it's the real thing, rose- or pistachio-scented from Istanbul or Lebanon

Select Bibliography

Andrews, Colman, *Catalan Cuisine,* Macmillan, 1992

Bareham, Lindsey, *In Praise of the Potato,* The Overlook Press, 1993

Beard, James, *American Cooking,* Little Brown, 1980

Bissell, Frances, *A Cook's Calendar,* Chatto and Windus, 1985

Bissell, Frances, *Sainsbury's Book of Food,* Webster's, 1989

Boxer, Arabella, *Mediterranean Cookbook,* Dent, 1981

Brown, Catherine, *Scottish Cookery,* Richard Drew, 1985

Brown, Lynda, *Fresh Thoughts on Food,* Chatto and Windus, 1986

Bunyard, Edward, *The Anatomy of Dessert,* Chatto and Windus, 1933

Child, Julia, *The Way to Cook,* Knopf 1989

Christian, Glynn, *Glynn Christian's Delicatessen Handbook,* Macdonald, 1982

Costa, Margaret, *Margaret Costa's Four Seasons Cookery Book,* Nelson, 1970

Crabtree and Evelyn Cookbook, Stewart Tabori & Chang, 1989

David, Elizabeth, *A Book of Mediterranean Food,* Knopf, 1980

David, Elizabeth, *French Country Cooking,* Knopf, 1980

David, Elizabeth, *French Provincial Cooking,* Michael Joseph, 1960

David, Elizabeth, *Summer Cooking,* Viking Penguin, 1988

Davidson, Alan, *North Atlantic Seafood,* Macmillan, 1987

Del Conte, Anna, *The Gastronomy of Italy,* Bantam Press, 1987

Freson, Robert, *Taste of France,* Stewart Tabori & Chang, 1983

Gavin, Paola, *Italian Vegetarian Cookery,* M. Evans, 1990

Graham, Peter, *Classic Cheese Cookery,* Penguin, 1988

Gray, Patience and Boyd, Primrose, *Plats du Jour,* Penguin, 1957

Gray, Patience, *Honey from a Weed,* Prospect Books, 1986

Grigson, Jane, *Good Things,* Michael Joseph, 1971

Grigson, Jane, *The Mushroom Feast,* Lyons & Burford, 1992

Grigson, Jane, *Jane Grigson's Vegetable Book,* Michael Joseph, 1978

Grigson, Sophie, *Sophie Grigson's Ingredients Book,* Van Nostrand Reinhold, 1991

Hambro, Natalie, *Particular Delights,* Jill Norman and Hobhouse, 1981

Hazan, Marcella, *Classic Italian Cookbook,* Knopf, 1976

Heath, Ambrose, *Good Dishes From Tinned Foods,* Faber, 1939

Heath, Ambrose, *Good Sandwiches and Picnic Dishes,* Faber, 1939

Heath, Ambrose, *Good Savouries,* Faber, 1939

Heath, Ambrose, *Savoury Snacks,* Nicholson and Watson, 1939

Holt, Geraldene, *Recipes from a French Herb Garden,* Simon & Schuster, 1989

Madison, Deborah, *The Greens Cookbook,* Bantam, 1987

Maschler, Fay, *Eating In,* Bloomsbury, 1987

Mellis, Sue and Davidson, Barbara, *The Born Again Carnivore,* Optima, 1990

Pomiane, Edouard, *Cooking in Ten Minutes,* Cookery Book Club, 1969

Rance, Patrick, *The Great British Cheese Book,* Macmillan, 1983

Roden, Claudia, *A New Book of Middle Eastern Food,* Viking, 1985

Roden, Claudia, *Picnic,* Jill Norman and Hobhouse, 1981

Ross, Janet, *Leaves from Our Tuscan Kitchen,* Viking Penguin, 1994

Round, Jeremy, *The Independent Cook,* Barrie and Jenkins, 1985

Sahni, Julie, *Classic Indian Vegetarian Cooking,* Morrow, 1985

Scott, David, *The Demi-Veg Cookbook,* Bloomsbury, 1987

Seeber, Liz and Gerd, *Simple Food,* Dorling Kindersley, 1987

Spencer, Colin, *Colin Spencer's Fish Cookbook,* Pan, 1986

Stobart, Tom, *Herbs, Spices and Flavourings,* The Overlook Press, 1986

Toklas, Alice B, *The Alice B Toklas Cookbook,* Harper Collins, 1986

Waters, Alice, *Chez Panisse Menu Cookbook,* Random House, 1982

Wells, Patricia, *Bistro Cooking,* Workman Publishing, 1989

INDEX

All cheese recipes are indexed under *cheese* rather than under the name of the particular cheese being used